by Simon Ramo

Introduction to Microwaves

Fields and Waves in Modern Radio,
with John R. Whinnery

Fields and Waves in Communication Electronics,
with John R. Whinnery and Theodore Van Duzer

Space Technology

Handbook of Automation, Computation, and Control,
with D. E. Wooldridge and E. M. Grabbe

Cure for Chaos

Century of Mismatch

Extraordinary Tennis for the Ordinary Player

The Islands of E, Cono, & My

*The Management of Innovative Technological
Corporations*

America's Technology Slip

*What's Wrong with Our Technological Society—
And How to Fix It*

Tennis by Machiavelli

The Business of Science

SIMON RAMO

The Business of Science

Winning and Losing in the High-Tech Age

 HILL AND WANG

A division of Farrar, Straus and Giroux

New York

Copyright © 1988 by Simon Ramo
All rights reserved
Printed in the United States of America
Published simultaneously in Canada by Collins Publishers, Toronto
First edition, 1988
Library of Congress Cataloging-in-Publication Data
Ramo, Simon.
The business of science.
Includes index.
1. High technology industries.   2. High technology
industries—United States.   I. Title.
HC79.H53R36   1988   338.4'762   88-4428

TO VIRGINIA

I should like to thank my publisher Arthur Wang
for his numerous helpful questions, constructive
criticisms, and editorial care.

S . R .

CONTENTS

The Business of Science

PROLOGUE

Being There

This century will go down in history as the century of technology. Of course, before our time, the wheel, electricity, the automobile, and numerous other technological breakthroughs had a great impact on civilization. But in the 1900s we created a technological civilization.

In these almost one hundred years we developed the ability to move people and things between any two points of the globe in hours and to keep those points in instantaneous communication. We sow, reap, cook, communicate, manufacture, travel, clothe, entertain, educate, research, manage, cure, and kill by highly technological means. Most important of all, it is in this century that we discovered how to release enough energy from the atom to destroy our civilization in minutes, this before we learned how to live together on the same planet. This is the century in which technology advance outstripped social advance.

Even in the resourceful and democratic United States of America we are not organized—and are not yet even deliberately engaged in organizing—to meet the challenges of the technological society that has so quickly evolved. Neither we nor any other nation has a culture and a government able to cope with the enormous imbalance, the mismatch, between accelerating technological development and lagging social-political adjustment. At worst, our civilization will end in a nuclear holocaust. At best, however, we could innovate to create a bright and calm future in which science and technology will be employed exclusively for the benefit of humankind. Life on earth, considering these two possible extremes, must be regarded as a race, a contest waged on the frontier where advancing technology and society interface.

My life has been spent on that frontier. My years have coincided with the century's span (give or take a few years at the beginning, when I was not yet here, and an undetermined period at the end, when I may be gone). First I was a quiet researcher, probing fundamentals in science, with little concern over how such knowledge might be applied and no concern with the influence of technology's advance on society. But World War II and subsequent events propelled me to the front lines of change, where science and technology, with tremendous force and speed, have been driving our civilization to new attainments and new dangers. While still deeply immersed in science and technology, I found myself, often with fascination, in the precarious world of business, finance, politics, government power, the founding of new companies, and the directing of huge projects. This book describes the frontier and the battles there for supremacy among companies and countries.

Although this is not an autobiography, it proved helpful for me to picture this exciting frontier by relating some firsthand adventures there. But I found myself unable to resist going beyond those experiences to connect what I observed with many less visible global influences in the political-social-economic spheres. I have drawn broad, often unprovable conclusions and engaged in predicting. It seemed sensible for me to do this stretching and linking, from past to future, from the technological to the humanistic, because all aspects of our world are remarkably interconnected and in the end we must know more than merely what has happened. We want to understand why, anticipate what might happen next, and try to shape those events.

The story that follows is in two parts. The first is about the past and the present; the second contemplates the future. It starts where I came in. When I was young, all technological advances—telephones, motion pictures, radio broadcasting, cars, home refrigerators, airplanes—appeared to me to happen because of us. We the people created their development and controlled their use. We knew they didn't fall from heaven or emerge from hell by themselves. Technological innovation, I thought, was never to be feared, because the system apparently made the right things occur. If attractive and useful new products were made available, the consumers bought them. If a development was a mistake, the market quickly sensed it and rejected it. For some important projects, like great bridges and battleships, it was our democracy's elected government rather than the free market that determined what would be built. All in all, however, technological advances in our society always seemed to me to be in response to our wishes, whether expressed through the marketplace or through the government we ourselves elected.

Gradually, however, I came to question whether technological advances have been happening *because of* us or *to* us. Look, for instance, at what television has turned out to be. In the beginning we expected the new invention would merely entertain, and as such TV is an overwhelming success. But now we know TV is much more than entertainment. Television dominates in the selection of the President of the United States. It has usurped so much of our children's attention that it is as influential in forming their minds as schools and parents. TV's impact on determining political leadership and indoctrinating our children was not foreseen when television first emerged as feasible. The public did not debate ahead of time the desirability of this tremendous influence. It simply happened, and that is typical of technology's impact.

It was well past the midpoint of the century before the majority of Americans began to suspect that the coupling of technology and society would not always be beneficial. We have not yet realized—despite the possibilities of a nuclear world war or a ruination of the

environment by man's technological activities—that matching accelerating technology advance with more rapid sociopolitical maturation is the challenge of the century.

The Depression confused things because it slowed the rate of
technological advance and focused our attention on efforts to mit-
igate the worst of the Depression's ills. Then World War II created
a massive expansion of technology. It put us on a steep climb to
an even more sophisticated technological civilization; and the disparity between technological change and lagging social adjustment
was masked by the all-out effort to win the war. After the war,
some realized that the atom bomb would demand fundamental al-
terations in international relations; still, the priorities to rebuild
Western Europe and Japan and exploit technology for economic
recovery pushed the issue of the relation between technology and
society into the background.

The 1950s and 1960s brought us Sputnik, the ICBM era, the
space race, and the weapons race. As the 1970s opened, the United
States, having landed its astronauts on the moon, held undisputed
first place among the world's technological powers. It was the high
point for America, but also the beginning of America's technology
slip. In the 1970s and 1980s, evidence poured in (foreign cars and
TV sets and unemployed steel workers) that technology has become
a global phenomenon and that other nations can do most things
as well as we can and some things better. Uncontrolled technological expansion is now seen as hazardous. It has become clear
that we cannot afford to go on escalating the military-weapons race.
Our space program has gone into disarray. Our trade imbalances
and federal budget deficits have become intolerable. Available resources are seen as insufficient to enable us to outdo potential
enemies and simultaneously to lead the world in civilian products.
Our system is wanting in the ability to choose national goals and
priorities; we seem incapable of mixing government control with
the free market to sustain high economic growth. The imbalance
between technology advance and sociopolitical progress can no
longer be ignored.

As we examine the past, we look for clues (particularly on the frontiers of technology) as to why things happened as they did and caused our present situation to be far from fully satisfactory. We then look to the future with an eye to discovering how it might be influenced for the better, if not the best. Of course, many important future events surely will come as a surprise; when they happen, we will wish we could somehow have foreseen and prepared for them. But the future impact of technology on society will largely be the natural consequence of trends discernible today. We can describe future possibilities and try to choose among them. We can aspire to control instead of being mere observers.

I have often been at the right place at the right time, sometimes by accident or luck and sometimes through deliberate forecasting and planning. I have seen enough of both the predictable and the unpredictable to be convinced that it pays to look both back and ahead. Of course, no matter how well we analyze the past and anticipate the future, we cannot design and create society as we would like it to be, even if we could agree on what it should be. But the relationship between technology and society does not have to be as bad as it often has been; nor need it be as bad as it might become. Thinking people have a high stake in trying to influence their future for the better.

ONE

The Violin
and Other Roots

In May 1925 I turned twelve, and for the first time in my life I heard a recital by a violin virtuoso. It was in the Mormon Tabernacle, in Salt Lake City, where I was born and raised, and the violinist was Jascha Heifetz. As a youngster I displayed talent in mathematics and in playing the violin, so everyone told me that I should be a scientist or a violinist. By intermission time at the concert, I had made an important decision: I would not plan to be a concert violinist. Years later I came to know Heifetz's playing intimately. (We became friends; he even played the Bach Double Concerto with me one informal evening, an act showing both his generosity and his sense of humor.) I could then confidently conclude that I had made the right decision. After that concert in Salt Lake City more than sixty years ago, my chosen field became science, but I could never have predicted that my music would be linked to the launching of my career in science.

When I was fifteen, I made another good decision involving the violin and my career. It was early 1929 and I was a senior in high school, planning to attend the University of Utah that autumn to study engineering. I was preparing to enter the Intermountain High School Music Contests, where I hoped to win first place in the violin category. In Salt Lake City in 1929, performing arts outranked even basketball in popularity. We had an opera company, a ballet corps, a symphony orchestra, and the famous Mormon Tabernacle Choir. This was before the era of airlines, and the premiere artists of the world came regularly to perform in the Tabernacle, breaking up the long train trip from the East to the West Coast with a night in the luxurious quiet of the Hotel Utah and an appearance before a large sell-out audience of true music lovers.

The annual high-school music contests were important events, especially so to me that year. By working after school, I had saved a little over three hundred dollars, enough to get my college education started, but I knew that financing it for four years would require steady after-school work. It would help me immeasurably if I could win the violin contest and receive not only free music lessons but a full scholarship to any department of the university and two hundred dollars in prize money. I noted also that there was another award and more cash for "best string performer." If I could win the violin contest, then I had next to beat out the violists and cellists. Finally, there was the "best performer of the day" prize, with yet another medal and still more money. Winning that last award, I remember thinking, would be improbable because I would be up against the piano and vocal performers and there would be many talented entries in those categories, more than the number who would compete as violinists. I also recall being apprehensive about the oboe, bassoon, and piccolo players. One of them might take the top honor just because of the spell those instruments, less often heard as solo media, have been known to cast.

I contemplated hungrily the possible booty that might become mine and decided to take my first investment gamble. I drew out my entire savings and bought a violin for $325. It was a genuine Italian instrument. Playing on it for the first time, I wondered how a Stradivarius, an instrument I had never been near, could possibly be superior. I learned much later that I had bought what experts would call a mediocre violin, but in comparison with its predecessor, a Japanese specimen that had retailed at twenty-five dollars fresh from the factory, the quality of the violin's sound and its respon-

siveness and volume over the entire range, from the lowest notes
to the highest, seemed tremendous. The instrument gave me a bold,
unwarranted confidence and I made a clean sweep of the May
contests. I ended up with my "expensive" violin and more funds
than I had started with.

The risk-taking I had engaged in was not exactly like shooting
dice. It was based on cool calculation. To begin with, I was established as the number-one fiddler of my own high school, one of
three within the city limits. In Salt Lake City there were many
insistent invitations for young musicians to perform, what with
several Mormon missionary going-away parties, in which we non-
Mormons were active participants, and numerous fund-raising charity events every week. If some spectacular student violinist was
living in town at the time, I figured I would have noticed that rival.
As to the out-of-town high schools anywhere around the state of
Utah or even in Idaho, Wyoming, Nevada, and New Mexico, all
invited to take part, there was always the chance that an exceptional
player from one of those distant spots might enter the contest and
win. But such contestants would have come from towns smaller
and culturally less well endowed than Salt Lake City and it seemed
improbable to me that really skilled teachers would have been
available to them. Also, those contenders would have been accus-
tomed to music performances in their communities well below the
quality of those regularly heard in Salt Lake and would have had
little inspiration to emulate the higher standards. I, fortunately,
had heard not only Heifetz but Kreisler, Paderewski, Piatigorsky,
Rachmaninov, and others of similar stature.

Every New Year's Day, a performance of Handel's *Messiah* took
place at the Tabernacle, with the Mormon Tabernacle Choir, the
great organ, and an augmented symphony orchestra. All the professionals and better amateurs of the greater Salt Lake area were drafted
to complete the large ensembles. The men wore dark blue suits and
white shirts and the women wore white dresses. At age fourteen,
being the youngest player in the broadened orchestra, and protesting
that I had not ever played with my jacket on and could not possibly
do so, I had been permitted to join the orchestra in white shirt

sleeves and dark blue trousers. My contest rivals probably had had no such experience, jacket or no jacket.

Accordingly, I reasoned that the odds favored my winning the violin contest. By investing in a superior violin, I estimated I had doubled my chances. Although it would be many years before I would become involved with founding corporations, the planning and risk-taking involved in my gambling my entire net worth to back the violin contest had similar ingredients, such as analyzing the competition, estimating the odds of success, and comparing potential returns on the investment with the risk of its loss.

It turned out that if I had not invested the money in the violin, I would have lost essentially all of it. The savings bank where the funds were deposited failed almost immediately after the October 1929 stock-market crash. Years later, depositors were paid less than ten cents on the dollar. If someone had suggested to me at the beginning of 1929 that I should consider the possibility of a stock-market collapse with dire consequences for my bank savings, un-insured in those days, I would not have known what to do. It was simply an accident that my decision to purchase the violin kept me from suffering a financial disaster. I had been lucky. Many years passed after that first deliberate gamble before I realized I had become a hybrid of scientist, engineer, and entrepreneur. Risk-taking, I understood well by then, was a major factor in my life. Perhaps, I have occasionally wondered, if I had not bought the better violin and then had lost the contest, followed soon by the disappearance of all my savings, I would never have had the confidence to launch new companies later.

The connection between the violin and my science-engineering career did not end with that key violin investment. As it turned out, my first real job, at the General Electric Company in 1936, might not have been offered to me were it not for my music.

Some things that happen to us are the result of discernible developments stemming from known beginnings or decisions. These occurrences might be characterized as predictable, based on a logical chain of cause and effect. Other events in our lives appear so unconnected that we label them unpredictable and attribute them to chance. When such things turn out to our advantage, we consider ourselves favored with good fortune. I was lucky in being born in and living the first twenty years of my life in a community of gentle, warm people. All my teachers were competent, responsible, and caring. That I finished college in 1933, when there were no openings for new engineers, seemed then to be a piece of bad luck sent my way to balance things out.

As I studied engineering during the Depression, it was easy for me to learn that advances in technology were not automatic and inevitable. They would not occur just because creative engineers with good ideas were available. The economic climate had to be favorable, and it clearly was not in the 1930s. It was also the era of Franklin Roosevelt's New Deal, so, like everyone else around me, I assumed it was up to the government to straighten out the economy. But stopping the Depression and stimulating economic growth (so a position would open up for me after I graduated) seemed to be terribly difficult. It was evident that no one—neither Franklin Roosevelt nor the managers of giant companies nor the big-name economists—had the expertise to couple government policies to the private sector's activities to bring about the nation's recovery.

Still, I remained optimistic. I enjoyed a simplistic belief that society could only benefit from science and technologic advance— the more rapid the advance, the greater the benefit. (In fact, it would take me years to realize fully that science and technology are only tools and that, even when used most skillfully, they could not solve all of society's problems.) I could see no flaws in my belief. If science and technology were applied to the fullest, then, as a side effect, new engineers would find good jobs. A host of new products would issue forth. These would be so useful and attractive to buyers as to ensure a strong demand. Factory work would boom. Investments in the new technology would bring high returns. This was the way to lick the Depression, but I had little interest in the details. Sooner or later, it would all work out. I hoped it would be sooner, but that it would happen I had no doubt.

Had there been no Depression, had the nation's economy been thriving, I would have entered industry upon graduation. My four-year bachelor-of-science degree in engineering would have been the last of my formal education. But such a course, it was clear later, would not have been best for me. Postgraduate study to expand my knowledge of science was far wiser. As luck would have it, the choice was made for me, because, of the two alternatives, only one was available. Postgraduate education had not come to a halt in the nation, as had new careers in industry. Graduate fellowships were offered to students with exceptional records. Among the engineering graduates at the University of Utah in 1933 (mechanical, electrical, civil, mining, metallurgical, and chemical), I was the youngest in the class by two years but had the highest scholastic point average. Hence, I could obtain a fellowship.

I selected the California Institute of Technology in Pasadena and arrived there in the fall of 1933, expecting to spend a few years learning a lot more about electrical engineering. I thought my study of science was behind me and what I needed was to become expert at applying science to the design of real-life electrical equipment and systems. But when I began my courses at Cal Tech I thought I had made a terrible mistake and come to the wrong place. At this institute, probing the scientific frontiers was the dominant endeavor. There were graduate courses listed under Electrical Engineering, but their main thrust was the science underlying the engineering. Physics, electrical engineering, and mathematics were all in one division. What I would be spending my time learning at Cal Tech, I now realized, was science and the mathematical tools needed to deal with science.

It was a year before I realized how lucky I had been to land at Cal Tech, particularly in the 1930s, when numerous discoveries were being made at the frontier between the known and the unknown in the laws of nature. My eyes were opened to a whole new concept of how to prepare for a career in the application of science. Innovative engineering consists in part of brilliant inventing by creative engineers of new ways to put well-established scientific principles to work. But a large part of what engineering is also about, I came to see, is the exploiting of new scientific knowledge as soon as possible after it is uncovered. It is like the difference between learning how to pump oil ever more efficiently from an existing well and finding new oil deposits. Cal Tech taught me how to discover oil.

I received my Ph.D. in electrical engineering and physics at Cal Tech in June of 1936. That spring, the engineering personnel recruiter from the General Electric Company, Maynard M. Boring, stopped in at the institute, even though recruiting by General Electric was virtually at a standstill. May was once again a critical month for me.

Mr. Boring started his visit with a talk in the Cal Tech auditorium. He had an overflow audience; unemployed engineers from the entire Southern California area showed up to learn what they could about the outlook for employment. Early in his presentation, Mr. Boring dropped the remark that scientists and engineers were a dime a dozen. (It occurred to me that this pronouncement might have been a deliberate overstatement of their worth, charitably put forth to cheer up the audience.) If G.E. should hire a few of the country's new graduates, he hinted, it would be largely so the company might stay in shape for real recruiting in the future when the Depression was over.

Mr. Boring made one point whose significance was most unclear. He said that since G.E. really had no need for more technical staff, anyone to whom he might make a job offer would have to be able to contribute something to the community besides science or engineering. I failed to see what that remark might mean for me, but it was caught by Dr. Robert A. Millikan, the eminent scientist who headed Cal Tech and had led it to its enviable position among the world's great centers of learning. Millikan was not only a world-famous physicist, a Nobel laureate; he was also a skillful executive and determined to place Cal Tech's Ph.D. graduates in good jobs. Soon after Boring's morning talk, I received a message from Dr. Millikan's office directing me to come to a luncheon for Mr. Boring at the Athenaeum.

What with Millikan's genius in fund-raising for Cal Tech and the philanthropic interests of some of the leading figures living nearby (Henry Huntington, the donor of the splendid Huntington

Library and Art Gallery, and Harry Chandler, publisher of the Los Angeles *Times*, among others), the Athenaeum was both a campus dining facility for the faculty and an exclusive, invitation-only social club for wealthy outsiders known as the Associates of the California Institute of Technology. Their high-priced membership dues were important in building up Cal Tech during the Depression, and individual associates made grants for facilities and endowment that financed the institute's growth. The superb architecture and furnishings of the Athenaeum made it a suitably elegant clubhouse for the Pasadena and San Marino aristocracy that built it. There were handsome rooms upstairs for visiting scientific dignitaries and more than adequate lodging for those graduate students fortunate enough, like me, to have been granted a teaching fellowship providing room and board and tuition. Alongside the Athenaeum's dining hall was the Hall of the Associates. This large room was used for concerts, lectures, and meetings and also for fancy dinners for the associates, prepared by a French chef. The Hall had a grand piano and a closet where I kept my violin. There it was handy for a bit of practicing when I could spare the time and the room was empty.

When I arrived for the luncheon, which I had imagined would be a large one, with Mr. Boring doing a bit more opining on the Depression and the nation's surplus of engineers before starting his afternoon job interviews, I was surprised to find only a single round table for twelve in the center of the room. If this was to be a small affair, with no speech, why had I been included? Why was the luncheon not served in the main dining hall, in the usual fashion?

Might this mean I had already been chosen for the finals in the contest for a rare invitation to join the General Electric Company? Wishful thinking. This could not be. The competition was too severe. There was no reason why I should be selected when there were so many other applicants. By 1936, with the scarcity of industrial openings, a much larger fraction than in the past of the best bachelor's-degree engineering graduates in the nation were going on to graduate school. Cal Tech itself had some dozen students who, like myself, combined the study of electrical engineering with physics in pursuit of a doctorate. All of us hoped either for an academic appointment, one combining research and teaching, or for a post in some large industrial organization that might still be engaged in research and development (R&D). In 1936, Mr. Boring could choose from a long list of strong candidates throughout the country.

My puzzlement grew when the party assembled. Taking careful inventory of the guests after we were seated, I suddenly realized that, in addition to eight members of the faculty, plus Dr. Millikan, Mr. Boring, and me, there was only one other student, really an ex-student. He had obtained his master's some two years before and was living in Pasadena, still without a permanent job. His presence was even more mystifying to me than my own. He happened, however, to be a good pianist and my regular accompanist.

Dr. Millikan had become acquainted with my violin playing early in my first year at Cal Tech. His typical weekend included being the guest for tea at the home of one or another of the many wealthy families who lived in the impressive estates bordering the institute. After tea was served, he would talk to the assembled potential donors about the research being carried on at Cal Tech and its significance for society. He held his audiences spellbound with his well-chosen subjects, excellent delivery, and personal charm. On occasion, he would have me come along to soften up the audience with a few violin selections.

Halfway through the luncheon (before the serving of my favorite dessert, the chef's specialty, caramel pie—which I remember with annoyance to this day because I was too nervous to finish it), I had finally guessed why I was there and why my accompanist had been invited. When lunch was over, Mr. Boring turned to me and in brusk, top-sergeant style said, "Ramo—I've been hearing what a whiz you are with a violin." (I figured he must have stopped at the University of Utah on his way West and picked up some exaggerated comments.) "Let's have some fiddling before I start my interviews."

"We have the time," pronounced Dr. Millikan, now clearly the mastermind of the affair. "It's only one o'clock and the interviews start at one-thirty." This meant I should play for about fifteen minutes.

I performed uncomfortably, bothered by the conviction that this act was the wrong thing to stage for Mr. Boring. He was not recruiting violinists and he could well hold the opinion that art and engineering do not mix. He would be seeking very practical people for General Electric. Musicians, like poets and painters, are often regarded as the opposite—dreamers. Besides, he was wearing a multibuttoned, double-breasted suit of unpatterned gray serge with very stiff shoulders and lapels that seemed to me like a military uniform. The shirt and necktie he had on were of solid gray as well, and the three separate shades created a clash of incompatible monotones. I was sure that anyone so overcommitted to steel gray on gray on gray and case-hardened clothing would not be big on music appreciation.

From the fall of 1929, when I enrolled at the University of Utah and the stock market immediately collapsed, to the spring of 1936, when I entered the room for my interview with Mr. Boring of the General Electric Company, I had lived with the knowledge that getting a job after graduation would be an enormous challenge. Any offer would have to be considered. To land a position in research and development would represent marvelous good fortune, since it would be very much against the odds. Across the nation, expenditures for research and development of new products were a low-priority activity compared with efforts at short-term financial survival. It seemed beyond expectation that an opening would exist for me at G.E. in the year 1936, until that luncheon.

The afternoon interviews proceeded in alphabetical order. Each lasted three minutes, and my turn came at four o'clock. Almost before I could sit down, Mr. Boring informed me that there was a symphony orchestra in Schenectady, New York, part professional and part amateur. With General Electric the backbone of Schenectady, most of the orchestra's musicians were General Electric employees, he added.

"Ramo, you will enjoy the orchestra," Mr. Boring tossed out

with an air of finality. I responded faintly with something like "I'm sure I would." I recall well that I didn't dare say "I'm sure I will," because that would sound as if I had presumed he was offering me a job. Before my confusion could do me in, he provided clarification. He consulted a little gray notebook that he pulled deftly out of a vest pocket, and named a Monday in August as the date for me to report. He said nothing about salary or travel expenses and called for no response from me. As he stood up to dismiss me, he remarked with continued efficiency, "You will be getting a letter from me."

"I'll look forward to receiving it," I replied, rising as fast as I could and trying to emulate his decisiveness.

The very first day I reported for work in Schenectady that August, I received a telephone call from the conductor of the Schenectady Symphony Orchestra to tell me the time and place of the next rehearsal. As I entered the auditorium later that week, the conductor spotted me immediately and seated me beside the concertmaster, based on a recommendation, I assumed, from Mr. Boring. I ran into that highly disciplined personnel recruiter some time later. He asked me how I liked the orchestra. It happened that I had been made concertmaster a week before. I said I liked it very much, mentioned that I now occupied the first chair, and asked Mr. Boring in return if he was enjoying the concerts. He replied that he never attended symphony concerts, since he didn't much enjoy music.

When I arrived at the General Electric Company in the late summer of 1936, I was in for a shock. My first assignment was in the so-called General Engineering Laboratory. Research and development activities were carried on not only in this laboratory but in every one of the numerous departments making up General Electric's engineering staff, each department devoted to a specific product line such as motors, generators, vacuum tubes, transformers, appliances, or turbines. All these engineering staffs consisted of people with the conventional (and, as I saw it by then, outdated) bachelor's degree. They had studied no mathematics or science beyond their sophomore years, just like me during my undergraduate years. The separate, famous, and rather isolated General Electric Research Laboratory housed a number of gifted ex-professors and others with doctoral degrees in science. For its engineering activities, however, G.E. preferred new recruits with only a four-year college degree. Biases against Ph.D.s were openly expressed. New employees with postgraduate education, being older, were considered difficult to mold to the G.E. ambience. Ph.D.s were, in addition, assumed to be prima donnas.

The Research Laboratory appeared to be as high-quality as I had imagined from its reputation. Still, it was small, with, at the most, only twenty researchers of prominence and many of them relatively narrow specialists. There was one Nobel laureate, Dr. Irving Langmuir. Most of the rest, if contributions in pure science were the sole basis for judging, would not have rated with the leading scientists at America's major universities.

The company's leadership realized that further education was important for its incoming engineering staff. But instead of seeking recruits with postgraduate degrees, the company maintained its own education program. Of the newly arrived engineering employees, those regarded as especially suited to the most technically difficult engineering tasks were enrolled in a so-called Advanced Course that lasted three years. One morning a week, this small and select group attended lectures by the company's outstanding engineers, who presented examples of their own work, explained the analytical techniques they were applying, and assigned problems for homework.

Unfortunately, few of these lecturers, twenty or so years removed from their universities, had been exposed to recent developments in higher mathematics and science. They were top practical engineers, but they possessed only a superficial awareness of the frontiers of scientific exploration and of the evolving mathematical methods needed to deal with the newly postulated theories in physics.

Admission into the Advanced Course depended heavily on doing well in a written examination. It had been designed for the typical new employee who had just earned his bachelor of science in engineering. The questions involved science and math of the freshman and sophomore college years rather than the engineering methods usually taught to the juniors and seniors. With my preparation (I was the only Ph.D. taking the exam that year), I was able to score unusually high, and so the supervisors decided to place me in the second year of the course.

A few months later, all second- and third-year students in the program were called in individually by the vice president of engineering and asked what they thought of it. I responded with blunt assertions that the Advanced Course was highly inadequate. It would not prepare G.E. engineers to apply the latest science in their work. Too young to understand that such criticism was brash, I delivered it with relish. I had no idea I was taking a risk; I could easily have been categorized as an arrogant upstart. Who was I, age twenty-three, in my first year there, to pan this proud company's prestigious educational system?

Quite by accident, however, my timing was just right. The top engineering executives had sensed that G.E.'s courses needed updating, and my severe criticism seemed to them quite appropriate, a not unexpected confirmation. They pressed me for specific recommendations, and I proposed that they use the classroom time to inform the students about recent scientific discoveries and teach them the mathematics needed to understand the new scientific principles. I was merely suggesting, of course, that they emulate a good university graduate school. They could teach, I suggested, those sciences where they felt new product ideas for General Electric would most likely originate. If necessary, scientists from outside the company might be brought in to give key lectures.

The lucky consequence for me was to be assigned to start a new branch of the company's courses, to deal with the emerging field of electronics. I handled the task in the only way I knew how. I arranged lectures and assignments concerned with the science underlying electronics engineering. I quickly received recognition that could not have come my way had I arrived at G.E. three years earlier with no graduate degree. It was my good fortune that the company's leadership had blundered in grossly underrating the value of hiring new engineers who had done serious graduate study and research at a major university.

My new status led to my being granted in 1937, immediately after the year I spent creating the new course, an opportunity to engage in R&D of my own choosing. If I had had the benefit of hindsight to help me identify the field of research and development most valuable to my career, I could hardly have done better than to choose the field I did. That choice stemmed from no special gift of intuition, but rather from a realistic recognition of my limitations. I counted my education in science as excellent, my engineering experience as zero, and my expertise in any phase of physics or electrical engineering as trivial. Every established category had its world experts, individuals decades older than I, who were the originators of the knowledge with which I was only scantily acquainted. I decided to find some new field where no one was yet an expert.

Electricity with an alternation rate of sixty cycles per second is useful for providing lighting and power. Let the frequency of oscillation be higher—say, in the millions of cycles per second—and electricity can be made to manifest itself as radio waves that make AM (amplitude modulation) radio broadcasting possible. Speed up the oscillations even more, so that the radio broadcast frequency is in the tens of millions of cycles per second, and the higher-fidelity FM (frequency modulation) can be carried. At one hundred million cycles per second, TV bands can be broadcast. By 1936, vacuum tubes and circuits had been developed to operate at even higher frequencies, a few hundred million cycles per second, albeit at so low a level of power as to be barely useful. Beyond this, on up the radio spectrum to the billions of cycles per second, essentially no capability existed in the mid-1930s. As there were no effective means to produce electromagnetic waves this high in frequency, there were also no corollary means to amplify, transmit, and receive them. It was a virgin field. There were no experts. It was perfect for me.

Extremely high-frequency electrical phenomena—microwaves—act much like the even higher-frequency electromagnetic wave action known as light. Microwaves can be focused and directed in a beam. Microwave antennas are not constructed of the long wires used for lower-frequency electrical emissions, but consist of metal reflectors in the shape of dishes and parabolas (like searchlights). One pioneering researcher at G.E. (Wiam Hahn) had shown that microwaves could be generated by creating waves in a stream of electrons, but the technology was embryonic. Fundamental inventions and thorough exploration of the basic physics and engineering lay ahead. Beneficial uses had always been found for electricity at all frequencies in the spectrum, so I was confident applications for microwaves would eventually be developed to justify the investment needed to learn how to produce such phenomena. I cared nothing at that point, however, about the applications. I approached the subject as a scientist; my aim was to contribute to the understanding of the key principles.

I lacked the insight and practical experience to conceive of something like radar, which turned out to be a prime application of microwaves. Hence, after I began to make progress in generating these waves, I was astonished one day when a company vice president, accompanied by a Navy captain in uniform, came around to swear me to secrecy, instruct me on how to handle classified information, and turn my laboratory into a securely controlled area, with access permitted only to members of my team and such others as had a formally arranged need-to-know. This had followed by less than a week a visit by two other Navy officers obviously very knowledgeable about electronics, whom I had been directed to brief on every aspect of my work. Had I been more sophisticated in such matters, I would have put two and two together in a hurry after their visit and realized that the research I was doing had military applications, and also that the period in which I had been able to write and talk freely about my laboratory results and theories was about to end.

What had specifically caused the laboratory director to bring in the military was the means I had come upon for generating microwaves. I was not an inventor of the Thomas Edison kind. He was remarkable in not needing to master the physical science underlying the inventions that came to his mind. In contrast, most of the patentable concepts I had begun to evolve stemmed from my attempts to understand the physics of the process. To generate strong electromagnetic waves in a stream of electrons, my studies indicated, the wave motion had to be synchronized with the motion of electrons: high-frequency waves in the stream required high-speed electrons. This necessitated applying a high voltage to accelerate the electrons. High voltage, in turn, would send high power into my experimental setup. I saw that I needed to apply the high voltage in a special way, intermittently—not steadily, because that would burn my laboratory apparatus to a frazzle. So I administered pulses of high voltage, each lasting only about one millionth of a second, repeating the pulses about a hundred times a second. The high voltage, thus, would be "on" only a tiny fraction of the time, and the net or average power I would be forcing into my apparatus would be modest and withstandable.

It happened that my doctoral thesis at Cal Tech had focused on measuring high-voltage electricity, including electricity in the form of simulated lightning; that is, high-voltage electricity occurring in pulses of short duration. Accordingly, I knew how to make a pulsed high-voltage generator and apply it to the electron stream. In this way, I was able to obtain the high electron speed needed to produce microwaves of high instantaneous power during the active short-pulse period. This would lead to understanding the principles.

The technique I was applying was precisely what was needed for radar, where a series of high-power, short-duration pulses of electromagnetic waves are produced and sent out in a directed beam, into the skies, for example, to search for airborne targets. Outgoing waves striking an airplane are reflected back to the source. The beam's pointing direction at the instant an echo is received discloses the target plane's angular location. The time elapsing between the emission of an outgoing pulse and the arrival of the returned pulse tells how far away the object is. This is *Radio Detection And Ranging*, or *RADAR*. Without having the slightest notion that I was doing so, I was extending radar into the microwave spectrum to create new possibilities for improved accuracy.

Until the secrecy restrictions were placed on my laboratory, things were going exceedingly well for me at the General Electric Company. Because the approach to research and development natural to me always seemed to require intensive study of the basic physics underlying the project, this gave rise to my publishing many articles on the fundamentals I would uncover. After Pearl Harbor, my books and articles had wide distribution because an understanding of the basics I had spent so many hours puzzling out was needed suddenly by thousands of engineers. They had been forced to learn about microwaves and other advanced electronics. General Electric encouraged me to accept invitations to speak on the scientific foundations of electronics engineering in universities and before professional societies. All these events made me fairly well known within the profession, and I received offers of employment from other companies and universities.

I was twenty-seven years of age in 1940 when I discovered (in a meeting called by the top laboratory executives to talk about the organization of the laboratory) that my group of some eight engineers and scientists was the largest R&D section in that laboratory. Very encouraged, I took this to mean that there was great respect for the proposals I constantly made for projects to pursue. (By then, I had added other experiments to my work with microwaves. To generate microwaves, I had to produce a controllable free electron stream, and it seemed sensible to employ that technology to achieve other ends. For instance, since electron beams can be made to act like light beams of extremely short wavelengths, this makes possible an electron microscope with magnifying power superior to conventional light microscopes. Proof of these principles had already been published by the Germans. I was permitted to develop electron microscopy; additional technical specialists were assigned to me to further such efforts.) But the real reason I had accumulated projects so rapidly was the underrecruiting of Ph.D.s in General Electric's engineering departments and laboratories. Had G.E. hired dozens of engineers with good postgraduate science educations, our individual efforts would have been concentrated on only one project and my work would not have stood out.

The directors of the engineering laboratories were aware that the low rate of hiring during the Depression had created a shortage on the R&D staff of scientists and engineers in their twenties and thirties, the most productive period for innovators. In order to allocate research-and-development funds, these executives wanted to know the views of the younger generation, and with few young staffers available, I began to be invited to meetings with the decision-makers, where I was urged to express opinions about how the R&D budget might best be spent. I expected to continue as a researcher for the rest of my life, but the laboratory directors were laying a foundation for a later substantial change in my career. Without being aware of it, I was becoming, at a very early age, an overseer of the work of others, a director of R&D, if you will. If I had thought to further my career in that direction, I would not have known how. Accidents of timing and location were on my side.

The year 1940, when I was ushered into the fraternity of highly classified advanced military technology, was the beginning of a period of intensive discovery for me. In the light of new experiences and new knowledge of what others had been doing in secret, I was forced to reevaluate what had gone on before: my work, the General Electric Company's productivity in R&D, the role of science and technology in fighting the war, the power of government, and the weakness of the industry's engineering in contrast with the strength of science in the academic world.

To my dismay, I found that the British had been generating microwave pulses by precisely the means I had independently evolved, but had started doing so earlier. As to realized peak pulsed powers, it appeared I held the lead in the United States, but scientists in Great Britain had gone beyond the power level I had achieved. Further, they had progressed so far in the detailed design of the apparatus that they were close to a production version to carry in airplanes. (England's sophistication in radar was the deciding factor in the Battle of Britain. The R.A.F. had the ability to observe the Nazis assembling their bomber squadrons, then to direct their fighter planes to take off at just the right times, and finally to reach precisely the correct path of travel to track and kill their targets.)

After Pearl Harbor, teams of scientists and engineers were quickly organized in the United States to attack all the important new military technologies: radar, computers, bombsights, communications, submarine warfare, improved firepower, airplane navigation, rocketry, and nuclear weapons. The total of this national effort soon dwarfed R&D at General Electric.

The General Electric Company, to the great credit of its management and employees, was an important producer of equipment for the military in World War II. It was a very minor player, however, in the research-and-development effort needed to create new, essential military technology based on recent scientific advances. G.E. was not alone in its shortcomings. In the American technological industry, executives with the management skill to organize for rapid progress on large-scale projects based on new science were in as short supply as well-educated scientists and engineers. Only by a mass draft of university researchers in physics and chemistry, individuals broadly based in science, were the R&D requirements of the war effort met.

I had begun to suspect shortly after arriving in Schenectady that General Electric was not, as I had earlier thought, the world's center of research and development in the electrical field. It was painful for me to let go of the image of General Electric I had held since my early teens. I had first become aware of General Electric when my first science instructor had arranged for the junior-high-school class to go to a "House of Magic" show. This was a public-relations presentation, assembled by G.E., which toured the country in the 1920s. Fascinating electrical effects were produced on stage, and each display constituted convincing evidence for me that General Electric was synonymous with leadership in electricity. My ambition, still strong as I earned my doctorate degree, had been to join General Electric and make a career with that company.

I finally accepted during World War II that a new evaluation of General Electric and my own career was in order. When I considered and compared my past impressions and predictions of the future, I knew even before World War II was half over that I would probably move elsewhere when it ended. The company had become bureaucratic. Creativity at the management level was modest. Being careful was adequate. The engineering executives of G.E. were badly out of date when I arrived in 1936, comfortable in their jobs, as secure as civil servants in government, almost unaware of the tremendous breakthroughs at the frontiers of science. Most of G.E.'s top R&D stars were well past their prime, their reputations based on work they had done some twenty years earlier. The famous G.E. Research Laboratory was really a very small unit when measured against the wide spectrum of emerging new science that could have been applied to enable G.E. to provide leadership in electrical developments.

The Depression could be blamed partly for the sparse drive and imagination G.E.'s management showed in the 1930s. If the prosperity of the 1920s had continued, expanding earnings would have provided funds for larger-scale probing of new phenomena. But I felt the Depression was not the whole cause of the trouble. I had no exposure to, and no competence to judge, the company's budgeting for developing new opportunities. I was sure, though, that if I could have analyzed earnings, cash flow, assets, and the like, I would have found a way to justify a far bolder R&D effort for this number-one company in electricity, the corporation with the strongest financial base and overall industrial position, the one certain to survive even if a continued economic slowdown eventually caused the bankruptcy of virtually every competitor. When the company found itself with sinking earnings in the Depression, it became even more conservative in investing in the future. The Depression was a dozen years old when the Japanese struck Pearl Harbor. The more cautious executives at General Electric had taken charge and they were not leaders with great determination to meet challenges and expand frontiers.

The prime movers of the nation's wartime R&D efforts did not come from industry but from the academic world. Statesmen of university science and engineering, like Vannevar Bush and Karl

Compton from M.I.T., Richard Tolman from Cal Tech, and James Conant from Harvard, created a national R&D organization for the war effort (Office of Scientific Research and Development, OSRD) that reported directly to President Roosevelt and worked closely with the government's top military men. OSRD quickly organized new laboratories, extensions of leading universities, and other units housed administratively within the U.S. government, places like the Los Alamos-based Manhattan Project to develop the atomic bomb under J. Robert Oppenheimer from the University of California and Cal Tech, the Jet Propulsion Laboratory at Cal Tech for rocketry under Theodore von Karman, and the Radiation Laboratory for radar development on the M.I.T. campus under Lee Du Bridge. Other world-famous scientists—Enrico Fermi, I. I. Rabi, and Harold Urey from Columbia, Hans Bethe from Cornell, Eugene Wigner from Princeton, Edward Teller from Chicago, John von Neumann from the Institute for Advanced Study, and Leo Szilard from Columbia—were recruited to take on specific tasks. Not one of the directors of R&D at the General Electric Company was drafted to head a major war laboratory.

The situation was different in production and procurement. G.E.'s president, Charles Wilson, was pulled away by the government and made head of the War Production Board, and many other executives from industry were given high rank in expanded military and civilian departments to handle production and procurement of military weapons for the government.

The speed with which the government and the academic scientific fraternity moved amazed me. I had been invited to take a leave from G.E. and become a staff member of the Radiation Laboratory at M.I.T. to go on with microwave R&D work there. The director of my laboratory convinced me that it would be a mistake to accept. This new laboratory of the "professors" would be only a small, minor activity, he said, one that might slowly improve the understanding of the underlying basic science but would not get into serious weapons work. The real microwave research and development, he was certain, would be done in industry at places like the General Electric Company. I discovered within a year that the relative size, effectiveness, influence, and overall contribution to microwave military technology would be the other way around.

After 1942, General Electric found it almost impossible to expand its R&D staff because the supply of scientists and engineers had dried up. No such problem appeared to exist for the pertinent government departments, the military, and especially the large laboratories created under the leadership of the academic scientists. They seemed able to acquire the personnel they needed, the engineering strength drawn from industry and the research Ph.D.s from the large number of small academic institutions as well as the large ones. I would continually run into individuals in their thirties and forties, with doctorates in physics and chemistry, who had spent years as teachers in four-year colleges where they had had no opportunity to do research. When relocated by the war, they suddenly found themselves in well-equipped laboratories and moved rapidly to apply their pent-up energy and talents to the R&D needed for the war effort. Also, many engineers had taken jobs during the Depression that required little technical education. The war opened up new opportunities for them. In the 1940s, I would come across numerous such engineers, now military R&D officers or engaged as civilians in engineering alongside the academic scientists in the new laboratories, who appeared to be happy, hardworking, and very effective. Most often, when one would mention the company where he had been previously employed, I had never heard of it.

The organizations that the government, the military, and the academic scientists pulled together cooperated well with industry's production engineers, so the volumes of apparatus needed were produced remarkably fast. Money was instantly available from the government. The goals were to achieve results quickly, not to maximize the returns on capital investment. Before we entered the war, I had looked upon government as having an extremely modest influence on technology, and regarded the military leaders as not competent in technology. (The government, I had thought, could affect citizens largely by offering relief checks to the unemployed.) This wartime government, both military and civilian, was entirely different. It was an impressive force promoting rapid advance in technology.

By the time the war ended in Europe in 1945, I had made up my mind that my postwar career was going to involve creating a new company. The nation, I was convinced, would never again be as it had been. We had been lifted by the war onto a higher technological plateau and would quickly reach still higher levels after it ended. General Electric would continue to be one of the country's largest technologically oriented companies, but it would be but one segment of a vastly enlarged industry that would grow rapidly. Among all the players, G.E. would not be especially distinguished for its high-tech contributions; it would be simply one of the crowd. No longer would I nurture the naïve belief that U.S. advances in technology were controlled by a small number of elite giant corporations. Companies mature in time; they change, become bureaucratic and arrogant, and miss new trends, leaving opportunities for new and small firms.

I began to read about the history of American corporations. I noted that, one hundred years earlier, Western Union had become the nation's largest corporation, this because telegrams were so superior to the Pony Express, smoke signals, semaphores, carrier pigeons, and the other forms of communication which telegraphy replaced. But those who ran Western Union failed to envisage and incorporate the next advance, telephony. Western Union's leaders did not even try to make a deal with Alexander Graham Bell when he invented the telephone. A new company was formed to exploit telephony, and it then became the nation's largest. General Electric was assembled by imaginative entrepreneurs who combined Edison's laboratory with other operations to achieve a position of world superiority. The companies that provided illumination for homes and factories (with gas and oil flames) missed the electricity revolution entirely. Similarly, the companies that produced steam engines to drive machines in factories with countless shafts and pulleys did not develop the electric motors that replaced them. General Electric was formed to develop the lighting and the electric power applications. These examples, I guessed, represented the natural cycle of change. I was determined to phase myself into the next cycle when the war was over.

My new company would be in California. If you had been born in the West, lived three years in Pasadena, California, in the 1930s, found your life's partner there, and then moved to Schenectady, New York, chances are you and your wife would develop a severe case of Californiaitis. This disease causes its victims to be in extreme pain unless they reside in Southern California and is an ailment for which the definitive cure, smog, had not yet been discovered. Living in Schenectady between 1936 and 1946 had its advantages, but weather was not one of them. It was not casual conversation during the war when my wife and I would discuss moving back to California when it was over, even though a satisfying career at General Electric seemed guaranteed.

In August 1945, when the United States dropped two atom bombs on Japan and V-J day followed quickly, I felt certain that the United States government would not relinquish its leadership in technology. Military procurement would be vastly reduced, of course. But a technological Pandora's Box had been opened and the atom bomb was out. Moreover, the Soviet Union and the Western powers had split Europe. The former allies would have to rely on continued military power to feel safe. The postwar world was going to be an insecure one, and the potential of new science and technology would forevermore exert a powerful influence on that insecurity.

I was fascinated with the new challenges I was certain military technology would offer in the postwar period. One day not far off, I was sure, President Truman would announce that the U.S.S.R. had successfully detonated its first atomic bomb. With that startling, frightening news, it would instantly become evident to all Americans that we were no longer protected by the oceans. The United States military was already planning the Strategic Air Command (SAC), a fleet of manned bombers that would be able to deliver our nuclear bombs anywhere in Europe and Asia; so the Soviet Union would rush to attain a similar capability. I was confident that the United States would feel compelled to mount a crash program to create a continental air defense system, and it would be greater than any military technical project in our previous history. It would comprise a complex multibillion-dollar ground-radar and communications network to detect and track Soviet planes on their way to North America and a means to intercept and destroy them.

The speed of jet airplanes when they were developed made it no longer sensible to imagine air battles in the sky in which our airmen, individually, unaided, would go up to find the Soviet bombers and then maneuver to shoot them down. Our pilots would not be able to spot the enemy planes early enough and could not determine quickly enough how to get on an interception path to shoot them down. Our interceptors would have to be guided by long-range ground radar and would employ airborne radar to lock onto the targets automatically in any weather, high or low visibility, day or night. In the future, the way to stop the bombers would be with guided missiles launched from interceptor planes. The missiles would be small, fast, and accurate. In the coming years, computers on our airplanes would instantaneously integrate their speed and altitude with our radar's incoming data about the movement of hostile bombers; this would permit us to direct our interceptors and launch missiles at the right time and in the right direction, without pilots being involved in handling data. The air-launched missiles, with much higher speed and greater maneuverability than the Soviet Union's heavy long-range bombers, would home in on the radar echoes from the intruders and annihilate them with direct hits.

The United States government certainly would spend many billions developing the basic technology, the microminiaturized electronic circuitry and components, guided missiles, airborne computers, radars, instruments, and the rest. This military technology would ultimately find its way into peacetime use: commercial computers, production controls and robotry in our factories. How marvelous it would be, I dreamed, to create an organization to be in the forefront of the exciting developments that basic science makes possible. Our company would provide vital protection for the nation against a nuclear attack, virtually guaranteeing that such an attack would never be mounted, and at the same time it would advance technology that would later benefit civilian society.

The major established electrical companies, it seemed more than reasonable to suppose, would give first attention to their civilian business, which had advanced only modestly during the Depression and which they had had to neglect during the war. They would feel pressed to incorporate the wartime technology into their communication, consumer, and industrial lines ahead of their competitors. Bell Labs and Western Electric would vigorously prepare for America's postwar expansion of telephone services, while General Electric, RCA, Westinghouse, Sperry, Raytheon, Sylvania, and the rest would fight each other feverishly to dominate in selling consumer and industrial equipment. They would all accord a low priority to military technology.

In the spring of 1946, when industry and the universities began reorganizing after the war, attractive overtures came my way from aircraft companies in Los Angeles and from Stanford, the University of California at Berkeley, U.C.L.A., and Cal Tech. I thought seriously about the university invitations; but the aircraft industry was not for me: its managers sensed their companies' future revenues would depend heavily on electronics yet they did not know how to organize and recruit for R&D.

The way the aircraft companies handled their engineering personnel was atrocious, I thought. Their rapid increase in factory workers had resulted in practices unsuited to high-grade R&D. Time clocks, essential perhaps in the factory, glowered on everyone, including professional teams. A whistle blew at twelve o'clock and that was when you left for lunch, not a minute before. If you tried to leave early, the guard at the gate would demand a special permit. He also would send a demerit slip to your supervisor if you returned after one o'clock, regardless of when you left. If you went to the company library to take out a book needed in your work, you had to go through a time-consuming, insulting procedure intended to make certain you were not going to steal it. To discourage idling, the men's lavatory compartments had no doors.

Demeaning to the engineers and a guarantee of inefficiency was the total lack of office privacy. These professionals sat at desks lined up against each other in a huge, unpartitioned area with no windows, each person allotted eight by six feet for himself, the furniture, and the books. There were no telephones at the desks; they were at stand-up stations about fifty feet apart. The phones rang constantly. A single clerk would answer the telephones and shout over the loudspeaker the name of the person being called, who would then leave his desk and go to the open phone station. When one engineer came to consult with another, a chair would be squeezed in alongside the desk. A table with a dozen chairs around it at one end of this cattle yard constituted the conference room where engineers might meet to consider a problem.

To round out the list of improper personnel practices, unions of engineers defined all engineering positions and each was assigned a specific hourly rate. One could advance, say, from Structural Engineer C to Structural Engineer B with a fixed, posted sixty-three-cent hourly rate rise, or make a parallel shift from Associate Senior Hydraulics System Designer to Deputy Electrical Integration Supervisor. I could easily envision this preposterous system continuing for years, appropriate only to government-administered cost-reimbursement regulations and the unions' involvement in negotiating the pay for each classification. A mountain of paper to record adherence to rules was considered by manufacturers as basic to peaceful relations both with government contracting officers and with labor-union leaders and was thought to be as important as turning out quality engineering or delivering equipment on schedule and without cost overruns.

The aircraft companies, I knew for sure, would expand into guided missiles, radars, and military computers after the war, but they would be severely handicapped by their management practices and their inexperience with electronics engineering and the frontiers of science.

An exciting opportunity existed for a new company.

TWO

Howard Hughes and National Security—the Odd Coupling

What proved to be an astounding high-technology research and development center was founded just after World War II in Culver City, California. It came to house the largest concentration of technical college graduates, including the greatest number of Ph.D.s, in any single industrial facility of that period, except for the Bell Telephone Laboratories in New Jersey, the research arm of the nation's then largest corporation, AT&T. By winning competitions, the new operation attained a virtual monopoly in certain critical military electronics and guided-missile technology. For decades, every airplane with the mission of intercepting enemy bombers entering North American air space was equipped with vitally needed radars, computers, and missiles developed and produced by that one source.

No military R&D effort received a higher priority in the postwar years than that to defend the continent against a nuclear air strike. No military weapons systems called for greater advances of technology. No group of scientists and engineers received stronger support of their efforts by the U.S. government. Yet the key organization involved was neither a branch of the government nor a publicly held corporation. It was the property of one man, an eccentric, uneducated, uninformed, virtually out of communication with the world, and not a participant in conceiving the program or in managing it. He did not have a security clearance and hence was only superficially aware of the company's projects. He never once visited the laboratories where the research was being done.

How these strange circumstances came to be, it is tempting to say, has some similarity to the improbable, but not impossible, tossing of a coin to turn up a succession of heads with no tails intervening. In its most important aspects, however, the creation and growth of this remarkable weapons-systems company under Howard Hughes's ownership was not at all like flipping a coin. It was not so much a statistical anomaly as the result of a series of discernible, though odd, events.

In April 1946 I came to the Hughes Aircraft Company to institute high-technology research and development. I knew perfectly well why I had made the decision to leave the General Electric Company and to form a new group. Right or wrong, I had thought hard about the move, which, as I saw it, rested on some surely sound premises plus some possibilities worth gambling on, with much attendant risk. What happened afterward was partly what I had envisaged, but the greater part was well beyond my imaginings.

I had planned to found a new high-technology company in California at the end of World War II, but I didn't know how. I had no model to copy. Successful new high-tech companies were exemplified for me by Dave Packard, whom I had known at G.E. and who had left years before the war to found Hewlett–Packard with his friend Bill Hewlett, and by a former chemistry professor at Cal Tech, Arnold Beckman, who had launched Beckman Instruments. Both had started by developing measuring devices which they could produce in small quantities in their back-yard garages. They knew a market existed for those instruments, and they could hire a few technicians and a salesman and be in business. The company I had my heart set on would be entirely different. To assemble a team of specialists and create the facilities needed for developing guided missiles, I would need millions of dollars.

I was acquainted with a number of Department of Defense

officials who handled weapons procurement for the Armed Forces. They regarded my personal technical capabilities highly, but I could not say to them: "I would very much like to start a new company, but I don't have any money or facilities or a staff just yet. Please give me a contract anyway. I will then line up backers to finance the company and persuade outstanding scientists and engineers to join me." The military services could consider proposals only from companies already in existence.

Early in 1946, on an assignment in California for G.E., I met some people who were working for what they referred to as the hobby shop of one Howard Hughes. I had heard him described as the nation's richest man, but I was a bit unclear about the source of the riches. They told me his father had died when Howard was eighteen and had left him the Hughes Tool Company with its strong patent-based monopoly of the most effective oil-well drilling tools. That inheritance not only had grown enormously in value but had been providing him with an annual cash income of several million dollars for twenty-five years.

They persuaded me to visit the Hughes Aircraft Company, legally not a separate corporation but merely an informal part of Hughes Tool, and view the mammoth flying boat the company had put together out of plywood. It looked like a wooden ocean freighter to which wooden wings had been added. The wingspan appeared to be the length of a football field (I learned it was actually 319 feet), and it had eight propeller engines mounted on the wings. I was impressed with both its colossal size and the lack of common sense which could have led to such a project. From this inspection tour, I picked up some impressions of what the peculiar Hughes operation was about, and an equally peculiar thought came to my mind. If what I was being told was even half accurate, then I should take seriously the proposal made by these Hughes folks that I join the fun.

Howard Hughes, I was informed, rarely came around. When he did show up, it was to take up one or another trivial issue. He would toss off detailed directions, for instance, on what to do next about a few old airplanes (of metal) decaying out in the yard, or what kind of seat covers to buy for the company-owned Chevrolets, or he would say he wanted some pictures of clouds taken from an airplane. An accountant from Hughes Tool had the title of general manager but was there only to sign checks. A few flying buddies of Howard Hughes were on the payroll, using assorted fanciful titles like some in Gilbert and Sullivan's *Mikado*, but apparently did next to nothing. A lawyer was on hand to process contracts, but there were practically none. In addition to the *Spruce Goose* flying freighter, there was an experimental Navy reconnaissance plane under development (which, with Hughes at the controls, later crashed, almost killing him). The contracts for both planes had been canceled.

Perhaps, I said to myself, this is one of those unforeseeable lucky opportunities. Why not use Hughes Aircraft Company as a base? In April 1946 I knew unspent war funds were available to the military services, money appropriated by Congress for that fiscal year and needing to be committed by June 30 or it would return to the Treasury (an option the services abhor to this day). If I were to write proposals on behalf of the company, might they not have a good chance of being accepted?

I took a trip to Wright Field in Ohio, where the Air Force procurement operations were headquartered. There they told me straightforwardly that, with the war's end, they expected it to be difficult to get the best engineers in the best companies to work on their projects. They could only hint, but did so strongly, that I would very likely succeed in obtaining some beginning contracts for Hughes Aircraft. This would enable me to hire a staff and get going. Of course, I would still be taking a big risk.

The major California universities had produced a large number of Ph.D.s in engineering and physics. Many of these worked in the East and I felt sure were suffering, like me, from Californiaitis. The prewar employment insecurity felt by engineers and scientists had been eliminated by the war. The technical fraternity had worked feverishly for five years on crash programs, always with a shortage of technical talent and had come out of this experience no longer afraid of being unemployed. Profits from war contracts had built up established corporations so they now had the funds to develop peacetime products, to which they would be giving priority. But many of the professionals I would be seeking would much prefer the challenge of the glamorous, difficult advances needed by the American military to spending their time applying the newest technology to mundane products. Moreover, they knew it was inevitable that the U.S.S.R. would develop nuclear bombs and that it was tremendously important to create a defense system to protect our country from possible nuclear attack.

It was on the strength of this line of thought that I resigned from the General Electric Company and joined Hughes Aircraft to build a new entity.

During the next few years, some things happened precisely as expected. I received initial contracts from the Air Force for advanced military-electronics and guided-missile R&D. Some outstanding engineers and scientists in the Eastern United States quickly heard what I was up to and contacted me. I was able to hire them with no interference from other Hughes "management." I found myself free to organize the venture as I wished.

One morning in 1949, President Truman made the announcement I had been expecting: the Soviet Union had successfully tested a nuclear bomb. This news made front-page headlines across the country and was the first item reported on the radio. (Not quite the first in every broadcast, however, because Rita Hayworth eloped with the Ali Khan at about the same hour the Russian atom-bomb story broke.) The U.S. government promptly stepped up the program it had begun in 1946 to develop an air-defense system against a nuclear attack by the Soviet Union. The contracts we had were expanded. I was on track, but events led me to uncharted territory.

My original plan was for research and development only. I thought the group would comprise around one hundred technical experts, all preeminent in their specialties, so that we would attract support for R&D on the most difficult facets of advanced military technology. We would point the way by working out the fundamentals. We might go as far as fabricating prototypes of missiles, radars, or computers to prove our concepts, but we would not venture into actual production. The results of our R&D would be made available to the large established industrial companies, and they would manufacture the equipment for the Armed Forces.

Many of the professionals I would recruit would be Ph.D.s, but not all of them. We needed experts, but their educational backgrounds and experience would vary. These senior staff members would be backed by others who would do the more routine tasks. Each expert would have a private office where he could work without being disturbed. Every office would have a telephone and windows, and would constitute the periphery of each floor, with the laboratories in the central area.

We would have a weekly "town meeting" where the scientists and engineers could voice their ideas about how to cut administrative red tape and maintain close communication and mutual stimulation to achieve the full benefit of each other's talents. We would be particularly strong in systems engineering (the discipline of the design of the whole, to realize a harmonious and effective ensemble, as distinct from the design of the parts). Our specialists' contributions would be tied together by our seasoned generalists, so that our final products, even though very advanced, would present thoroughly practical answers to the military's requirements.

As word spread about our existence, our aims, and our approach, inquiries about joining us came from outstanding scientists and engineers all over the country. The staff began to grow much more rapidly than I could have imagined. With each new arrival came more ideas, more proposals to the military, more contracts, and a greater capability for carrying them out. After the staff of experts exceeded one hundred, every one of them of the highest caliber, I thought maybe two hundred would be the proper ultimate size. When we exceeded four hundred and were clearly heading for eight hundred, I thought maybe sixteen hundred would be ideal. After seven years, when I left Hughes, the organization included three thousand engineers and scientists and a supporting staff of technicians, mechanics, draftsmen, purchasers, secretaries, librarians, accountants, contract administrators, guards, janitors—but this is getting ahead of my story.

The team established itself quickly as exceptionally qualified in military technology, worked with unprecedented enthusiasm and morale, and made rapid progress. As I had thought, we usually competed against second teams from established industry, their first teams being occupied with the nonmilitary products which their companies chose to emphasize. Simply put, we were well above average in the stature and zeal of our staff and in smoothness of operation, and we competed against groups whose average individual competence, quality of organization, and motivation were decidedly inferior. We did not lose a single competition. Often, other projects were canceled when we presented better alternatives for meeting the military's requirements.

In the summer of 1946, a few months after the start of the operation, my former classmate and close friend at Cal Tech, Dean Wooldridge, telephoned me. He was then one of the most valued staff members of the Bell Telephone Laboratories. That call, in which Dean inquired whether there might be a spot for him in my fledgling endeavor, was for me the strongest possible guarantee of future success. Dean had been one of those rare Cal Tech graduates who had earned a Ph.D. in physics summa cum laude. He was my age—two months younger, in fact—but when he entered the institute for graduate work at age twenty he already had a master of science. He had obtained that degree, which usually required five or six years of university study, during his four years as an undergraduate, while his classmates were earning a bachelor's degree. When I came to know him well, I didn't wonder how he had managed to complete the work for his master's so quickly, but rather, in view of his enormous intellectual gifts, why it had taken him so long. (He had shifted major a few times before settling on physics.)

Dean and I became partners in building up the new organization. We thought so much alike on management principles that either of us could handle a policy issue alone, confident that the other would have done it the same way. We divided between us the directing of the effort and constantly conferred about problems and progress. Our working relationship became a model for cooperation throughout the organization.

A significant difference between my original forecasts and the way things actually turned out was the fact that we were forced to broaden our objectives. Instead of limiting our efforts to research and initial weapons development, it became necessary for us to manufacture the equipment required by the government for actual operational implementation. We had to design and create servicing equipment and set up maintenance facilities. We had to produce spare parts and provide for their distribution. Airplanes to use in testing our products were allocated to us by the Air Force, and we employed test pilots who worked closely with the development engineers to evolve procedures for test-flying the systems under close-to-operational conditions.

We could not avoid this expansion. We tried to pass our initial developments on to other companies so they could perform the production role. We brought in manufacturing experts from Westinghouse, General Electric, Philco, RCA, and others and gave them extensive presentations and demonstrations to help them get started in the manufacturing. They would respond enthusiastically but would estimate that it would be years before they were ready and could reach the production rate required. The military services deemed the proposed schedules too slow. They would decide, for instance, that they needed one hundred radar-computer-missile systems for operational testing that year, and only we could produce them that soon. We did so in our laboratories' model shops, with our engineers directly supervising the construction and our laboratory technicians and model-shop mechanics, not regular factory workers, providing the assembly labor.

During that time, as those first systems were being produced and flight-tested, our scientists and engineers would observe the system's shortcomings. They would introduce improvements, always with the strong urging of the military. These modifications steadily mounted, and the estimates from other companies as to when they could deliver the product would stretch out and the prices would increase. Eventually they stopped even trying to keep up. We were forced to turn our informal fabrication and assembly activity into a full-fledged manufacturing operation. We had to construct factories and hire factory workers, set up training programs, and develop specialists in test-equipment design and construction, cost-reduction engineering, and factory quality control.

When we realized that we had to develop an extensive production capability, it was also clear that we had to organize the company so that one chief operating executive would oversee both the R&D and the production, the overlap between them making a tight connection under a commonly directed program of action a necessity. I assumed this post, with the title of Vice President and Director of Operations. All in all, we researched, developed, designed, and manufactured a parade of continually improved models of our airborne radars, computers, controls, and guided missiles. Because, with full capability, we provided by far the fastest and cheapest way for the government to get what it needed, we became a large, broadly based company in military technology.

The work was accomplished under "cost-plus" contracting, with all expenses applicable to the effort reimbursed by the government, and with a fee, a gross profit, added on top. It was essentially impossible to lose money. The operation would have had to incur substantial "disallowables" because of expenditures that were entirely inappropriate, obviously wasteful, and irrelevant to the contract's objectives. Special facilities, buildings, laboratories, test equipment, etc., needed to meet the contract were all chargeable to it, if not as an expense paid for immediately, then as a capital item that would be written off quickly through depreciation charges covered by the contract. Working-capital needs were minimized because the government made generous cash payments as the work progressed. If more cash was needed, it could be readily borrowed from the banks because the government provided loan guarantees. Thus, the Hughes Tool Company took on only infinitesimal financial risks from the mushrooming business of Hughes Aircraft. The profitable return, in proportion to the small real investment, was extraordinary. Many millions were added to Howard Hughes's fortune. (Meanwhile, in the hangars on the Culver City property, the airplane projects, the personal fancies of Howard Hughes, had passed out of existence.)

To carry out the technical tasks of R&D and manufacturing, we hardly needed the corporate framework that existed vaguely over us. Legal approval by the Hughes Tool board of directors was required, of course, for such actions as borrowing from the banks, signing contracts, or breaking ground for new buildings. These consents initially were readily obtained from the Tool Company's headquarters in Houston by way of the accounting and legal representatives of the parent corporation in Culver City. Sometimes I would accidentally receive a memorandum containing a few excerpted sentences from records of meetings of the board of directors of the Tool Company that had voted the required resolutions. I noted that Howard Hughes, the board chairman and president, was never present.

In late 1947, Hughes hired General Ira Eaker, who had just retired as Deputy Chief of Staff of the United States Air Force. His responsibilities were never made clear to us, but we assumed he had been employed to keep an eye on the Aircraft Company and would have access to our elusive owner. Eaker in turn brought in several others. We seemed to have gained a "corporate management" that would handle legal and financial matters above and beyond what Wooldridge and I could properly assume was within the authority given us. It turned out that Mr. Hughes had delegated little corporate power to this management layer, which in addition to Eaker included retired Lieutenant General Harold L. George as the general manager and Charles B. Thornton* as George's assistant.

When this group looked around at what was going on under the aegis of the Hughes Aircraft Company, they concluded that the future lay in electronics and missile development. Eaker, George, and Thornton were capable and well motivated and quickly

---

* He was the "Tex" Thornton who later left Hughes Aircraft, where his exceptional entrepreneurial talents could not be applied, and built Litton Industries into a giant conglomerate.

began to do whatever they could to support Wooldridge and me.

Anyone with experience of how human beings relate to one another would readily have predicted that the upper administrative echelons of the Hughes Tool and Hughes Aircraft structures would eventually clash. As Hughes Aircraft attained an important national position, the senior Tool Company executives naturally wanted to be in on the success; Hughes Aircraft was, after all, legally just a part of Hughes Tool. The executives at Hughes Tool who dealt with the bookkeeping, financial commitments, fund transfers, legal obligations, and the like and those at Hughes Aircraft reporting to General Eaker and expecting to cover the same terrain found it difficult to sort out their overlapping responsibilities.

This territory of corporate administration was at first of no interest to Wooldridge and me, and we were unconcerned with the contesting fiefdoms. As far as we knew, our scientific, engineering, and manufacturing activities dominated the scene and were the substance of the company. No one made any effort to interfere with our projects or tried in any way to boss us. Getting the accrued costs of R&D and manufacturing down on paper and the payroll accounting executed properly, sending bills to the government, arranging for bank loans, obtaining legal sanction of incoming contracts from Hughes Tool Company—being involved in any of these functions was not at all attractive to us. We were developing advanced technology that we were proud of, winning competitions, and earning plaudits on the performance of our equipment. Our reputations grew rapidly in science and engineering circles, and the cream of the crop of university graduates interested in our kind of work most often would accept our offers over those of competitors. *

A basic problem for the administrative executives in both the Aircraft Company and the Tool Company was that neither group could exert real company leadership. That had to stem from a solid knowledge of what we were doing and why, and that would involve

---

* A particularly conspicuous example was Ruben F. Mettler, regarded (judging by the attractive offers he received) as the most promising graduate with a Ph.D. in engineering at Cal Tech in 1949. He accepted our invitation over others, soon became our youngest major project head, and later rose to be chairman and chief executive officer of TRW Inc.

a participation in the relationship between the government's military personnel who were setting the requirements and our engineers and scientists who devised the ways to meet those requirements.

The limitations of a company with an absentee owner, legally the chief executive of the company but exerting no executive control, gradually became too great to ignore. The rival administrative teams finally became bitter adversaries. Accusations of serious misdeeds flew back and forth. (Years after I left Hughes, one libel suit was still working its way through the courts.) With no top executive in charge to curb this harmful competition and distrust, our organization's future became endangered. I was not willing, for instance, to give up the ambition I had had from the beginning that the organization would encompass civilian products. In fact, I had begun to do some formal planning in the hope that after a reasonable period of development we might market commercial electronic computers, factory automation systems, industrial process controls, and perhaps even some advanced electronic consumer products. Such ambitions could never be realized unless something was done about the loose (nonexistent) management structure. We were generating profits, but—to list only one conspicuous example of an administrative blockage—we had no authority to reinvest those earnings in civilian-product R&D. We had no structure to obtain such authority. Spending Hughes's money was very different from incurring expenses against a cost-reimbursed government contract.

The probability of further corporate-level chaos soared when Howard Hughes developed serious difficulties with other principal investments. It was the middle of 1950, as we were engaged in the challenging task of doubling our size, when his problems with TWA and RKO began to make front-page news. Hughes's long interest in movie-making was centered in his control of RKO; his interest in commercial airline operations was evinced by his owning a majority of shares of TWA. Both these large companies had public shareholders, so Howard Hughes had to obey government regulations created to protect their interests, and he did not always comply. Through apparently random and generally incompetent actions, Hughes encouraged legal suits by minority shareholders and attracted the attention of the government's regulatory agencies.

When it appeared that many of his management actions at RKO might be deemed in violation of the law, of minority shareholders' rights, of SEC regulations, and of rules for listing shares on the New York Stock Exchange, Hughes tried to buy up the minority shares, to own the whole company and then sell it. But he put himself in further difficulty by deciding to unload his holdings to a syndicate that was itself under suspicion, if not indictment, for violating the law. When that group's bad reputation, probably not previously known to Hughes, was described by the press, he canceled the deal.

TWA was even worse for Howard Hughes. After much litigation, in which through arrogance or lack of understanding Hughes ignored the court's orders to appear at hearings, the court took away his right to vote his own shares and, treating him as a child, a legal minor, ordered his stock into the custody of outsiders appointed by the court.

Many people sophisticated in high finance knew of Hughes's problems and had heard of the success of our organization and the esteem in which our talented group was held. They thought Hughes might be willing to sell Hughes Aircraft Company and were prepared to pay handsomely for it. Several large corporations (Westinghouse, Lockheed, Convair, Thompson Products, and others) and a number of investment banking firms put together proposals and endeavored to lay them before Howard Hughes. The principals of such prospective purchasers always made contact with Wooldridge and me first, because they were not interested in the company unless the technical team went with the purchase. They eagerly mentioned their desire to include us personally (and extremely generously) in their financial plans. We were kept up-to-date, then, on who was trying to buy the company, and learned some Wall Street fundamentals as well.

One other issue was even more important than the possible sale of the company, or the name calling and accusations by the administrative staffs of the Hughes Aircraft Company and the Hughes Tool Company, or Howard Hughes's problems with his other investments. This was the growing concern of the United States government. As publicity grew about Hughes's personal performances at TWA and RKO, Defense Department leaders stepped up the frequency and vehemence with which they expressed to us their alarm that so large a fraction of their most urgent military-technology projects were in the hands of a company owned by Howard Hughes.

One high government official who thought very poorly of Howard Hughes was K. T. Keller. In 1950 President Truman appointed Keller, then chairman of Chrysler Corporation, to be his special assistant for guided-missile programs. Because of the broad powers given him to control fund allocations for missile R&D and production, Keller had to be catered to by both the Department of Defense and the industry. Without his approval, a project was doomed, and he quickly earned the reputation of being extremely tough. We were suddenly informed one day that in a week Keller would pay his first visit to Hughes Aircraft Company to see where we stood on the very important Falcon air-to-air missile being developed to intercept Soviet bombers. We were also told that he had expressed strong criticism of the Air Force for assigning so vital a project to an entity owned by Howard Hughes.

We naturally were nervous as we awaited his arrival. It happened that we were just then preparing for the first realistic demonstrations of the complete missile system. The Falcon had been partially tested in many ways, but in this full-scale test the missile would be launched from an airplane instrumented like a real interceptor and would be directed at a target plane similar to an enemy bomber. The interceptor plane's radar would lock on and illuminate the target airplane. On-board computers and control equipment would be employed to direct the pilot of the interceptor to so control his plane as to send the missile off in the right direction at the right time. Launched from a few miles away, the Falcon, if all went well, would close in on the target bomber. This plane, a "drone," was an old vehicle newly equipped to take off, fly a useful course, and land, all by remote control, with no human pilot aboard.

In these first tests we expected that, at best, the missile would merely pass close to the bomber. The missile carried proximity-measuring devices, as did the target bomber, and the instantaneous miss-distance readings would be radioed to the ground, so we would know precisely how close the missile came to a hit. Of course, if everything worked extremely well, the missile might even collide with the bomber. Operational missiles would carry warheads to explode at the optimum moment, hit or miss, but in these first tests a dummy warhead was used.

We knew that K. T. Keller would take with a grain of salt our recitals of partial tests and analytical work proving that the system should work. The program would be under threat of cancellation until we showed him "kills" in actual flight tests. I decided we should take a big gamble and speed up the test program. A few hundred miles away in the desert, two drones and a launching plane carrying two missiles were in the sky as I was starting the presentation to K. T. Keller. While I was enumerating in chronological order the testing so far accomplished, the interceptor moved into position against one drone and then released the first of its two Falcons.

The launched Falcon homed, as it was supposed to, on the radar echoes emanating from the drone. But it did not miss the target! The guidance accuracy at four miles proved to be so excellent that the Falcon penetrated the target airplane, damaging enough critical control equipment that the drone crashed and was destroyed. Within moments, a news bulletin was handed to me at the presentation podium. On reading its succinct but dramatic message, "One bird launched one drone destroyed," I speeded up the presentation and reported the successful hit. As I was doing that, the second Falcon was launched against the second drone. It also was penetrated and brought down. (Afterward, the Air Force asked me whether it might not have been more sensible to call a halt after the first hit and consider some revision of the testing so as not to lose both drones, but I found it difficult to criticize the flight-test director.)

Keller was ecstatic about our missile program's progress. He invited Wooldridge and me to have dinner with him that evening in his hotel suite. We thought it was so he could pat us on the back some more. What he had in mind, however, was to tell us of his deep concern that the Falcon missile program was being worked on in a Hughes company. He said it was a miracle that we had managed so well despite the eccentric Howard Hughes and he doubted that we could be successful much longer. I don't remember exactly how we responded, but I do recall that he worried us more than we reassured him.

K. T. Keller and other high government officials faced a dilemma. They could deliberately set out to rein in Hughes Aircraft by placing new contracts elsewhere. This would strengthen the competition and cut the risk that the ignorance and capriciousness of the company's owner might suddenly result in critical harm to national security. Yet they knew such an action would destroy Hughes Aircraft. Its best people would leave, and failure to perform would result. The government leaders themselves would have precipitated the disaster they were so anxious to prevent.

This led the Department of Defense repeatedly to hint that it would be well if a few of the key people were to establish another company to create the competition that was needed—provided the departures did not get out of hand. Another alternative the DoD favored was for the company to be bought by some acceptable entity. If some stable, well-led organization were to purchase Hughes Aircraft Company, that would be satisfactory to Wooldridge and me. Unfortunately, to accomplish such a sale, someone would have to negotiate with Howard Hughes. But, in view of his unavailability and his indecisiveness, the sale might take years. Many had tried to talk with him about a purchase and had been solidly turned off by the way they were treated.

One prominent Wall Street investment firm's chief executive officer, Ben Pepper of Pennroad Corporation, sat in his room at the Beverly Hills Hotel in early 1953, waiting for four days for the return call he was told daily to expect from Hughes. When he was on the point of leaving town in disgust, he received a telephone message that he would be picked up in thirty minutes at a designated street corner a few miles away. He took a cab to the spot. One of Hughes's Chevrolets arrived and took him back to a cottage at the very same Beverly Hills Hotel. From there Howard Hughes himself emerged to take over the wheel. The visitor, hardly believing his eyes, assumed that at last—as he thought he had been promised, although he had never spoken directly to Hughes—he was about to confer with the billionaire. Instead, Hughes, with only a nod in place of a handshake and without a single word, drove to a nearby residence, and after first donning a yachting cap he produced from a rumpled brown paper bag he was carrying, he went to the door and fetched a "blond starlet" (to use the financier's words). The three then drove to a boat harbor in further silence. Here a Hughes Tool executive awaited their arrival. While Hughes and his date walked off toward the moored yachts, the Tool Company executive announced to the New Yorker that he was there to hold a "short courtesy meeting" with him and that Hughes would not be returning.

I will delay no longer in relating the most important part of my deliberations as to what I should do next about Hughes Aircraft. It was imperative, I decided, that I see Howard Hughes personally, and not depend entirely on others. So I began to work toward generating an opportunity to talk with him.

My impressions of Howard Hughes will be described in two steps. First, I will summarize what I had been told about him by others. What did those who knew Howard Hughes best say about him? The pilots said he was an incompetent aviator. The accountants said he did not understand even elementary accounting. The lawyers said that he steadily pressed stupid suggestions on them about how to handle his legal affairs. One Hughes Tool executive, whose seniority made it reasonable to believe he had dealt with Hughes often, warned me never to try to explain anything to his boss. "Howard is interested only in girls and airplanes—in that order," he cautioned.

The pilots who had flown with Hughes attributed his inadequacies as an aviator to laziness and indifference, which kept him from doing the necessary homework. As they described it, Hughes would exploit his unique status to bully others into allowing him to try out planes against the regulations, which required that a pilot must receive detailed instructions before taking the controls of an airplane new to him. When he was almost killed in a crash landing (in which the plane's wings were sheared off as he flew between two houses in Beverly Hills while trying to reach the fairway of the Los Angeles Country Club), the company pilot engaged to do the flying of that experimental plane remarked that what had happened was not surprising, considering Hughes's lack of familiarity with the plane. Typically, pilots who had co-piloted aircraft with Howard Hughes at the controls would say freely that they always lacked confidence and sometimes were scared to death.

The accountants reported mainly on the need they continually experienced to revise the way in which data were presented following queries from Howard Hughes. None of the accounting professionals I met had ever sat down and discussed things directly with Hughes. His handwritten notes in the margins of their data sheets were their sole means of evaluating his comprehension of accounting. One favorite comment (I assumed an exaggeration) from the accountants was that he found it terribly hard to accept that he could have a liability, a difficulty that peaked at income-tax time. Because he automatically rejected the idea of paying a tax bill, he would disbelieve their figures stating how much he owed.

While the accountants described a man whose reasoning was akin to superstition, the lawyers considered it virtually impossible to serve him professionally. Their frustrations had many dimensions. This is well illustrated by an example in which I had a tangential involvement. Hughes was very anxious that the Hughes Tool Company not declare dividends, because if he received any, he would be liable for a high-bracket personal income tax. If a corporation with a single owner elects not to pay dividends, however, the government has the right to step in and force tax payments. Howard Hughes would regularly issue orders to his attorneys to preclude such government actions. When they could not do so, because no basis in law existed for his not paying taxes, he would badger them with ludicrous notions of his own. They would respond with detailed written explanations of why his ideas were unworkable or illegal, whereupon he would change attorneys. Often, those dismissed would have difficulty receiving payment for their services. Of course, there were plenty of other attorneys who had not yet dealt with Hughes who were eager to capture this world-famous ultra-wealthy eccentric as a client.

One attorney contacted me because he was working on a concept on which he assumed I would be helpful. The government's rules permit temporary dividend deferral if there are demonstrably clear and pressing needs for a single-owner corporation to use its available cash in the business. The attorney had the idea that since Mr. Hughes was buying land in Nevada it might be claimed that the land had to be purchased so that the company could do mandatory guided-missile flight testing on it to fulfill government R&D contracts. The attorney told me he had tried this idea out on Mr. Hughes, who responded enthusiastically. The reason for dragging me in was not to ask if the land (some of which was right in or close to Las Vegas) was truly required for guided-missile testing. Instead, it was to obtain my help in preparing the petition by providing backup rationale for the claim.

I explained that only the DoD, never a private entity, operated guided-missile testing ranges. These were tremendously expensive facilities, huge in committed acreage and equipped with numerous observation, communications, launching, and measurement installations, airfields, flight towers and hangars, airplane and equipment maintenance facilities, housing for the operating staff, and various large-scale systems to maintain secrecy and control security and access. These flight test centers always were remote from population concentrations, to minimize the risk of missiles going out of control during a test and endangering civilian lives or damaging private property. Under no circumstances would flight tests of the military's guided missiles be permitted on private land, especially in the vicinity of Las Vegas.

The attorney was very disappointed to hear this. He said he could not relay these facts to Hughes, who would not accept them and would insist that the attorney concoct a way to make the idea work. The lawyer suggested that I should conduct a few guided-missile experiments on Hughes's land that might appear to the Internal Revenue Service as necessary, even if they were really meaningless. My refusal to comply probably caused that attorney to lose his client.

Hughes's special position in life may have allowed him to circumvent rules when it came to piloting airplanes. Unfortunately, that same disdain showed up elsewhere. Clearance for access to secret information, for example, was necessary for Hughes to participate in decision-making. This required that he be fingerprinted. But Hughes would never allow that. He was not interested in putting himself out a tiny bit to gain understanding of projects in his own company.

Let me now relate my direct personal contacts with Howard Hughes. The first was an accidental encounter in early 1947, after I had been at Hughes Aircraft Company for less than a year. I saw him leaving the office of an attorney, Howard Hall, as I was walking toward that office. The tall, slim figure with the mustache was instantly identifiable from his photographs. He looked more gaunt, but then those photos I had seen were old ones. His face was small for his stature, something I had not expected from his pictures. He had on a plain blue shirt open at the neck and a pair of thin, light beige flannel pants. His trousers were too short. The sun's rays filtering through the window at the end of the hall hit his cuffs, so I could see that the pants had been lengthened; the horizontal creases left from the previous cuffs were visible. Still, he did not look sloppy, and he was not wearing the tennis shoes that rumor had it he wore all the time. He glanced at me as we passed and I nodded and smiled. His expression indicated that he was wondering if I was somebody he should recognize but didn't.

I went in to discuss with Hall a contract for a project we were about to take on. I had been there about five minutes when I heard the door open behind me. Hall rose with sudden, clumsy speed and his face broke out in a stiff forced smile, so I had to turn around to find out what had brought on this behavior. Seeing Hughes, I also stood up hurriedly, almost knocking over my chair. Hall introduced me with the words, "This is Dr. Ramo, Si Ramo. He's the one who designs your guided missiles, Howard." The attorney had raised his voice to a high level, confirming that Mr. Hughes was hard of hearing.

Hughes turned to me, somewhat reluctantly, I thought, and we shook hands. I immediately asked Hall if he would please give me a call later and started to walk out. Hughes raised one hand a bit, however, and before he said anything, the attorney indicated I should wait.

I looked at Hughes and he looked at me, the three of us still standing, and it seemed that Hughes was trying to find words. Eventually a question came forth: "How can a missile know which way is up? If there's no pilot to see the ground—how does the missile fly right?"

Mr. Hughes watched me with a grim expression. I was anxious to talk with Howard Hughes about guided missiles. But his question took me by surprise and I did not know where to start. Surely, as a pilot, he had flown on instruments in many a black night or storm when he could not see the ground. Gyroscopes are used in missiles (as in airplanes) to maintain spatial orientation. I brought up gyros. I also made clear that the guided missile is fired from an airplane instrumented to maintain stable directional references. Upon launch, the missile is given an initial, correct direction and it then proceeds to home in on radar echoes from the target plane. The missile, as it flies, has very little need in its computer brain to "know" where the earth is, but every reason to keep its "eye" on the target airplane. In principle, the target could head for the ground or soar vertically and the missile would follow, gain on it, and intercept it. I tossed off four or five sentences about these facts, but I could see as I spoke that they were contributing little to his understanding. I was annoyed with myself for not doing a better job somehow.

He obviously was wondering how the missile took gravity into account and I was slow to realize that he thought of the target as an object not susceptible to a downward gravity force because the aerodynamic forces on its wings and body were holding it up. He thought of the missile, in contrast, as being dropped like a bomb. It would need to "know" where earth's pull was coming from or it would fall to earth, despite its being driven by a rocket engine. After another question, I realized that, like many other laymen, he thought of a rocket engine as discharging high-speed gas which, when it exits from the nozzle at the rear, pushes against the air behind the rocket and thus generates forward thrust. He wondered how the rocket could produce appreciable thrust at high altitudes where the air is so thin. I told him right away that the missile obtains its force forward as a result of ejecting gas (produced in the rocket by the fuel's burning) backward, in line with one of Newton's laws of motion that says "for every action there is an equal and opposite reaction." Shooting gas out the back would propel the missile forward even in a vacuum. This was high-school physics.

For days after that meeting, I mulled over the conversation*— what Howard Hughes had asked and what I had said in reply. Why had I handled my end of the discussion so poorly? On dozens of occasions I had had to explain to laymen how an air-launched guided missile can lock onto and hit an airborne target. Secretaries and under-secretaries in the Defense Department usually were lawyers or ex-business executives with no scientific training, and few congressmen possessed any. I had quickly found ways to describe the basics simply and adequately for their purposes. Why had I been so inept with Hughes?

Finally, I decided what the problem was. It was my preconceived, incorrect notion of Howard Hughes. Despite the derogatory comments I had heard about his ability as a pilot and his amateurish tinkering with engineering ideas, I foolishly had thought of him as an engineer—not a formally educated one, to be sure, but a man who had lived with flight apparatus and flown airplanes and so possessed a good sense of three-dimensional geometry, instrument action, and the like. I was too slow to appreciate from his questions how little he understood of the fundamentals involved.

The experience netted me one valuable reading on Howard Hughes. I had no firsthand knowledge of whether he really was a

---

* I did extensive "mulling over" after every conversation with Howard Hughes, so our words became embedded in my memory almost enough to justify using direct quotes, as I do for the sake of clarity.

bad pilot, as the pilots reported; did not understand accounting, as the accountants claimed; and was a simpleminded legal client, as the lawyers said. But I did know now that his comprehension of science and engineering was minimal.

The next time I found myself with Howard Hughes, the meeting was longer. The topic was administrative, not technical. It was even more of an eye-opener.

We had heard one morning in 1949 through the corporate grapevine that certain additional laboratory and office buildings already scheduled to be built would not receive approval unless they were erected in Las Vegas. This, we were told, was an irrevocable order from Howard Hughes himself. At first, we did not believe it. Periodically, we would hear that Mr. Hughes absolutely wanted this or that, usually something silly or impossible, and we discovered that if we ignored the edict nothing would happen. There was, for example, the scholarship incident.

We had inaugurated a program of scholarships at leading universities to sponsor outstanding students working toward Ph.D. degrees in fields critical to our long-term success, fields in which there were not enough graduates. We did not require that the scholarship recipients join Hughes Aircraft after graduation. Almost all accepted our offers, however, as we had hoped; and the reputation of our organization was enhanced by the scholarship program. The expenditures for the scholarships were fully reimbursable as overhead expenses on the government contracts, so they were not philanthropic contributions from Mr. Hughes; they cost him nothing. Still, one day the word came down that we must terminate the scholarship program, because "Mr. Hughes did not believe in that kind of philanthropy." (He appeared not to believe in any kind of philanthropy, no one around being able to cite any donation from Howard Hughes to the numerous educational, social, cultural, medical, and other causes in Southern California or elsewhere.) Next, we heard that the scholarships would be abolished unless we made certain the scholarship winners were "loyal Americans." The procedure was to give the funds directly to the universities, who chose the recipients, and anyway, we did not know how to conduct "Americanism" searches.

Wooldridge and I decided to ignore the directive, which we weren't sure was authentic, in any case. We felt on safe ground because we were not giving away Mr. Hughes's money.

But this new order, to locate future buildings in Las Vegas, was infinitely more serious. We had just won a competition for a major new project and the contract spelled out exactly what we were to do, including building certain additional facilities. The contract plan was that key experts would divide their time between existing programs and the new one. Most of the new construction would merely enlarge existing laboratories. Slowed communication would result if some of the staff were moved; even if certain laboratories were duplicated, schedule slippage and increased costs would be certain. We polled our key professionals and found that they regarded it as laughable to imagine that they would pick up their families and move to Las Vegas. The new work was not even remotely a project for which we could recruit from scratch an entire separate staff to work in Nevada.

This silly situation turned into a crisis very quickly, because if we could not proceed, the government would have to be informed. We knew we must seek a face-to-face meeting with Howard Hughes. We had often heard there was a specific procedure to follow to reach him. A few nondescript offices in a modest building in the heart of the Los Angeles motion-picture district, Old Hollywood, housed an equally modest office staff for a company called Hughes Productions. In addition to secretaries at that office, Hughes maintained a group of young men around his hotel lodgings to chauffeur him about, buy his socks, secure the guards to station around his rooms, and track down people he wanted to reach. These aides were in constant communication with the Hollywood office. It was understood that the only way to arrange a conversation with Howard Hughes was to leave a message at that office. This method presumably was used by the executives of Hughes Tool, TWA, and RKO. So we left messages. There was no word back.

We had no problem in letting General Eaker know the seriousness of the Las Vegas building directive. Unless we obtained immediate approval to go ahead as we were obliged to do, we would have to report to the U.S. Air Force not only that we had to turn down the job but also why. This would confirm the Defense Department's suspicions that they could not depend on a Howard Hughes organization. Unfortunately, General Eaker also was ignored when he tried to get a message through.

Nervous days quickly became weeks. Finally, when we felt we had reached the absolute deadline beyond which default on the contract was certain, we went to the Air Force and told them sadly that it appeared we would have to turn back the contract. Naturally, Wooldridge and I were aware that, having done this, we might be fired. If that happened, many others would resign. It was suddenly conceivable that this gem of a company might collapse—which would be penalizing to the nation as well as to Howard Hughes.

We could not assume that word would reach Hughes. We did tell General Eaker, however, and he promptly left a new message. That got us our meeting with Mr. Hughes.

It was held in a two-room cottage, a part of the Beverly Hills Hotel complex, which turned out to be his residence at that time. We were there for about an hour. I was determined not to make the mistake a second time of assuming a higher capacity for comprehension than Hughes actually had. Wooldridge and I took turns describing what was bothering us, but I had to do most of the talking, simply because I was capable of producing a higher level of acoustic power than Wooldridge. Naturally soft-spoken, Dean had to strain to speak loudly, and the effort made his face tight and gave him a look that could be misinterpreted as anger.

Howard Hughes told us in halting mumbles that he owned a great deal of property in Las Vegas and hoped to acquire more. We tried to explain why we could not split our group and still meet our contractual commitments, because of the subsequent communications delay, the interdependence of the experts, and the impossibility of separating the new work. We said that our people would not move to Las Vegas, that they regarded Las Vegas as an isolated, uncultured gambling resort and not a place where they would want to rear their children. He did a good deal of silent nodding. He looked more mystified than annoyed.

From some of his widely spaced remarks, I gathered he found it difficult to understand why we would pay any attention at all to the wishes of mere employees. Perhaps Mr. Hughes customarily employed obsequious individuals, sycophants or lackeys anxious to hold on to their jobs and ready to do anything he commanded. It seemed strange to him to "build an organization around the idea of democracy" (his exact words).

We explained that close communication was vital to our technical teams of specialists, so that the resulting weapons system would constitute a highly coordinated, compatible configuration of the many diverse pieces of equipment. He asked why we could not use radio facsimile to do our coordinating. We replied by describing the engineering challenge we would face in creating a communications system that would send words, numbers, and diagrams between people by radio while simultaneously meeting secrecy requirements. We pointed out that the Federal Communications Commission could hardly be expected to push everyone else aside and assign us an exclusive wide-band radio channel for coded messages. We commented on the limits of transferring information by facsimile through the telephone system. He suggested we should develop some entirely new communications system that would bypass all such limitations. We replied that perhaps we could, but it would be a long and speculative project, and the government would neither pay nor wait for it.

After about an hour, Wooldridge and I decided it was time to say unequivocally that, if we did not secure immediate approval, the consequences would include the important contract's being returned to the Air Force, probably a first in U.S. military procurement history. The government, having to turn to others, would blame him for the loss of time on a vital project. We expressed the certainty that many of our people would leave to go to other organizations. It would become, I remember calling it, an unprecedented national-security scandal.

We had to bring the meeting to a close, yet it was not clear that he realized why a decision had to be made immediately. His wandering comments often had no direct relevance to the meeting. So I took the risk of putting words in his mouth. I said we assumed that since he now understood the problem, he was agreeable to our going ahead with the buildings as originally planned and as described in our signed government contract. I repeated this, saying it three or four different ways. Since he did not dispute it, I thought we should take that to mean he was accepting our position. When we left we knew, whether Hughes did or not, that we would break ground on the buildings—unless somebody stopped us. No one did.

That meeting spelled out for me that I could never again allow myself to be in so dangerous and nerve-racking a situation. I would have been out of my mind to imagine that by some brilliant stroke we could recast Howard Hughes as a sensible executive. Yet I had a tiny glimmer of hope that we might somehow devise a way to live with the handicap of his ownership. Here we were, after all, building the new buildings, not in Las Vegas, as he had wanted, but in Culver City, as we had insisted. We must not stop with this first step. So I set out to try to meet with Hughes to discuss general management and long-range strategy. I repeatedly left messages at the Hollywood communications center. Months passed with no response.

Wooldridge and I then sent him a memorandum stating that we could not go on working for him if we were not able to confer with him when necessary. We were ignored. So a month later we sent him a joint letter of resignation, naming an effective date two months hence. This brought a response. Hughes, Wooldridge, and I met at the Desert Inn in Las Vegas, where he had recently moved.

When I remarked on the many policemen standing around, the young man who came to escort us to the meeting said Hughes was renting half the floor, from the central elevators to the building's end, keeping empty the rooms on both sides of the hall and a similar half of the rooms on the floors immediately above and below. Police were posted throughout the three stories and the stairways. We were led into our meeting place, one of the regular twin-bedded hotel rooms along the hall, from an adjoining room. I noted that Hughes, concerned that our loud talk might be overheard in the hallways, had stuffed towels all around the door to the hall; he requested that we sit facing away from that door.

His face had the unhealthy color of fireplace ashes. (During the meeting he remarked at one point that he no longer went out in the daytime.) The twin beds of this meeting room were covered with piles of envelopes and folders. This was his office, the tops of the beds his filing cabinets. The door into the adjoining room, the last one along the hall, was ajar and I caught sight of an unmade bed and a milk carton on the floor beside it. Here was this strange billionaire's two-room home—an impersonally furnished pair of hotel rooms, one his workplace, the other his bedroom. In this, his castle, the halls and rooms all about him vacant and guarded, he was about to be assailed by two visitors from another world. I suddenly felt very sorry for him. I wanted to phrase everything I had to say carefully, to avoid the slightest harshness.

Dean and I had prepared well. First we explained why we thought it necessary, in the national interest, to leave his employ. Then we made clear what would have to change if we were to stay. Our proposal contained nothing Dean Wooldridge and I judged startlingly creative, but we knew it might appear revolutionary to Hughes. We suggested that our operation be separated from Hughes Tool and made into a new corporation. We put heavy emphasis on his delegating authority in the new corporation to an outside board of directors. We asserted that in view of the respect our operation enjoyed from all pertinent communities—from the science and engineering fraternity of the nation to the leaderships of industry, Wall Street, and the government—it would be possible to attract high-grade board members. The board would have the responsibility of appointing appropriate corporate management and setting goals and strategy. It would be empowered to make commitments and invest available capital. Hughes would not be a member of the board. (As the owner of the shares, he could always call a shareholders meeting and dismiss the board.) We went on to say that the corporation's health and growth would require reinvesting earnings to start civilian commercial activities capitalizing on the high technology we were developing for the nation's security.

Instead of a list of complaints, we offered a positive presentation. He would only have to agree to an intelligently organized and managed company that would deserve a high rating from the government or anyone else. We were aware that our proposal required his thinking of himself as nothing more than the principal owner of the shares, with no function in the company other than to reap two benefits of ownership, pride and high returns on his investment. We knew that our proposal was demeaning. Nevertheless, we felt it was the proper recommendation for us to make.

We got the chance to say our piece without interruption. Again, I was not sure from watching his facial expressions whether he heard all of Wooldridge's words, but we indulged in enough redundancy so that if Howard Hughes heard most of what I said and half of what Wooldridge said, he could not have missed what we came to tell him. We took great pains to be courteous and sensitive, granted the unavoidable arrogance inherent in our telling him what he would have to do for us to stay. He showed no irritation at any point.

When we finished, I asked, "What is your reaction to our proposal?" From our previous experience, I expected it to be a long time before he said anything and I did not want to sit there wondering if he thought we were finished.

Laboring to find words, Hughes said he could not consider a plan in which there would be "public" directors. That had not worked out for him in the past, he said, and he did not want to be subjected again to public humiliation. I assumed he was thinking of RKO and TWA.

I immediately pointed out that his past experiences could not be compared with the problem he now faced. I was surprised by his immediate rejoinder: "What do you mean?" This was not said in anger. He seemed quite simply not to know what I meant. I explained that the company had become a highly important national resource. Since he cared about the country, shouldn't he consider approaches that he might not necessarily choose for ordinary companies he might own?

He responded by going on at length about his personal difficulties. What Wooldridge and I were doing exemplified his true goals in life, he said. Losing us would be terrible because no other involvements had come close to bringing him the satisfactions our accomplishments had. He realized, he stated quietly, that he didn't know how to deal with people and was regarded as an eccentric. All these confessions of his personal shortcomings threatened to become the focus of our meeting. Wooldridge made several efforts to bring the discussion back to our proposal, while I simply looked at Howard Hughes sitting there so forlorn.

We had to find a way to bring the meeting to an end, so we repeated that Hughes should not make the mistake of assuming we were less than a hundred percent serious about leaving. From everything he had said, we had no choice but to conclude, we said, that he was not interested in our proposal to set up the operation as an independent corporation with a prestigious board of directors to whom he would relegate authority. We thanked him for meeting with us and rose to leave. I was concerned that he had not fully heard our parting remarks, because he looked surprised when we stood up. But we left.

I was amazed to receive a call from Howard at my home the next evening. (It was early evening, not the middle of the night, when Hughes was reputed to make his calls.) He asked me to return to Las Vegas alone to see him. He said I was sympathetic to his unusual personal situation and he did not think Dean Wooldridge was. He thought that perhaps the two of us could work out a way in which Wooldridge and I could continue with the organization as we desired. He said he had not yet conveyed to us the intensity of his desire to keep us. He desperately feared that Hughes Aircraft would fall apart if we left.

Dean and I wanted to be sure no one could ever say we had behaved irresponsibly. So we concluded that I should return to Las Vegas alone, as requested. In this next meeting, he would be the one to make a proposal. I had only to listen, making no commitments. When I returned, Dean and I would consider what Hughes had to say.

The meeting turned out to be the first of two, which helped Wooldridge and me feel that we had proceeded properly. And they enabled me to acquire a firsthand understanding of Howard Hughes, which I had believed essential. But they did not lead to our remaining with him.

The first meeting dealt with two topics, both brought up by Howard. He had bought a new shirt and trousers for the occasion. The precise creases on the shirt showed it had not yet been laundered; the cheap tan cotton slacks, worn without a belt, showed evidence that a label had just been removed from the waistband. The pants undoubtedly had been bought for him by his errand boys and he had not made himself available for a proper fitting. To get an adequate trouser length, they had purchased a large size that was overly expansive at the waist, and the waist had been taken in so much at the back that the two front trouser crease lines did not center over his shoes but angled widely off to each side when he stood up.

He first discussed what would happen to Hughes Aircraft Company if Wooldridge and I did indeed start a new company. All our associates, he predicted, would leave with us, so Hughes Aircraft would have to close down. It was worth a great deal of money now. He could easily sell it if we stayed, he said, and he would reap an enormous profit.

I was sure his assessment was correct. On the basis of the accumulative inflation over the thirty-five years since then—specifically, in costs of producing weapons systems—our earnings of $10 to $20 million in 1953 would represent $100 to $200 million in 1988 currency. In view of the company's growth and the potential for further growth into commercial fields stemming from the powerhouse of talent we had assembled, the stock market in 1953 would have put a high multiple on the company's earnings. The price for the company, if it had been sold then, would have been two or three billion of today's dollars.

Hughes Aircraft, he said, would come to be worth nothing if we left, and therefore he was prepared to make it worth our while to stay. Ever since he was eighteen years old, he had known that everyone has a price. He was careful to point out that he did not mean a price to do something wrong, unethical—"indecent," was how he put it. But to stay and run the operation in the national interest. He wanted me to name in dollars what it would take for us to stay.

Wooldridge and I had anticipated such an offer and I knew what to reply. (So it will not appear that the two of us considered ourselves above temptation, it should first be noted that we understood full well that our circumstances did not allow us the privilege of being paid to stay.) I explained that if Wooldridge and I were "bought" by him, without any of the changes we proposed, we would be letting down our military customer and our associates. We would destroy our reputation and with it the company. In no way would our getting rich solve the fundamental problem. This time I had to emphasize that he was that problem.

If he would simply act on the organizational ideas that Wooldridge and I had already proposed, I said, the company would not fall apart after our departure, as he feared. I assured him that our concern and that of the government for national security would keep us from accepting as employees in our new firm more than a small fraction from Hughes Aircraft, which might preclude its being able to continue competently in defense work. The company, I said, had outstanding technical specialists and executives. There was bound to be some movement of top talent from Hughes Aircraft to competing companies that would make offers too tempting to be refused. But a very strong organization could be preserved. The government, having come to rely on it for essential technology, would grant it substantial new contracts in the future, if he took the steps we outlined. These, I repeated, were to: (1) create a separate corporation, thus eliminating the feuding at the administrative level; (2) install a strong board of outside directors; (3) rely on that board to select top management; (4) be personally content with silent ownership. If he could just bring himself to do these things, I assured him, then this national asset would be preserved and he could hold his head high.

Hughes quickly shifted to his second topic. He said he had been afraid he was going to get a negative response to his offer of money, even big money. Wooldridge and I, he commented, were "overly independent types—no justification for it—idealists." If we were determined to start our own company, then we would need backing, he remarked, launching his next proposal.

"You will have to raise money—tens of millions—to do what you will want to do, and the government will want you to do. You can get it, of course. All those who've tried to buy the company from me—any of them would certainly finance you. But you're worth more to me than to them. I'll be your financial backer. I'll give you a better deal. Then I won't be publicly embarrassed by your leaving."

This we had not expected. I did not want to say anything to him that would be rude in its frankness, but to consider his proposal seriously would be crazy. Here we were, ready to solve the government-relations problem by setting up an independent source of military-weapons R&D. It would not merely vitiate the solution if we allowed Hughes to get in the act; it would make things worse. Howard Hughes involved in the existing company and in the new one, too?

I took the easy way out. We had been talking for almost two hours. I suggested that I think about our conversation and come back. When he seemed delighted, I was concerned that I had given him false hopes, when in truth our relationship was over.

Nonetheless, I returned to Las Vegas a week later. Wooldridge and I had decided meanwhile that we should tell a very few people inside and outside the company that we were leaving. Getting out was going to be a touchy business. We had to ensure that Hughes Aircraft would continue to be strong and that the Defense Department would respect us for the way we handled our departure. Until we actually left, we were still responsible for managing the organization and we needed to do it competently. I would not be going aimlessly to Las Vegas. My next meeting with Hughes would be the last. I did not see how it could be a pleasant one.

This time, his air-conditioned hotel room was icy cold and I shivered visibly a moment after sitting down. Howard said, "You're cold," and he stepped over and slid open the closet door. There I saw hanging one baggy pair of khaki trousers, three freshly laundered shirts on wire hangers, a zippered tan cotton windbreaker, and a dilapidated, fuzzy brown wool sweater. He reached for the sweater and draped it over my shoulders.

As I feared, he looked to me to start the discussion. Hesitantly, I said something like, "I regret to have to tell you again, Howard, that the Department of Defense doesn't see you as appropriate for a major ownership position in a really important defense company."

He replied at an even slower pace than in previous meetings. It saddened him to hear that, he said, but he appreciated my frankness. He went on intermittently, haltingly, adding more personal information about what he called his missed life. He said, for instance, that he was terribly disturbed, and when disturbed, he could not eat. He said the only food he had had for several days was milk. He looked thinner, his face even more drawn and pale than usual. He told me that, contrary to what most people thought, he was really like others and he worried about what other people thought of him. I needed to be more patient with him, he said, to get to understand him. He was ten years older than I was, but I found myself thinking of him as still only eighteen, the age when he was orphaned.

We were making no progress, and I was increasingly uncomfortable. Fortunately, he said he wanted to think about it all some more and would call me. He did telephone every few days to invite me back to Las Vegas. Each time, I told him firmly that it made no sense for me to make the trip again.

Wooldridge and I submitted formal letters of resignation and on Friday, September 11, 1953, we left the Hughes payroll. But I found I was not yet finished with Howard Hughes. He reached me at the office the morning of that Friday and said he was coming into Los Angeles to meet with me the next day, since he now realized that I would not go to Las Vegas.

In 1953, there still remained on a prized portion of the ocean-front in Santa Monica the elegant beach house built for actress Marion Davies by William Randolph Hearst. It had stood vacant for years, until a new owner named it the Ocean House and made it available for rentals. It was eventually torn down. I had once attended a charity function at the Ocean House. It was more a mansion than a cottage on the beach, with a heavy-looking exterior and a huge formal swimming pool of black marble. The high-ceilinged rooms were beautifully finished. There were many expensive chandeliers. Anyone walking about in swimming trunks would have looked out of place.

I was picked up at my home on that Saturday morning by the customary Hughes messenger-driver in the customary Chevrolet. When we entered the beach house, no furniture was to be seen, just fragments of newspapers and packing cartons scattered about on the terrazzo floor. Dust was everywhere, the windows very dirty, and the chandeliers gone. Telephone equipment was being installed feverishly by three telephone men, who were being watched over by two policemen and two messenger-drivers, whom I recognized from Las Vegas. We went up the stairs to the top floor, where I was ushered into Howard's presence.

He was standing in a large corner room, its two inside walls mirrored, the two outside ones of glass, and the floor carpeted wall-to-wall with fluffy, thick white wool. Probably this had been the actress's bedroom. I guessed it was the only room in the house in use that morning, and the only furniture in it was a single folding cot. That army canvas bed with its little ecru pillow and gray-brown blanket, and no sheets, made me think of a movie scene of a berth in a prison. Beside the cot, on the floor, were two quart-size milk cartons, one of them open.

Two folding chairs were brought in by the young man who had driven me to the beach. Hughes placed them alongside each other, so that we would both face an inside mirrored wall. (Howard obviously feared our being overheard by someone down on the beach.)

It was a comical side-by-side position, Howard looking despondent, his elbows on his knees and his chin in his hands. I sat as he did, except that, instead of looking at the floor, I stared into the mirror at the two of us, wondering which looked more ridiculous. I was no longer working for him; the Howard Hughes chapter in my life was finished. Wooldridge and I had already talked with our Wall Street law firm by phone. We were flying to New York on Monday, we would spend Tuesday with the attorneys, and on Wednesday the Ramo–Wooldridge Corporation would come into existence. Whatever happened here was not going to change that. Yet here I was, seated alongside the legendary Howard Hughes, gazing into a mirror in the empty bedroom used by Hearst's mistress, pondering how to preserve an organization critical to the nation's security.

In his telephone call to set up the meeting, Howard Hughes acknowledged that he had lost us. But he had a new idea, he said, one so well suited to our requirement for absolute independence that he had to discuss it with me. He said he hoped I would feel enough sympathy for him that I would give him Saturday if he came to Los Angeles. He said, "Believe me, you will not regret it, Si."

First he told me that he had had a line of thought which he had rejected but still wanted to tell me about. Recently, he said, he had had nothing but humiliations. He was not sure how he would survive our leaving him, and he had been thinking that, if he wanted to, he could stop us. "Suppose you get your financing from any one of those outfits that wanted to buy Hughes Aircraft from me. Now, I've been studying those companies," he said, still looking at the floor while I looked in the mirror at him looking at the floor. "I could start buying the shares on the market of any company that backs you. If I used everything I have, I figure I could get control of any one of them. So, Si, if I did that, you would end up still working for me."

I turned to him, suppressing a smile. He turned to me and took his chin out of his hands. To my amazement, he suddenly dropped his sad expression and grinned.

"But then I thought about it a little more," he added with an actual chuckle, "and I figured you'd leave me a second time and I'd own control of still another public company that I would have trouble with."

This time, it was I who laughed. Howard was not close to committing suicide after all. He might even be rated a good actor. Now, feeling very relaxed, I said, "That's not the way we're going to go about financing our new company, Howard. The way we're going to do it, you won't be able to get control of our company without dealing with us. You really ought to forget it."

He nodded and after a moment resumed his pitiable, chin-in-hands posture. Then he brought up his new idea. It had always been his plan, he said, to donate all his wealth to medical research when he died. For that purpose, his will would set up the Howard Hughes Medical Research Institute. In his will he would name me as "a principal trustee" of the institute.

While I knew that my reaction to this proposal was not going to hinge on it, my ego caused me to note that he had slowed down as he uttered this title and that he had not said "*the* trustee" or "*the principal* trustee," but rather "*a* principal trustee."

"Think of the good you could do with that money. So, here is my proposition. Together we will make two announcements: that I am backing your new company, and the plan for the institute and your future role in it. Then you will not really be leaving me. You can be independent and an idealist. I'll be only a capital source for your company. I don't need to own any of your stock. I can just make you a long-term loan. Just so you haven't left me. Then, some years from now, maybe not too many, you can put my fortune to good use."

Howard had been doing some inventing. He was trying. That I found surprising and even impressive. I had no desire to speak negatively to him about his proposal. I wanted rather to work on it positively. It needed to be modified a bit.

I told Howard his idea was good but should be revised.

"First, set up your Medical Institute right away. Second, at the same time—you'll see why in a minute—make the Hughes Aircraft Company a separate corporation. Shift no assets to the Hughes

Aircraft Company. They now belong entirely to the Hughes Tool Company. Leave them there. Merely have the Tool Company *lease* to Hughes Aircraft Company the buildings and land and all the equipment and facilities that it is now using, and, similarly, lend it the working capital it will need."

He looked at me suspiciously. I imagined he was saying to himself, "I don't know what this scientist is getting at, but I'm not going to like it. I'm supposed to be the eccentric one, yet here he is, not interested in the proposition I just put to him that I thought for certain he could not turn down."

"Now, Howard, this is very important," I continued. "Take that separated corporation, the new Hughes Aircraft Corporation, and donate it—right now—I mean a hundred percent of the shares— to your Medical Institute."

Hughes turned fully to me, startled. I purposely waited, matching his serious look, inwardly excited by the thought that I might succeed in selling him on the idea.

"You see, you will donate to the institute only the future profit stream. You told me that, after Wooldridge and I left, you expected there would be no earnings at Hughes Aircraft Company. So you will be giving away nothing.

"That earnings flow—why wait until you're gone to put it into medical research? You can direct Hughes Aircraft's earnings into the Medical Institute immediately. The institute can start operating at once. It can benefit humanity next month instead of when you go, which might be ten or twenty or thirty years from now. Install an outstanding board of trustees at the institute, all eminent citizens. With the institute the sole owner of Hughes Aircraft, the institute's board, not you, would have the job of selecting the management to run the company.

"Do all these things and announce them together. If you do, Howard, you will immediately be a national hero. Those now at Hughes Aircraft Company would not walk out on an opportunity to continue contributing to the nation's security while also creating earnings that will be used for medical research to benefit society. The U.S. government will be delighted. Suddenly you will be a philanthropist of the Rockefeller class, an admirable supercitizen who puts the nation and society first."

If he had some paper, I added, I would gladly write out the gist of the public announcement he should make. He called down the stairs for an errand boy, and soon a pad of paper showed up. Still sitting there facing the mirror, he chose to become a stenographer while I slowly dictated the steps I had outlined. He fussed about every word but did not try to alter the meaning.

That Saturday evening, thinking back on this last of our meetings, I felt there was a real chance Howard Hughes might follow my suggestions. And within a few months, he did initiate enough of them so that the Hughes Aircraft Company did not collapse. Many key people left during the next year, but others stayed on, and Hughes Aircraft is to this day one of the most important resources serving the Defense Department in military technology.

Howard telephoned me almost daily over the next few weeks. No matter how he started the conversations, I kept stressing the same things: establish the institute, make the Hughes Aircraft Company a separate corporation, donate all its shares to the institute, appoint strong trustees, etc. Instead, the first step he took was a disaster. He actually went to Culver City, called the senior people together, and pleaded with them not to quit. This meeting with some twenty-five of the top directors of research and development had, of course, an opposite effect. The brilliant scientist-executives wanted to know his policies and goals for the company, his plans for management, and how he saw his own role. He could not handle the questions and only displayed his general ignorance and lack of objectives for the company, which heightened his listeners' disrespect for him and made them resolve to leave his employ as soon as possible.

He was greatly disturbed when he called me after that session. I had already heard about it from some of those present and I again urged him to take the steps I had suggested. Finally, one day the newspapers carried an announcement from Howard Hughes that he had set up an institute for medical research, made the Hughes Aircraft Company a separate corporation, and donated all its ownership shares to the institute. He did not, however, appoint a board of trustees made up of distinguished individuals. Instead, he named himself the sole trustee. A bit later, he hired a capable executive, Laurence "Pat" Hyland, to run the company—a name at the top of the list I had recommended. He gave Hyland the job and then let him alone. Howard's telephone calls to me stopped and I was thankful.

From then on, Hughes Aircraft Company was owned by the Medical Institute. After Howard Hughes's death in 1976, no will could be found. What the news media described as a rough memorandum in his handwriting was discovered, however, and it appeared to describe intentions that he later carried out. It listed setting up a medical research institute and establishing Hughes Aircraft Company as a separate corporation, with all the shares of that company donated to the institute. It makes me feel good to hope, as perhaps I can be forgiven for doing, that what was found was the very memo he wrote in my presence in the Santa Monica beach house that Saturday afternoon in September 1953.

If the Hughes Aircraft Company had not been incorporated as an independent entity and its ownership given totally to the Medical Institute in late 1953, then, years later, in the chaos surrounding Howard Hughes's death without a will, the company, even if it had survived, would have been just another item in the contested estate. The once spectacular outfit would have shrunk quickly to a small mediocrity. It would not be the valuable company it is today, whose sale to General Motors for $5 billion will provide hundreds of millions of dollars a year for medical research.

Looking back, I am glad, of course, that I had a part in building Hughes Aircraft. It is satisfying to know that I played at least a small role in arranging for the largest part of the Howard Hughes fortune eventually to be employed for research to aid society. Back in the fall of 1953, however, as I departed Hughes Aircraft, my mind was not at all occupied with pride in my involvement in the way Hughes's vast wealth might be used. Other things dominated my thinking, such as the reverberations from the just-experienced management crisis. I knew we had done something remarkable at

Hughes, but I was not sure how to describe and rate it. I could not easily distinguish events that resulted from our actions from occurrences that were accidental or unplanned. Despite this, I was optimistic as the Ramo–Wooldridge Corporation was being formed. The experience Wooldridge and I had had at Hughes Aircraft had familiarized us with enough pieces of the technological-corporation jigsaw puzzle so that we ought to be able to assemble a company that would stand up against the unforeseen and be its own master. But the ink was hardly dry on the papers creating the new corporation when events we had not predicted took charge.

On the Monday immediately following the Saturday when I had my last meeting with Howard Hughes, Wooldridge and I traveled to New York to set up the Ramo–Wooldridge Corporation. Dean and I completed the legal formalities with our Wall Street attorneys on Tuesday and arrived in Cleveland early that evening to invite the Thompson Products Company* to become our financial backer. They accepted and we signed on Wednesday at noon. That afternoon, the attorneys informed us that we were officially the founders of a new, privately held Delaware corporation. We returned to Los Angeles that evening.

In September 1953, the average American understood—only superficially, certainly, but with awe and fear—the threat of a nuclear war and was mindful (what with the Korean War experience) that serious American military involvement at any time anywhere on the globe was not to be ruled out. The general public neither possessed nor needed knowledge of the details of the science and technology underlying these matters, and they had no familiarity with the men managing projects vital to America's national security. The buildup of Hughes Aircraft Company was well known, however, to many people in industry, government, and the universities. When Wooldridge and I left Hughes, the story spread

---

* Thompson Products had been one of the many prospective purchasers of Hughes Aircraft. Its chief executive, J. D. Wright, impressed Dean and me greatly with his intelligence, warm personality, and straightforwardness. Our confidence was not misplaced. Five years later, Thompson Products and Ramo–Wooldridge merged to form Thompson Ramo Wooldridge, later to be named TRW, with Wright as its founding chairman.

within hours to that professional circle and almost immediately afterward to the media, who pursued it instantly because any news involving the phenomenal Howard Hughes received full attention. Early in the evening of the Friday we left the Hughes payroll, our home telephone receivers had to be taken off the hook because of the barrage of calls from reporters. *Fortune* magazine put one of their top editors immediately on the story of "The Blow-up at Hughes," as they called it. *Time, Business Week, The Wall Street Journal, Forbes*, and others quickly prepared stories of our separation from Hughes.

On Thursday morning after we returned from Cleveland, the two telephones in our temporary headquarters were so jammed with calls from engineers and scientists interested in positions at the Ramo–Wooldridge Corporation that the Secretary of the Air Force, Harold Talbott, could not get through and dispatched a local Air Force major to our office to ask us to come to Washington for a meeting. Taking the night flight, we were in the Secretary's office on Friday noon, meeting with him and his R&D assistant, Trevor Gardner. When the afternoon ended, we had a letter contract calling for the new corporation to provide science and engineering analysis to back up a DoD strategic-missiles evaluation effort just begun by Gardner. It was nice to know that the new company would have only a week of start-up expenses and would become profitable in its second week. But this first task for which we had a contract was but the tip of the iceberg. The project that was coming our way was far bigger than we could possibly have imagined.

THREE

The ICBM

During the last quarter of 1953, when Dean Wooldridge and I were busy with the start-up of our new company, a group of top intelligence analysts in Washington was startled by new intelligence data that would dominate that start-up. When the pieces of intelligence arriving over several weeks were fully integrated, they added up to the astonishing, but unavoidable, conclusion that the Soviet Union was well along in the development of an intercontinental ballistic missile (ICBM). This proved to be the military intelligence of the greatest consequence since the end of World War II. It triggered a major shift in the nation's national-security plans and brought about a crash effort to develop an American ICBM, a project that became the largest technical development ever attempted by the U.S. military, even exceeding in assigned resources the wartime Manhattan Project to develop the atomic bomb.

When we founded our corporation, we had no inkling that a United States ICBM project would be launched shortly thereafter. Even if we had had some clue about the Russian ICBM, we would not have guessed that in a few months we would be asked to take on the job of directing the science and engineering for the American

ICBM effort. In hindsight, the events and their timing no longer appear so unpredictable.

The Department of Defense's reaction to news of the Soviet Union's ICBM program was one of enormous alarm. If the Russians completed their program, they could deliver nuclear weapons over the United States with total disdain for the multibillion-dollar air-defense system we had installed to protect North America from a manned-bomber attack. The frightening prospect of hydrogen bombs arriving from the U.S.S.R. on a high ballistic trajectory involved not only the short flight time (twenty to thirty minutes) but also the enormous velocity of the incoming warheads as they zoomed down from the sky at a steep angle. The speed would exceed by many times what any manned bomber could attain, and the high-angle trajectory would cause the missile's nose cone, the container of the bomb, to go unnoticed by the radar tracking systems in existence or capable of being designed at that time. Such systems could detect a large bomber traveling at nearly constant altitude for several hours over thousands of miles of land from which in-terceptors could be launched to attack it. A surprise strike by a large fleet of Soviet ICBMs carrying nuclear bombs could destroy the United States in half an hour. .

The U.S.S.R. could not be allowed a monopoly of such awe-some capability. If the Soviet Union were indeed moving rapidly to perfect an ICBM, then the United States also had to develop one and make it operational, if not earlier, then not much later than theirs.

It was amazing to the DoD that the U.S.S.R. could have jumped into an early lead on such an advanced weapons system. A nation as powerful and competitive as the Soviet Union, it is true, should not have been expected to be second to the United States in every development; this is recognized today by anyone even slightly knowledgeable about such matters. But the Soviets had been rated far behind until that intelligence report awakened us. (Even in the past decade or two, when its defense efforts have soared, the Soviet Union has seldom held a significant lead over us in military tech-nology. Where the Soviet Union is superior in armed power, it is mainly a superiority measured by quantity. For example, the Soviets have more land-based ICBMs than we do, and their warheads are heavier and more powerful. They have many more tanks in Europe than the NATO forces have. In certain classes of airplanes and submarines, their inventories exceed ours. None of their present military advantages is the result, however, of their having reached scientific plateaus substantially beyond our abilities. Even the spectacular achievement of putting Sputnik in orbit in October 1957 involved little advance over the available technology in the U.S. at the time. They launched Sputnik when they did because they chose priorities different from ours.)

The U.S. Department of Defense position, before the intelligence information was received, was that the ICBM possibility merited only a small, leisurely research program. Our modest effort was intended to indicate what advances in science and technology would be needed before a complete weapons-system development would deserve serious support. It was not a program to guarantee that an ICBM would be achieved at the earliest possible date.

For an intercontinental ballistic missile to make military sense, several key technical problems would have to be solved, and in 1953 they seemed close to insoluble to the DoD. To begin with, the technology then available for guiding an ICBM was so inaccurate that a target five thousand miles away would be missed by twenty or thirty miles or more. Of course, an H-bomb would pack great explosive power and do considerable damage even if detonated far off its target, but the early H-bombs were also extremely heavy. Further, the enormous heat generated by the payload during its streaking reentry into the atmosphere after the lofty trip above it would ruin the bomb unless it were protected from the heat by a thick blanket of material. But such a covering would add even more weight. Hence, it appeared that rocket engines of absurdly gigantic size would be required to boost the heavy reentry vehicle into space. A ballistic missile of intercontinental range, as envisaged in DoD circles in 1953, would consist of a giant cylinder full of fuel and oxidizer, with a modest warhead in the nose cone and a colossal rocket engine on the other end. The warhead and the other required apparatus (guidance and control gear, pumps, valves, instruments) would have to undergo terrific acceleration, particularly near the end of the rocket-thrust period, when the emptying fuel tank would become relatively light and offer little inertial resistance to the powerful rocket engine's thrust. The vibration alone could be expected to lead to inaccuracies in control and to equipment failures. All in all, in the early 1950s a ballistic missile to deliver bombs over the Soviet Union was considered a farfetched idea by the airplane pilots running the Air Force. They already had the "right" means for bomb delivery, the manned bomber.

The Russians were deemed to be fanatics in the supersizing of everything they created, from standing armies to steel mills. So, when the intelligence report was first received, some skeptics speculated that the Soviet Union might merely have decided to build an experimental mammoth ICBM even if its small-yield warhead and poor accuracy of aim would keep it from being of operational value. This might have been their way of making a start on an indefinitely long R&D program. But the majority of DoD's leadership quickly ceased indulging in the American habit of taking our permanent superiority for granted. They decided, instead, to put the most pessimistic interpretation on the intelligence data and to assume that the Soviet engineers had worked out solutions to the innumerable technical problems we had considered too difficult to overcome. The DoD took seriously that the U.S.S.R. might indeed have succeeded with a priority program begun at the end of World War II, seven years earlier.

Now, it happened that in July 1953, a few months ahead of the intelligence report, Secretary of Defense Charles Wilson* shifted to a fast lane in his determination to cut Defense Department spending. High on his list was to reduce redundant projects. At that time, since the military's established means of delivering nu-

---

* He was "Engine Charlie" Wilson, the former chairman of General Motors, so labeled to distinguish him from "Electric Charlie," the other Charles Wilson, the chairman of General Electric and the head of the War Production Board during World War II. "Engine Charlie" was the one who became famous for his remark during his Senate confirmation hearings that there could be no conflict of interest in his retaining his General Motors stock while serving in the cabinet because "what is good for General Motors is good for the nation."

clear warheads to the Soviet Union was by manned airplanes, a continuing effort to improve them seemed amply justified. It was reasonable, however, for Wilson to ask whether we were funding too many alternatives.

The Navy, for example, was pressing for increasingly large aircraft carriers. Critics believed this to be due in part to the Navy's desire to accommodate heavy planes suitable for delivering nuclear weapons anywhere in the world. The Army, starting with short-range German V-2 missiles (and making use of German rocket engineers who had developed the V-2 rockets used against England and who had been brought to the United States after the war), was working to increase their range. While such an extension of cannon fire did not constitute a duplication of the Air Force's strategic bombing mission, it was related to it because missiles with nuclear warheads and ranges of hundreds of miles could be stationed along the eastern borders of West Germany, where they could deter a Soviet nuclear attack by threatening quick nuclear retaliation.

Finally, and especially stimulating Secretary Wilson's skepticism, there were a group of intercontinental unmanned bombers; that is, long-range, ground-to-ground, guided missiles, under development by the Air Force. The subsonic versions were essentially conventional airplanes automated so as not to need a human pilot. They were to be smaller and cheaper than SAC's manned strategic bombers, since they would only perform one-way missions and would not have to carry personnel. The autopilot was to be coupled to an accurate terminal guidance system still very much in the research phase. The supersonic versions of these missiles required unconventional engines whose performance at supersonic speeds would have to greatly surpass the then existing jet engines. The eventual success of the R&D on these engines was far from assured, but if success was achieved, the higher speed of the supersonic missiles would make it difficult for the Soviet Union to design a defense system to intercept them.

The total American (pre-ICBM) strategic-missile R&D program in progress would require billions of dollars annually during the 1950s (the equivalent in the 1980s of tens of billions). If that R&D

was completed satisfactorily, ten times larger sums then would be needed to build substantial numbers of missiles, supporting equipment, and bases which together would constitute an operational capability. Wilson believed we could not afford and did not need so many alternatives for dropping nuclear bombs on the U.S.S.R. He wanted a smaller, more selective program. He handed the assignment to evolve it to the Air Force's Trevor Gardner, a very bright and energetic industrial executive who had joined the Office of the Secretary of the Air Force.

Gardner had been a new engineering recruit at General Electric during my second year there in 1937–38, and as further lucky coincidence would have it, we happened to live in the same small Schenectady apartment house. We took a liking to each other and started to develop a close friendship. But he deemed General Electric and himself to be wrong for one another and left after only a year.

Gardner was Assistant Secretary of the Air Force for Research and Development. In that position, he had to become acquainted with the activities at Hughes Aircraft Company, and so he and I became reacquainted. When appointed by the Secretary of Defense to evaluate the strategic-missiles program, he began by collecting preliminary judgments from a few individuals he trusted. He came to Culver City and asked me for crude estimates of the money and time needed to advance each of the missile approaches to operational capability and wanted to know what I thought the nation would get for its money. I remember well that visit from Trevor Gardner because my final meetings with Howard Hughes were going on at the time. Gardner was highly complimentary about weapons-systems development at Hughes. He compared the "focused and forceful" way, he called it, in which we developed defense systems with what he characterized as the "loose, uncoordinated, and wandering" management of the strategic-missile projects at other companies. Our management of Hughes Aircraft, he generously remarked, should be a model for the rest of the military-technology industry. These comments were welcome and yet very discomfiting, since I feared Hughes Aircraft might be heading for a management disaster. So I concentrated on trying to respond to his request to evaluate his plans for developing strategic missiles.

He was anxious that his effort not end as was usual with a DoD study, with a report that is filed essentially unread and has no effect whatever. I started by suggesting that even though more could be done to improve the economics, reliability, survivability, accuracy, and other aspects of strategic manned-bomber missions, there were fundamental limitations to that approach. Hence, it was sensible to ask if a radically superior nuclear-warhead delivery system could be created. To justify a strategic guided-missile program, however, in view of the fact that it would make a heavy demand on the nation's technological resources, it had to promise a major increase in military capability. It should be able to deliver nuclear warheads more effectively, its immediate readiness and reliability should be higher, and it should be harder to defend against than manned airplanes. Moreover, the total cost (research and development, production facilities, a fleet of missiles, launching bases and necessary auxiliaries, communication and command systems, annual maintenance, operational alert), when figured over the system's lifetime, should be substantially less than the cost of delivering payloads by bombers.

Could these military and economic criteria be realized with guided missiles? The answer surely would have to hinge in great part on the status of the sophisticated science and technology basic to the guided-missile approach. Accordingly, I urged Gardner to set up a blue-ribbon science and technology advisory panel to assist him in his deliberations. The panel would study such fundamental problems as missile structure, propulsion, flight control, heat generation and dissipation, guidance accuracy, nuclear-warhead match, command systems, reliability, possible enemy countermeasures, and other technical issues for each strategic guided-missile alternative. The individuals selected for the panel should be highly qualified and of unquestionable integrity, so that if they said that great improvements in performance were unlikely, or, conversely, that the potential was surely there and had only to be developed, the Defense Department from Secretary Wilson on down would listen.

Gardner had first to choose the right scientist as chairman, one not connected with any industrial company interested in contracts. I suggested several names, reserving the highest recommendation for John von Neumann. Von Neumann, educated broadly in science, was a mathematician whose contributions were so remarkable that he was often compared to Einstein, the latter considered the physicist, and von Neumann the mathematician, of the century. By 1953, von Neumann had demonstrated a breadth of abilities well beyond pure mathematics. He was both a key consultant to the Atomic Energy Commission on the U.S. nuclear-weapons program and a heralded pioneer in the basic architecture of computer systems. An active member of the faculty of the Institute for Advanced Study in Princeton, New Jersey, he was also involved in advising the Department of Defense. Moreover, von Neumann was extremely articulate and unusually amiable and considerate, exhibiting easy maturity in his relationships with others despite being described by co-workers as the most "cerebrally dazzling" thinker they had ever met. He would be a wise leader for a panel of distinguished scientists and engineers consisting of world experts in their fields. Von Neumann would be sound and judicious, able to put the pieces together. He would be trusted.

When Wooldridge and I were called back to Washington by Secretary of the Air Force Harold Talbott in September 1953, two days after our corporation became a legal entity, we did not know why we had been pressed to be there. It was at the urging of Trevor Gardner. We learned at the meeting that Gardner had taken my advice and had invited John von Neumann to associate himself with the challenge of evaluating and shaping the nation's strategic-missile program. What Gardner requested of Wooldridge and me was a commitment to assist him in putting together the task force and to provide it with detailed analyses. At that meeting, intelligence information about a Russian ICBM program was not even mentioned.

In those days, everything related to intelligence was extremely hush-hush. You didn't pry. Either you were in on certain intelligence activities and data, or you were presumed not to have a need to know and were not informed. Gardner, I learned later, had been privy to the initial intelligence on the Soviet Union's ICBM program. It was weeks before the incoming data led to the conclusion that the U.S.S.R. was rapidly developing an ICBM. At the time of the meeting in Talbott's office, Gardner already had a sense that such a conclusion was imminent. He apparently had decided that he wanted the Ramo–Wooldridge Corporation to become immediately involved, and to get us started without divulging anything, he had thought up the idea of enlisting our support for his task force. Wooldridge and I, not knowing what he was really up to, thought the initial contract was welcome but hardly vital from the business standpoint.

Because of the wide publicity about our leaving Hughes and starting a new company, we found ourselves overwhelmed with applications from would-be employees. We had the luxury of being able to hire far more outstanding scientists and engineers than we could immediately take on board. To aid Gardner's evaluations, we had no difficulty assembling a staff of the highest quality. We laid out the technological details to be considered, and then tracked down the top specialists and arranged for their participation in our deliberations. We used the Air Force's influence, expressed forcefully through Trevor Gardner, to arrange short leaves of absence for them from their employers. Personal contacts from von Neumann's prestigious associates, who recommended strongly that our urgent requests be supported, also helped. Great emphasis was placed on the critical nature of the panel's secret studies and their potential importance to national security.

We had just begun to work intensely when the intelligence about the Soviet Union's ICBM was disclosed to us. I hope we would have arrived promptly at the right evaluation of the ICBM approach without that knowledge. However, we were now led to give priority to the ICBM.

Then, about a month later, two breakthroughs in United States classified activities accelerated our deliberations. One concerned the bomb itself. Key tests had just been completed which confirmed the validity of the designs being developed to reduce the weight and increase the explosive yield of hydrogen bombs. The other concerned missile-guidance accuracy. Dr. Charles Stark Draper at the Instrumentation Laboratory at M.I.T. had achieved huge improvements in guidance accuracy with a so-called inertial guidance system in which an ingeniously rugged design gave missiles unusual precision and also made them capable of withstanding rapid acceleration.

A much smaller and lighter bomb with a very big bang would allow the use of substantial insulation around the bomb to protect it against the heat of reentry. The higher guidance accuracy would allow a decrease in bomb weight. The overall weight of the nose cone now called for a reduced and practical rocket-engine size.

Still needed were extensions of the art by a factor of ten for other ICBM design requirements. Thus, ICBM rocket engines would have to produce ten times more thrust than any rocket engine in existence. Nothing in the laws of physics precluded attaining this, but it would be immensely difficult to achieve in a hurry. Merely to test such a rocket engine, for example, thousands of firings on the ground would be needed, as well as test stands substantially larger than any previously built. They would have to hold the engine down and permit measuring the thrust, but the rocket's enormous blast of hot, high-velocity gas would burn everything nearby unless a technique was developed to prevent this. To fire the rocket engine, the fuel and oxidizer would have to be pumped into it at unprecedented speed from tanks that could hold such corrosive substances, some at cryogenic (extremely low) temperatures. Plumbing would have to be developed to direct these exotic liquids as they are thrust forward under powerful pressures. Research would be needed to learn the principles for controlling with great steadiness the flow into the rocket chamber and the attainment of stable chemical reactions despite the turbulence in the chamber. Essentially, we would be containing a continuing explosion, and new materials would be needed to accomplish that.

Similar major advances in metallurgy and structural engineering would be required if we were to build missile structures stronger yet lighter than any ever flown before. They would have to hold the high pressure of the fuel tanks and keep the payload, controls, and rocket engines in precise alignment even though the forces acting on the structure during flight would be far more destructive than ordinary airplanes have to withstand. (In one design, the structure was essentially a cylindrical balloon made of literally thin-as-a-dime but very strong steel; the structure had to be kept under pressure at all times on the ground or in flight lest it collapse.)

Controlled flight of the ICBM would require path-breaking innovations. The missile, in its early rise, would be at too low a velocity for aerodynamic surfaces to generate useful forces the way rudders do on airplanes, so the big rocket motors would have to be swiveled deftly and accurately to ensure stable missile motion. The missile then would pass through the potentially destructive sound barrier and into its supersonic-speed phase as it reached increasingly rarefied atmosphere. During this powered flight, the structure would have to be kept from excessive yawing, pitching, rolling, and twisting. At the same time, the engine's thrust would need to be constantly monitored to cause the missile to attain a tightly prescribed magnitude and direction of final velocity. The acceleration and vibration would be well beyond anything that flight-control instruments had previously been required to handle. We would have to test on the ground the equipment's ability to operate in the severe environment of powered flight. We would be pioneering even as we created vibrations in the laboratory to simulate the rocket engine's acoustical impact on the structure of the missile and its components.

Gyroscopes, accelerometers, computers, radios, and radars involved in guidance and control of the missile and the transmission of information about its operation during a flight test would also have to be enhanced by factors of ten or more over the proven art in accuracy, range, strength, lightness, reliability, and speed of response.

And finally there was the reentry problem. Here we would have to start from scratch. Knowledge of how heat is generated by very high-velocity flow through air was nil except for some modest theoretical beginnings. The ICBM's velocity of several thousand miles per hour would create conditions well beyond our experience. The basic aerothermal chemistry of such phenomena would involve much more than extremely high-speed airflow. The solid material of the nose cone would be abraded, boiled or burned off by the heat created during reentry, so its surface would face a complex and unfamiliar mixture of atmosphere and emitted gases chemically reacting at enormously high speed, pressure, and temperature. The nose cone would have to be made of some unusual material. (I stooped to giving that material the name of "unobtainium.")

Still, the known principles of physics did not dictate that designing for successful reentry would be impossible. By devising R&D programs to understand the molecular dynamics, we expected to discover ways to cope with the problem. The solution would involve assigning weight for insulation that otherwise could go into a more powerful bomb, or accepting a reduction in reentry velocity by shaping the nose cone so it would slow down substantially before reentry at high altitude and produce less heat when passing through the denser air below. We could find a way to reenter, we were confident, and we had to figure out a way to do it while suffering only tolerable penalties.

These were only the R&D challenges. Realizing a thoroughly practical ICBM system, however, would of course go well beyond the R&D. A large amount of hardware would have to be produced. It would be one thing to make a working laboratory model of a critical component under the careful supervision of the master engineers and the Ph.D.s who had conceived it and quite another to manufacture acceptable components on a factory production line. We would not be blessed in this project with the usual luxury of being able to tolerate large reductions in performance of the factory-manufactured components. They would have to be close to the best that could be created by hand, one at a time, or the ICBM would not work. A manufacturing industry did not exist that could supply this kind of advanced, precision hardware in volume. We would need to create it by arranging for the top manufacturing outfits to achieve this ability. They would have to develop the production technology and then build and shake down new manufacturing equipment. They also would have to start programs to recruit and train highly skilled workers.

We would need a large flow of hardware not only for the ultimate operational capability but also for the indispensable experimental aspects of developing the ICBM. Every tiny component and every assembly of components would have to be put through simulated operations many times on the ground and eventually proven out in the skies. Only after conducting many full-scale flights over a range of five thousand miles and more, with confirmed high accuracy of arrival of the reentry vehicle at the target, could we say that the development phase was finished.

It was at once clear that we would fly our test missiles out over the Atlantic Ocean from Florida to take advantage of Earth's easterly rotation. To design and construct in a short time the extensive launch and flight facilities needed would in itself be a heroic engineering achievement. Cape Canaveral in Florida would undergo vast development, and in addition, we would have to obtain rights to install instruments on the islands (under other nations' control) stretching east from the continental United States. That would enable us to watch the missiles performing and learn what was going on inside them through telemetered information broadcast from within the missiles to recorders strategically placed on land. (During the test flights we instrumented 150 points in each missile and telemetered the data to the ground by fifty radio channels.)

Finally, for the missile to become operational, a basing system would be needed. The missiles would be located in silos spread over many thousands of square miles in the central and northern United States. A tight security system for the silos, a substantial degree of hardness and invulnerability, means for ensuring and monitoring readiness, a foolproof and fail-safe communication-command-control system not readily susceptible to jamming or destruction in a precursor attack—all these would be required, and would break new ground.

How could such a program be completed in the shortest possible time? By 1954, military R&D had become leisurely. To bring to fruition a mere two-to-one improvement over prior art, eight or ten years was par. At this sluggish pace for new weapons acquisition, it might easily be a dozen years before completion of an ICBM; the U.S.'s defeat in the race with the Russians would be guaranteed. A special management scheme was called for. Gardner made this critical issue clear to Secretary Wilson, and Wilson asked Donald Quarles, a former Bell Laboratories top executive who had become the Defense Department's Assistant Secretary for R&D, to join the search for a solution. Gardner also arranged for a highly rated Air Force officer, Bernard A. Schriever, to study the management problem.

Wilson—aided by his assistant, Quarles, pressed by Gardner's determination, and backed up by the von Neumann task force's science and engineering evaluations—made the formal recommendation to President Eisenhower in early 1954 that the nation must launch an ICBM program on a crash basis. Eisenhower agreed and assigned to it the government's highest priority. The plan was to create a project management office within the United States Air Force and to give the director an exceptional degree of authority, cutting out many review and approval channels and the corresponding red tape. General Schriever was assigned to head that office and take on the awesome overall responsibility for the ICBM program.

His first task was to form an organization that would encompass all facets of a program that would be spread across the country in industry, government, and the universities. Most tasks could be described only inadequately at first, so revised instructions would have to flow continuously to the participants. The efforts of all would have to be locked into a single integrated project and a single integrated design of the ICBM missile and system.

Quickly rejected by Schriever was the practice that had become standard for the Air Force on guided-missile programs. Considering missile programs to be similar to airplane procurements, the U.S.A.F. had given each project to an aircraft company as a prime contractor. For the ICBM program, the aircraft companies of that era were judged to be too limited. Their capabilities lay in assembling flyable structures, and they obviously would be given such a role in the

ICBM program, but they were thought unacceptably weak in systems engineering and electronics and in their ability to direct a program that would extend the underlying basic science over so broad a spectrum.

A second way to organize the program, also rejected, would be to use a leading university, or create a unit managed jointly by several leading universities, or form a laboratory similar to Los Alamos (the nuclear-bomb laboratory managed by the University of California) or the Jet Propulsion Laboratory (the rocket center managed by the California Institute of Technology) to pursue the underlying fundamental science of the program. But this would still leave the need to integrate the science with practical engineering and the vast industrial expansion essential to the required flow of hardware. For this aspect of the program, the key management personnel needed to be highly experienced in directing large-scale engineering programs.

A third approach would be to create a strong technical direction and systems engineering staff within the government, the Air Force recruiting the necessary civilian technical talent through civil service. General Schriever (and Trevor Gardner, Donald Quarles, John von Neumann, and others advising the general) viewed this possibility as beyond serious consideration, deeming it unrealistic to expect that the government could attract the needed technical expertise in peacetime.

There was one more scheme that General Schriever and the other decision-makers could not avoid contemplating. This was to use the recently formed Ramo–Wooldridge Corporation. The building and operating of the large and successful Hughes operation had provided the two of us with strong records in systems engineering and electronics and a reputation for competence in technological industry management. The DoD had no doubt that we were considered sound by the science and technology fraternity and by the leadership of industry. The likelihood of our being able to attract exceptional science, engineering, and management talent to the project seemed high both from our Hughes Aircraft Company performance and from the recruiting we had done at the new corporation.

Dean and I realized that we might be asked to take on the technical direction and systems engineering role for the ICBM program, but we hoped that such an invitation would not come. To be sure, we were anxious to participate in the nation's most urgent and technically challenging project. Our free choice, however, would have been to compete for a principal contractor role developing guidance systems for the ICBM. That would fit better with our goal to be an outstanding producer of advanced electronics. Also, we wanted to balance the company's activities by combining work on military technology with peacetime electronics in the computer-communications-control field. Being drafted for the overall technical responsibility of the huge ICBM program might keep us from engaging in any other activity.

As it turned out, our personal preferences were not of great interest to the government. The DoD made the decision to press us into service as the systems engineers and technical directors of the ICBM program. General Schriever and his carefully selected team of outstanding Air Force officers would be stationed in Ramo–Wooldridge buildings, where they would wear civilian clothes to help keep the project under wraps. I was to give up other Ramo–Wooldridge activities and plans, leaving those to Wooldridge, and was to become the project's chief scientist (or chief systems engineer or technical director, as the function was variously called). These responsibilities were detailed formally in a sole-source contract signed between the Air Force and the Ramo–Wooldridge Corporation in June 1954.

Benny Schriever and I then immediately fell into a pattern of close cooperation—exchanging thoughts and ideas face to face virtually every day—for five years. Almost at once we concluded that to win the ICBM race against the Soviet Union, a parallel, instead of the conventional slow, serial, step-by-step, program was mandatory. We decided to risk paralleling the R&D with action on all other aspects of the program (hardware manufacture, ground testing, test flights, operational capability), without waiting for the ICBM design to become firm. If there was doubt about the success of any new technology, at least two parallel approaches would be started. Thus, two independent contractors would be used to develop the large rocket engines and each developer would be asked to prepare to manufacture a substantial number of engines even before the final design of the engine could be determined. Similarly, the design and construction of testing facilities would begin before details of the test program were determined. The assembly, checkout, and launching facilities at the Cape in Florida would be started before the missile's size, shape, performance, and operating characteristics were fully established. Several promising approaches to the reentry problem would be researched simultaneously.

This strategy of parallel development was based on the optimistic assumption that the project would succeed. We would immediately lay out a crude picture of every part of the missile system and the agenda for the program to develop it. We would elect to gamble that when the actual, detailed definition of any component or subsystem emerged, we would quickly be able to modify everything else in the system and program influenced by it, arrange compatible match and consistency, and not be required to throw out other components already developed or in process and completely start over. As the research and development proceeded, it would gradually become clear how each piece of the ICBM must turn out, what should constitute the test programs, what specific items of hardware would need to be produced in what quantity at what time, and how to base and control the operational system. Properly managed, all aspects of the missile and the program would mature at the same time and come into sharp focus.

To skip a few years in the story for the moment, in June 1957, the Atlas, the first United States ICBM, was tested in a short (600-mile) maiden flight out over the Atlantic with a dummy nose cone. We had completed enough prior ground testing to be confident that we had licked enough of the main technical problems to be able to benefit from that first flight. The rocket engine had been tested at full thrust and for the full duration required for powered flight while it was held down firmly on the ground. All the guidance and control components and instrumentation to be used had been operated in simulated tests which included subjecting the components to extreme vibrations. Ingenious models and simulations had been created in the laboratories, and flights of individual pieces of equipment on small short-range missiles had furnished convincing evidence that the complete missile would operate properly during a full, long-range flight. Through highly innovative experiments, new theory about what goes on to generate and remove heat during reentry was checked out. We learned how to choose and shape materials for the reentry vehicle's outer structure to protect the bomb without unduly slowing the final speed before detonation.

We expected, of course, that the flight tests would turn up additional problems that would only be evident in actual flight, and such problems indeed surfaced. Also, as we had hoped, we were able to make and incorporate design modifications quickly to handle those shortcomings.

By November 1958, the Atlas had been flown successfully over six thousand statute miles, with the nose cone separating and landing accurately on target. Large units and tiny components of the ICBMs were all being fabricated by then in industrial plants that had increased their versatility, precision, and quality control to fit the manufacturing needs of the program. The timing of the production buildup was almost perfect, providing the parts first in the quantity needed for the exhaustive ground testing, then for the beginning flight tests, and finally in a volume to match the needs for operational implementation of a complete ICBM system, with many missiles and spare parts ready for operational deployment.

When the first ICBM flight tests began, the race with the Russians reached a new level of excitement for those of us running the program. The anguish was triple-barreled. First of all, the question hung over us: Would the flights prove out our ICBM design? Remember, we had elected to parallel the important steps of the program, and we knew that was risky. Our first flight tests might disclose that we were not at all ready, that we were way off in our design assumptions. The launching pads and their auxiliaries and the instrumentation to follow a missile in its flight could turn out to be a collection of malfunctioning junk. Even if we had a sound missile design, it might be badly implemented, with parts mispro-duced in the factories, this condition discovered only in flight tests. It would be awful to have to face up to major debacles in the parallel-design approach and be forced to retreat to a slow, series approach.

The pressure as we approached flight testing was especially high because we were dealing here not with modest advances of the art in one or two dimensions of the overall ICBM design. The project depended for its success on achieving many simultaneous advances, all in the ten-to-one range. A lot of creative engineering had been applied to circumvent design bottlenecks that could have added years to the program. Had we skipped too many steps? Were there major flaws we had overlooked that test flights would show up?

The second source of nervousness was that we were racing with the Soviet Union, and they had started much earlier. Their first long-range ICBM flight, in June 1957, was six months ahead of ours. We knew that they had ground-tested large rocket motors before we had. We felt certain, however, that we were ahead in bomb design and that they were forced to make a heavier bomb to get the necessary yield to make their ICBM practical. We also were confident (from intelligence information on their testing of guid-ance equipment in the sky with airplane simulations and smaller specialized rockets, just as we were doing) that our guidance ac-curacy should prove superior to theirs. But what if the flights showed our guidance performance to be far poorer than we expected?

Third and last, we were concerned in a way we never had had to be in the previous four years about the public's reaction to the race. Until the flight tests began, the United States ICBM program had been remarkably secret. The project personnel had adhered strictly to the nondisclosure rules. Congressmen and congressional staffs (smaller than today's), who possessed classified ICBM knowl-edge, knew they were supposed to keep their mouths shut and they did. But we knew that the secrecy was bound to collapse as more and more people became involved in the huge program. Flight testing was too dramatic and newsworthy to be ignored by the media.

We flew intermediate-range missiles (from a few hundred to a thousand miles) in early 1957. They were each powered by one of the three rocket motors the ICBM required, and some of the ICBM's control equipment was proven out on these smaller missiles, as was our tracking equipment on the islands in the Atlantic and at our Florida base. At first there were no uninvited observers, but then the media began informing the public that we were flight testing. Floridians, determined to observe missiles in flight, got as close as they could to the coastline near the launching pads. Boats and ships of all sizes and descriptions and from many nations, including the U.S.S.R., all appeared in those waters. The audience built up, and by mid-1957 it was clear that the program could not be kept under wraps. Schriever and I campaigned hard, going right up to Secretary Wilson, to try to get major changes in policy about disclosure to the public. We wanted DoD to announce that we were engaged in an ICBM program and we wanted to be able to explain our flight testing to some extent. But we were turned down.

All doubts about coverage of our flight tests and the existence of the ICBM program were dispelled by the sensational launch by the U.S.S.R. of their first Sputnik in October 1957. That flight had a world impact, affected U.S. policies and plans in both national security and scientific research, and, quite apart from the race to achieve an ICBM operational capability, led to an entirely new contest between the superpowers: the space race. We shall discuss the remarkable consequences of Sputnik and the important space field in the next chapter. As a substantive indication of the status of the Soviet ICBM program, however, Sputnik was not overwhelming. We knew it was possible to put a payload in orbit, given the rocket-propulsion capacity of an ICBM with a range of several thousand miles, and we knew it could be done with only a crude guidance system. A useful ICBM needed more precision, and our first six-thousand-mile flight test, a success achieved only a month after Sputnik, demonstrated we had it. The Soviets had not yet matched that precision.

We were especially concerned about one problem that we knew would develop as we began ICBM flights. We had made the decision to start those flight tests with available, but not yet fully developed, apparatus. That was part of our paralieling strategy. For example, we were still in the debugging stage with our rocket engines. They might run perfectly during some tests but develop intolerable instabilities or hot spots during others. So we had a choice: to launch a missile only when we had attained a high probability of perfect performance during the entire flight, or to launch (in order to learn) engines having a substantial probability of failing in flight. Similarly, a malfunction in the control equipment might cause a missile to go dangerously out of control, requiring that we destroy it in the sky. (We had only to push a button; we had incorporated a destruct system in each missile.) Further, we might want to check out the strength of the ICBM's structure by subjecting the missile to maneuvers more severe than any encountered in an operational flight. Such dynamic motion, which could result in the missile's breakup in flight, might be the most effective means to get the engineering data we needed.

With great trepidation, we imagined the public watching our early ICBM flights on television, observing explosions or crazily swerving missiles, and concluding that the American ICBM was an utter failure!

During 1958 and 1959 we experienced some of just this kind of flight performance—explosions and crazy twists and turns—all in public view. Fortunately, in 1959 and just in time, Secretary Wilson retired as Secretary of Defense. He was replaced by Neil McElroy, who had been the chairman of Procter & Gamble and had once headed that soap manufacturer's rather extensive advertising activities. Highly trained in public relations, he immediately understood our plea for more open communications. He encouraged General Schriever and me to talk to the media. We appeared on national television and in magazine cover stories, discussing where we stood in proving out our designs. We still had to hold back details, of course, and it was a challenge to include only declassified facts when answering questions from interviewers. But the ICBM program turned out to be well regarded by the public during that period—aided probably by the fact that by March 1960 we had had twenty-one successive successful launches. In May 1960, one ICBM, equipped with an operational nose cone, was flown perfectly nine thousand miles to beyond the southern tip of Africa.

Where did we stand in the race with the Russians during these flight tests? Which of us was in the lead? On what respective dates did the two rival ICBM programs reach their objectives?

There should have been straightforward answers, but in fact it was a much more complicated race than such questions suggest. It was very difficult for us to determine who was ahead, until 1961, when we became certain we were. For a project with the objective of dropping an A-bomb on Japan, or landing an astronaut on the moon, a specific act can be readily associated with success on a specific date. In the creation of a complex system like the ICBM, no single event settles anything. What deviation from perfection in a test flight can be tolerated and the missile design still considered proven?

If our ICBMs have a ten-percent chance of exploding during a powered flight, is the design good enough to base an operational system on it? Is it a true operational capability, granted only an initial one, if only ten missiles are ready to retaliate for an enemy nuclear attack? Or should we set the minimum at twenty or one hundred missiles—such figures corresponding to later dates? When is a command-and-control system considered to have reached adequate readiness, security, and survivability? Since the whole idea of our ICBM is that possessing it will deter the Russians from launching a nuclear strike, at what stage in our buildup would it seem to the Soviet Union that they should rationally rule out such a strike?

During 1958–60, the two competitors performed meaningful flight tests of a comparable nature within weeks, or at most a month or two, of each other. It was in September 1959 that our first flight took place from an operational base (Vandenberg Air Force Base in California) under the control of SAC (Strategic Air Command) personnel in place of our R&D team. It was a totally successful five-thousand-mile flight with accurate missile guidance. This was a few weeks before the Russians' similar flights, or more precisely, their almost similar flights, because we learned that their guidance accuracy was inferior to ours. In January 1960, President Eisenhower disclosed to Congress that we had completed fifteen launches, each with a range of more than five thousand miles and with accuracy within two miles, substantially superior to the Soviet's ICBM flight performance.

In 1960, during the campaign for the Presidency, John Kennedy often cited the "missile gap" as an indication of the Eisenhower–Nixon Administration's failures. That Administration, he noted, had allowed the Soviet Union to get the jump on us in ICBMs. Immediately after Kennedy's election, Robert McNamara, his Secretary of Defense, received his first review of the U.S. and Soviet ICBM programs. It left little doubt that the missile gap of the election campaign had never existed. We were safely ahead in ICBM technology and implementation, a lead we held for about a decade. After that, the U.S. essentially paused, while the Soviet Union continued a major effort to manufacture and install improved ICBMs.

The American ICBM effort not only defeated the Russians in the race to a first operational force, it also was remarkably free of major cost overruns, schedule slippages, waste, and fraud. Of course, the performance of the principal industrial contractors, of whom there were about twenty, and by the hundreds of second- and thousands of third-tier contractors, was not perfect. But there were no abysmal failures and no scandals. The DoD and military contractors in the 1970s and 1980s, as the public knows full well, did not do as well. Recent military projects—fighter planes, bombers, missiles, ships, tanks, guns, and even toilet seats—have been of a smaller scale than the ICBM program and have typically called for more modest advances in technology. Moreover, in comparison with the ICBM program, these projects have not involved the need to coordinate so many parallel steps in R&D, production, testing, and operational implementation. Yet they typically have cost twice their original estimates and have taken far longer to complete than promised. Further, recent weapons have displayed severe shortcomings in performance.

Disappointing weapons-system developments in the 1970–80s have not hinged on any one factor. But there is a significant difference between recent years and the early ICBM era: it is "business as usual" today in the government; it was "mission impossible" on the ICBM project in the decade from 1954 to 1964. That some very large and complex project of high urgency and priority will arise in the future is virtually certain. It is difficult, however, to conceive of the government's being able to set up the tight, closely integrated systems management that proved so effective on the ICBM program. What exactly did we do that is so unlikely to be duplicated today? Why did we fare so well?

Of course, we had an outstanding team. Take first the project's overall leader, General Bernard Schriever. Schriever possessed remarkably strong aptitudes for the post: determination, superb leadership and organizing talent, excellent grounding in science and engineering, intimate knowledge of the workings of the Pentagon, the Congress, and the government as a whole, and an uncanny sense for evaluating and managing people. President Eisenhower and congressional leaders had only to be with him for a short time to become totally convinced of his competence, objectivity, and devotion to the task.

Generals in the U.S. Air Force, like the top members of other professional groups, are not average people. But they vary greatly in the breadth of their talents beyond their particular expertise. Gardner told me in January 1954 that a comprehensive search turned up at most a half-dozen Air Force general officers with the requisite background in science and engineering for the ICBM job. The education and training of most were along other lines. A larger number were strong leaders who had learned management by directing flight operations, logistics, or procurement in WWII. Few of those had been deeply involved in the planning and analysis of complex military technology and weapons systems. Still fewer,

Schriever included, had dealt intimately with leading scientists or had an understanding of how they think and what motivates them or were known to the scientists and enjoyed their confidence.

Had General Schriever not been available, some other Air Force officer would have managed the ICBM project. Very likely, he would have had only some of the talents with which Schriever was endowed, and the program simply would not have gone as well. He matched the need perfectly; the availability of Schriever was fortuitous.

Next, consider the science and engineering team. We were fortunate at Ramo–Wooldridge in being able to bring together an unusually competent group to supervise the scientific and engineering aspects of the program. I constantly marveled at the combined skills of the top members of our team. I called them our 20–20s. (The twenty principal technical executives on the program happened to have averaged twenty years of distinguished experience in related science and engineering endeavors at the time we started the project.) It was highly unusual to assemble so many stars in technical management in one company. *

Aside from the several hundred professionals assembled at the Ramo–Wooldridge Corporation for the ICBM project, the program had the active support of a remarkably large number of the best scientists and engineers in American industry and academic life. It would be very difficult today to pull together a concentration of such talent on one project. In fact, it could hardly have been assembled at any time in the past two decades. The development of the ICBM happened during a unique period from the middle 1950s to the middle 1960s. Let me explain why.

---

* Some examples, in alphabetic order: Richard DeLauer, who later became the Under-Secretary of Defense; William Duke, who became executive vice president of ITT; Louis Dunn, who had headed Cal Tech's Jet Propulsion Laboratory; James Fletcher, who became head of NASA (and as such became controversial, but there was no controversy about his superb abilities as a scientist-engineer); Ralph Johnson, who had been Associate Director of Research of the Atomic Energy Commission; Ruben Mettler, who rose to head all TRW's defense and space work and later became its chief executive and chairman; George Mueller, who later directed the Apollo manned lunar-landing program; George Solomon, who became executive vice president of TRW; Albert Wheelon, who became chairman of Hughes Aircraft.

I commented earlier that the technological industry of the United States in 1946, other than the defense-dominated aircraft manufacturers, had compelling reasons to assign the highest priorities to consumer products so badly neglected during the war and the Depression before it. Further, most of the best university physical scientists and engineers, who had been enlisted for development of military technology during the war, had returned to their university research, glad to be free of wartime pressures. As our experience at Hughes Aircraft showed, however, some engineers and scientists were keenly interested in the new military technology of missiles and complex electronic systems, and we were able to attract a substantial number of the nation's creative specialists. But the ICBM program needed a cast of stars and supporting players ten times greater than we had assembled at Hughes. Had the ICBM project arisen as early as 1946, 1948, or 1950, the lack of available talent would have created a severe bottleneck. Fortunately, the ICBM era started eight or nine years after the end of World War II, not earlier. By 1954, the mood of the academic scientists and engineers had changed considerably. Many began to consider the Soviet Union a serious threat. They were established in their university jobs and occupied with their research, but were willing to devote some time to advising the Department of Defense or to accept DoD funds for research.

John von Neumann's availability to the ICBM program in late 1953 is a prime example. By 1954, not only was he chairing the Gardner task force (renamed the von Neumann Committee and made the official advisory committee for the ICBM program), but he took a leave from academic life and accepted an appointment to the Atomic Energy Commission (AEC). All nuclear matters in the 1950s were under the control of the AEC, which had five full-time commissioners. Traditionally, one of the commissioners was a recognized statesman-scientist, and von Neumann filled that role. As such, he was able to ensure that the AEC would give top support to the ICBM program, with warheads tailored to fit the program's needs. The AEC had a rather special position with academic scientists, since the original Manhattan Project had brought a substantial fraction of its most gifted physical scientists into the American nuclear program. Von Neumann's close personal identification with the ICBM made him a powerful force in attracting former Manhattan Project people to the ICBM.

There was a tragic aspect to von Neumann's involvement with the ICBM. Not long after he joined the government, it was discovered that he had cancer. The disease was already so advanced that he was given no hope. He retained his position on the AEC and continued as chairman of the ICBM Science Advisory Committee until the final days of his life. We even held two meetings of the Advisory Committee in the Walter Reed Hospital in Washington, where he was treated during the last months.

I will never forget the last meeting, in the fall of 1956; it was held just after surgery had been performed with the hope of delaying the end. He was brought to the meeting room in a wheelchair, from which he ran the session of several hours' duration, his intellect as strong and his personality as charismatic as ever. His determination to go on contributing, even in his fatal illness, to what he felt was the nation's most important project earned him unbounded respect. During the last year of his life, a phone call about the project from Dr. von Neumann to people within and outside government was highly influential in eliminating bottlenecks.

I know that the others, like me, felt an immense desire to prove out our ICBM design before von Neumann's death. We failed in that. But he told me, before his death in February 1957 (four months before our first test flight), that he was certain the race was won. He had to leave the project, but he had helped to get it started and he knew that.

Turning from people to companies: by 1954 the American technological industry had completed much of what it had regarded as its first priority, to reestablish its lines of civilian products. Moreover, industry realized that the technology being developed under DoD funding was extremely bold, and it seemed mandatory to lay the groundwork for future civilian products by engaging in military R&D. Any company lacking military contracts in 1954 feared it might be handicapped by being unfamiliar with new and promising technology.

Thus, the interest and availability of technical experts in both industry and the universities were great enough in 1954 to handle major technological developments. Simultaneously, the Soviet Union's head start on an ICBM was widely recognized in the technological fraternity as a terrifying, unacceptable threat to U.S. security. The timing was fortuitous to develop the ICBM program.

The availability of top talent lasted for over a decade. Then, in the middle 1960s, the Vietnam War lessened the willingness of many scientists to work on military projects. By the early 1970s, most leading scientists and engineers in universities had become unresponsive to invitations to engage in military R&D. President Nixon, angry with the academic scientists for their failure to support the war in Vietnam, stopped the annual awarding of the National Science Medal, the country's top science award, and in January 1973 fired his science advisor and disbanded the President's Science Advisory Committee. Congress equally foolishly banned all DoD funding of basic research in universities, and the universities began to ban classified work on campus; the breach between academia and DoD widened.

Antagonism toward military projects continues in much of the academic world to the present. I see some university scientists and engineers almost weekly, either on campus or in advisory boards, professional societies' symposia, national academy gatherings, or socially. A large number want nothing to do with classified work. They think the military and the Administration have exaggerated defense needs and that selfish interests are overriding objectivity and common sense in the allocation of resources for national security. Half the time, I agree with them. They want greater emphasis on education and on wide-ranging pure research that holds promise for major benefits to civilization. Here I agree all the time.

Today, the U.S. technological industry views the future as offering possibilities for highly profitable, commercial exploitation of new advances; it is simultaneously worried about increasing worldwide competition. Business leadership is not anxious to watch Japanese and Western European companies take over consumer and industrial markets while we assign so many of our best professionals to military programs. Managers of American technological industry still seek military contracts because they can help establish a foundation for future and novel civilian products. Overall, however, these executives look today for a balance of military and civilian efforts; they no longer automatically favor the nation's military needs as they make their plans.

Contrast this with the 1954 situation. At the beginning of the ICBM program, some twenty-five principal executives of America's top technological corporations were summoned to the Pentagon, where they heard Secretary Wilson state why the President felt it urgent to win the ICBM race and why industrial leaders were needed toward that effort. Present to support this view were such celebrities as Charles Lindbergh and Jimmy Doolittle. Details were presented by insiders such as Schriever, von Neumann, and me. In addition to the industry executives, the presidents of universities with the strongest engineering and science departments were invited. Pressure from the government, together with the strong credibility of the case as presented that national security was at stake, led immediately to a phenomenal degree of cooperation.

Consider one example. To launch our attack on the reentry problem, we set up a six-week brainstorming session immediately following the Pentagon briefing. As chairman I was able to recruit Dr. Robert Bacher, then head of the physics division of Cal Tech, one of the most prestigious physics groups in the nation, often rated academe's number one. Invited to join Bacher for the full period were several scientists, the most brilliant in the country equipped to deal with this problem. Six were drawn from the universities and three from industry. All accepted, even though doing so interfered with their plans.

The Bacher group laid out a program which included several parallel elements. By 1955, a special vehicle had been designed, fabricated, and shot by rocket ten miles up into the thin atmosphere. As it was on its way back down, two additional rockets were fired to build up speed, causing the nose cone, as it entered the dense lower atmosphere, to endure even higher temperatures than an ICBM nose cone would encounter. The rocket was highly instrumented so we could gather critical data on the heat buildup and the way heat was transmitted to the passing air or absorbed in the outer material encasing the nose cone. The Bacher panel also proposed setting up the so-called shock-tube laboratories, where air held under high pressure was suddenly released and discharged at the very high speeds typical of reentry conditions. The airflow was caused to impinge on model nose cones, and again the temperature buildup and its consequences were studied.

Through aggressive follow-up of the important beginnings the Bacher group had provided, the reentry problem was solved. When long-range flight tests of our ICBMs began, the reentry vehicles performed precisely the way the theory and experiments preceding those tests had indicated.

To illustrate how different the environment is today for a high-priority project, let us do some imagining. Suppose the President of the United States were to announce in great secrecy to a small group of influential leaders in Congress that the United States must undertake a huge crash program or the consequences to the country would be disastrous. What would result?

First, the meeting would be leaked to the public and the reasoning behind the President's proposal would be disputed by politicians, media commentators, and scientists. The need for the project would be seen by some as exaggerated and as nonsense by others—in part because of the poor track record of earlier claims. The bigger the proposed program, the greater the opposition, because various interests would see that it might involve a reduction in other programs they favored. If the President were to include executives of industry and presidents of universities in our hypothetical meeting, pleading that they assign their outstanding scientists and engineers to this supercritical project, the executives would hesitate to commit themselves. They would fear handicapping their company's competitiveness in the world marketplace if they shifted their talented scientists to the President's project. The university presidents would know that few of their best professors would leave their chosen research to work on a military project.

In recent years, the voters, too, have become skeptical about the need for new, expensive weapons systems and have come to appreciate, to their credit, that national security involves much more than weapons systems. To be secure, the United States needs economic strength, social stability, skill in formulating foreign policy and negotiating with other nations, a healthy industrial infrastructure, assured availability of resources essential to national strength, and, finally, adequate military forces. This list is long, and the military is only one factor. That component, adequate military forces, includes a rather varied set of sub-requirements, one of which is weaponry. (Another is trained manpower, for example.) And weaponry includes not only complex weapons based on radical advances in technology but also much mundane and simple military hardware.

The state of the economy is very sensitive to overall efforts in science and technology. We must not place emphasis on sophisticated weapons systems alone and inadvertently deny ourselves the resources to create technologically advanced civilian products, because economic strength and international competitiveness are also requisite for national security. This would not be a matter of concern if we had resources to spare and a clear superiority over other nations in all technology. Unfortunately, such overwhelming preeminence no longer exists. Launching a huge crash program without controversy and delay is now impossible.

There is another important reason why the ICBM program went well. To cut the costs and time to complete any major project calls for a streamlined administration. Today, bypassing layers of red tape is out of the question; approval must be granted every step of the way. Every conceivable factor in a bureaucracy now seems to have an active part. Contrast this with the ICBM program in 1954.

Dwight Eisenhower was President, and not since George Washington had we had a leader in the White House in whom the public placed such confidence on military matters. With Eisenhower as President, the ICBM program could be launched with only a few members of Congress fully informed. If Ike said the program called for exceptional delegation of authority to its management team and a forgoing of the usual congressional reviews, Congress assumed that backing his recommendation was in the nation's interest. In 1954, the late Senator Henry "Scoop" Jackson, a Democrat, was a principal figure in the nonpartisan effort that enabled the ICBM program to move without congressional delay. He put in writing strong private advice to President Eisenhower that the program be established with the highest priority and the usual review process be waived. He did this even though he was called the Senator from Boeing, and Boeing, the major defense contractor from his state, was at that time the principal contractor on the U.S. manned-bomber program which the ICBM might replace, with no guarantee that Boeing would win any ICBM contracts.

Even in 1954, the defense bureaucracy was so strong that it was difficult to speed a project through. It is far worse in the late 1980s, but the overlapping review system that grew quickly after WW II would have been enough then to force the ICBM project to move at a snail's pace had it not been for Trevor Gardner's disdain for lower-level military and civil-service personnel. They were determined to get in on the ICBM management and Gardner was just as determined to deny them that opportunity. Again and again, the bureaucrats found that while they were still studying an action—perhaps to approve it, perhaps not, or more likely to demand more information and stall—it had already been implemented by Gardner. Were they then to insist on being involved, they would have had to seek a decision reversal, something they were loath to do because they might be accused of standing in the way of progress. They would give up.

Only rarely do appointees risk making enemies of the established bureaucracy. They may start their terms of office with great determination, but they usually temper it greatly when the entrenched bureaucracy threatens to overwhelm them. Every bureaucrat has countless allies. It was thus a conspicuous accident of timing that the irrepressible Gardner appeared on the scene in his particular post just when the ICBM program needed aggressive launching.

Considerable credit for Gardner's effectiveness belongs to Sec-retary Charles Wilson, whose instincts were always to cut red tape. Secretaries of Defense in the 1970s and 1980s have had, instead, to tolerate red tape—so that enough checks will minimize errors and hence a bad press. More recent Secretaries of Defense have had to devote much more time than Wilson did in the 1950s to defending DoD programs to the Congress and the media. I doubt if Wilson had to protect the huge ICBM program from either group of critics even once. Immediately after the Russians orbited Sputnik in 1957, *Meet the Press* wanted to quiz Wilson on TV on what that sensational accomplishment might mean to our nation's security. Wilson declined and actually got away with sending me instead.

One incident will illustrate the difference between then and now on this issue of defending government programs from its critics. After the ICBM contractors had been working furiously for a year, Secretary Wilson asked Trevor Gardner, General Schriever, and me to accompany him on a visit to each of the top dozen corpo-rations responsible for ICBM hardware. We covered the nation in the Secretary's plane, always going to the facility where the work was being carried out. Each meeting would start with Wilson's making certain that the chief executive, who would be present, was fully aware that, until the race with the U.S.S.R. was won, he must regard his company's part in the ICBM program as the most important mission of his organization.

On that trip, the Secretary brought with him a large briefcase full of internal Pentagon memoranda to read on the plane. Some-where between Washington, D.C., and Minneapolis, he handed me, with no comment, a memo prepared by some of his advisors on congressional relations. It warned that political woe (congres-sional investigations, for instance) was inevitable, because the pro-gram was so big. The paper insisted, in an ominous tone, that the management of the ICBM program always be prepared to defend itself. It suggested that detailed documentation accompany every act of management, to show that all alternatives had been thor-oughly examined and that each decision was clearly the best. Oth-erwise, the memo warned, there would be no way to handle the certain-to-arise accusations of incompetence, carelessness, blundering, waste, and perhaps illegal, even criminal, actions.

Secretary Wilson wanted my reactions. Were we adequately documenting our decisions? The question was not new, and I hated to be asked it by the Secretary. There was a seeming infinite number of technical decisions for which I had prime responsibility. The big decisions were highly documented, but I knew that if we did this for each and every item, we would have time to do little else. We would surely fail in attaining an operational ICBM system ahead of the Soviet Union. In truth, we often had to choose between two things: completeness in setting down why we were doing what we were doing, and getting on with doing it.

I decided to tell Secretary Wilson that good management seemed always to involve a contest between reducing risks to our necks and achieving success. "If we are successful," I blurted out, "if we get the ICBM designed and working in the shortest possible time, if we beat the Russians, then I feel confident I'll survive any attack on me that may come. On the other hand, if our project should fail, then the last thing I would want is to be associated with a *well-documented* failure!"

I had been concentrating so hard on how to express straight-forwardly what was on my mind that I was completely taken aback when he laughed loudly. Later during the trip, he asked if I would write down precisely what I had said. Since his request was flattering, I have always been able to recall the wording. As it turned out, the program was never accused of incompetent management or waste or worse, and I was never asked to appear before a congressional committee to defend my performance. If it had been otherwise, I might also recall my remark to the Secretary on the plane, where I sounded facetious but was entirely serious, but the memory would be less pleasant. The real point, of course, is that my reply, if given in the 1980s, not the 1950s, would not have been rated clever, but, rather, naïve and irritating. In today's environment, Schriever and I would have been forced to document and justify our every act—and it would have done us little good. We would have spent half our time defending the program and ourselves before

Congress, on TV, and in numerous government, industrial, and academic gatherings.

We were not greatly handicapped by political problems in the ICBM program, but we encountered a few. Harold Talbott was Secretary of the Air Force when the ICBM program was begun. At one point early in the program, a rocket-engine contractor who had lost out in the competitions succeeded in gaining Talbott's support to reopen the decision and elbow his way into the project. Talbott came to Los Angeles for the purpose of changing the contractor, a West Coast company, which the Project Office had chosen. The small meeting included Trevor Gardner, General Schriever, and me. The Secretary made the argument that the contractor for that particular task should be situated in the middle of the country (as was his candidate) because, in case of war, the two coasts would be bombed the most and the Midwest would be the safest. This was the "dispersal" policy Talbott had mandated for Air Force procurements.

It made a very weak rationale for reopening the selection process and dictating the use of his chosen contractor. The acknowledged paramount priority was for the United States to attain an ICBM capability before the Soviet Union. We were absolutely certain that the contractor Talbott was pushing, who had been properly evaluated against competition, was of marginal competence. It was critical to Gardner, Schriever, and me not to tolerate pressure to include unacceptable contractors who had used political influence to gain what management wouldn't give them.

Each of us was reluctant to challenge the Secretary, and we sat there speechless at first, each gauging the effect of bucking a high-level Presidential appointee. Schriever was an outstanding young general whose career might be ruined if he chose not to cooperate with the Secretary of the Air Force. I was the chief scientist on the program, but I was an employee of a private corporation, so the Secretary could not fire me. But could I refuse to cooperate with the Air Force's top executive and expect my company to go on doing business with that service? I was protected, of course, by the fact that my role did not include selecting contractors. General

Schriever, not I, represented the government in its contracting with industry. Yet I felt I should say something to oppose Talbott, because, unless he withdrew his directive, he would badly damage the program.

Trevor Gardner was a member of that Secretary's staff, reporting to him directly. Talbott could not dismiss Gardner unilaterally because Gardner was a Presidential appointee, but the Secretary's recommendation for his removal would be acted on within hours. Knowing Gardner as I did, I knew he would make a strong statement. His position in the government was in jeopardy, but not his life.

It was General Schriever, the one with the most to lose, who beat us to the draw in replying. He told the Secretary that complying with the directive would impair the program and very coolly explained why. Gardner and I immediately backed up Schriever. Talbott glowered, then lost his temper. He was a handsome, well-built man, elegant in attire and seemingly always poised, so it was scary to see him come apart, get red in the face, and with an ugly expression yell at Schriever: "Before this meeting is over, General, there's going to be one more colonel in the Air Force!" He had given Schriever an order, he ended his tirade by saying, and expected it to be obeyed.

"I can't accept that directive, Mr. Secretary," General Schriever said calmly, quietly, but with very clear enunciation, "because I have a prior and overriding order. On being handed this assignment, I was directed to run this program so as to attain an operational ICBM capability in the shortest possible time." His manner displayed no challenge or disrespect. He added, after a pause, that perhaps Talbott might wish to put in writing an order specifically naming his choice of contractor to replace the one already selected, and at the same time lower the priority of General Schriever's assignment and put industry dispersal above the need for speed in developing the ICBM.

The redness left Talbott's face and he turned pale. He made no comment and began to stare at the table, vigorously tapping a pencil on it and trying to pull himself together. He undoubtedly was thinking that if he put his directive in writing, he might have to cite more of his reasons for it than he would like. Also, Talbott's action would not go unnoticed. If the contractor was changed on Talbott's orders, it would be the talk of the industry. And there was Gardner to contend with. Talbott could expect Gardner to go have a talk with Secretary Wilson. Talbott would have to get Gardner removed from his job. He could not fire me directly; he would have to eliminate our company's involvement with the program.

In a few moments, his face returned to normal. With the fewest of words, he said to leave the contractor decision as it was, and left. I sat there wondering what Talbott would do next. If Talbott had been of a mind to do so, he could have harmed the project and all three of us personally. He chose not to. In fact, he went about singing the praises of the ICBM program's management team. Schriever had passed a vital test. If he had given in, he would have retained his title but lost control of the project. He was now firmly in charge.

Not too long afterward, Talbott's resignation was requested by Secretary Wilson because it had suddenly come to light that Talbott, using his Air Force letterhead, had been importuning government contractors to employ a firm he still owned. Perhaps the ICBM program benefitted because it was lucky enough to have certain players on the team, but also because it lost the participation of certain others.

FOUR

Heroics and Humility at Frontiers of Space

"What will we do next?" I found myself asking in 1956. We had assembled a remarkably capable team of scientists and engineers for the technical direction of the ICBM program, and it was now impossible to ignore that question. Of course, I knew the ICBM effort would not suddenly end after we had achieved a first operational capability. Second-, third-, and fourth-generation ICBMs surely would be developed, because the U.S. and the Soviet Union would feel compelled for decades to surpass or catch up with the other. The performance of successive ICBM systems would be steadily improved by advances in guidance accuracy, bomb yield, reliability, command and control, and survivability. Both superpowers would deem it vital to have the capability to retaliate with such severity, no matter how strong any surprise attack might be, as to deter any such attack being seriously contemplated. A continuing, if not an increasing, ICBM program seemed assured. But I knew that to continue to improve ICBMs over the years would be insufficient to motivate the brilliant group developing America's first ICBM. Once the system's capability was fully demonstrated, they would want to engage in new challenges, and they would not necessarily want to be limited to military technology.

One possibility was the exploration and utilization of the space surrounding Earth, both near in and far out. We were learning how to loft a heavy package of complex equipment high above the atmosphere and to cause it to travel several thousand miles around the globe to descend on a precisely designated area. The planet's being spherical meant that if we were careless in guidance accuracy and allowed the payload to reach a higher speed than intended, it could easily overshoot its target, miss Earth, and become an artificial satellite.* While developing the ICBM, it was very clear in 1956 that we were automatically also creating the entire range of technological tools needed for orbiting Earth: large rocket motors and matching fuels, light yet strong structures, electronics for control and guidance, test instrumentation, production lines turning out quantities of reliable hardware components, and large-scale launching and tracking facilities.

Many promising applications opened up. Thus, a satellite could be designed to serve as a communications relay. A radio signal could be sent up to a receiver in the satellite, and a companion transmitter in the spacecraft could direct the signal back down to a receiver elsewhere on Earth. A high satellite could put any two places on the planet in direct communication. It would become practical to broadcast radio and TV programs intercontinentally and to send telephonic communications and industrial, financial, medical, and every other kind of data all over the globe via satellite.

Satellites could be placed in highly stable orbits, their locations at all instants predictable with great accuracy. They then could act like instrumented artificial stars to create a breakthrough in airline navigation and traffic handling as to reliability, economy, and safety. Similar techniques could improve navigation of ships at sea.

Instrumented satellites could examine Earth and transmit observations to ground stations. This would have obvious application

---

* In fact, by substituting a lightweight radio transmitter in place of the heavy payload, we were able to orbit an entire Atlas ICBM (minus its booster) on December 18, 1958, and as a ploy to partially counter the Soviet Union's psychological victories in the earlier orbiting of their Sputniks, we broadcast taped holiday greetings from President Eisenhower to the world.

to military intelligence and reconnaissance and arms control; Earth-probing spacecraft also could benefit the mining, agriculture, petroleum, fishing, and forestry industries and aid in locating water supplies and improving flood and pollution control.

During the 1950s, even as the ICBM program was creating the foundation for the use of space, computer-technology advances were making it possible to process a tremendous amount of information quickly and economically. Space-, atmosphere-, and surface-based instruments could instantly report on worldwide environmental conditions (temperature, moisture content, pressure, tides and ocean-wave conditions, wind velocity, ice, snow, rain, fog, chlorophyl distribution, etc.) that affect weather changes. Great progress in weather forecasting could eventually result.

There was a strong possibility that the Ramo–Wooldridge ICBM team could find exciting outlets for its talents in a future U.S. space program. There would be such a program, I felt sure, and it would be big. As a result, in January 1956, I asked the company attorneys how we might protect the name Space Technology Laboratories for our possible future use. The answer was: to create a corporation with that name. Space Technology Laboratories was incorporated in early 1956 as a wholly owned subsidiary of the Ramo–Wooldridge Corporation. Of course, Space Technology Laboratories at that point was just a name; it existed only on paper. My plan was for the unit to begin operations in 1960 or 1961, after the ICBM program had achieved a first capability.

The Soviet Union's Sputnik was launched on a Saturday morning, October 4, 1957. I had missed predicting the start of the space age by an embarrassing three years or so. Every Saturday during the ICBM development, Benny Schriever and I would arrive at project headquarters early and spend the entire day (we called it Black Saturday) in a review of where everything stood on the program. Schriever and I arranged this review so we might uncover problems and, it was hoped, home in on opportunities for saving time. All day, we would list items that needed decisions or investigation during the week ahead. On this particular morning, the review was interrupted when we were given the news that the Russians had placed an artificial moon in Earth orbit. Black Saturday suddenly became black-and-blue Saturday. The American response to the accomplishment of the Soviet Union was comparable to the reaction I could remember to Lindbergh's landing in France, the Japanese bombing of Pearl Harbor, and Franklin D. Roosevelt's death.

I was furious with myself for not having predicted this Russian feat. Belatedly, I realized that anyone in the middle 1950s who had seriously pondered the Soviet Union's future technical activities should have expected it. Indeed, the United States had announced it would place a very modest instrumented capsule in orbit in 1958 as part of the International Geophysical Year, the IGY. The question had arisen earlier of assigning the production of that IGY satellite to the ICBM team. We had so large an assembly of engineering talent and apparatus and facilities that it would have been but a tiny chore to loft that small package. But when the IGY plans were being laid, America's ICBM program was still young and under tight security wraps. The military's priorities precluded delaying the ICBM's operational date even slightly to accommodate what they saw as a minor science experiment. Moreover, the IGY was an unclassified, open, international program. Putting the IGY satellite project into the ICBM organization might lead to leaks of classified information. At the time, it was a carefully guarded secret that the U.S. even had an ICBM project.

Intelligence reports indicated that the Soviet Union was behind us in the efficiency of its nuclear bombs and so had to design their ICBMs to carry heavier payloads, thus requiring correspondingly larger rocket engines. Their ICBM could consequently boost a greater weight into orbit than ours could. This might not have been enough for me to call out a Sputnik launch as a possibility. But there is more.

Although the IGY was an international program, it really had been planned under United States leadership. The Soviet Union's contribution was expected to be relatively minor, befitting a nation backward in science and technology. I should have known they would resent that. I should have put high odds on their finding it attractive to shame the United States' IGY instrument package by orbiting a much larger payload and doing it earlier.

If we ICBM insiders in the U.S. had foreseen in, say, 1955 that the Russians might put equipment in orbit in 1957, with enormous international implications, we could have asked that our team be given the job of trying to beat them. Had we done so, an appropriate U.S. space program would have been started earlier. As it was, Sputnik surprised the world and shocked the United States. We recognized that the Russians excelled in ballet and caviar, but we expected to be the first to launch an artificial moon. The Soviet's Sputnik offended and alarmed us. We responded to the challenge and the fear, and by early 1958 the space race was underway. Virtually all U.S.-government-sponsored research and development was accelerated, the President appointed a science assistant in the White House (James Killian, president of M.I.T.), and money was provided to the universities to expand education in science. Within a year, the United States created a new government agency to take us into space that reported to the President, the National Aeronautics and Space Administration (NASA).

The Soviet Union sparked our space program. Had they launched their Sputnik later, our space program would have begun later. If there was no space race with the Russians, the emphasis of the U.S. program might have been on orbiting an unmanned spy satellite, or creating a commercial project with immediate return on the investment, such as intercontinental television or telephony by satellite. Anyone with scientific curiosity about how biological matter (a man, for example) might respond to a gravity-free environment would have had to wait his or her turn in line along with researchers inquisitive about other frontiers of knowledge.

In a less competitive space program, the moon would have been kept in its proper place. But immediately after Sputnik, hawks, alarmist columnists, military zealots, and nervous scientists insisted that the moon must be captured at once and turned into an American platform from which to bomb the earth or to use as an invulnerable hiding place for nuclear weapons. They cited the moon as the military high ground (strangely overlooking that, to a man on the moon, Earth is the high ground) and warned that whoever controlled the moon would thereby control Earth. "What will we find when we land on the moon?" they asked. "If we delay, the Russians!"

This was foolish forecasting. Thirty years later, the moon still has no military role. Space has become highly important for certain military functions, but the moon is not a practical military base. Its potential ranges from uneconomic to irrelevant, its orbit around Earth is too far out, and its back side as a safe place for storing nuclear weapons is neither necessary nor advantageous. If we insist on extremely expensive and inhospitable weapons-storage sites, confusing such conditions with invulnerability, we might first look to the North and South Poles.

That we were so surprised by Sputnik and then responded in considerable confusion struck me as further evidence of the importance of engaging in competent prediction. My priority during the weekend of the Sputnik launch, however, was to press an idea with my associates. With their concurrence, I came into the office very early Monday morning and wrote an announcement changing the name of the Guided Missile Research Division of the Ramo–Wooldridge Corporation, the part of the company devoted to the ICBM program, to the Space Technology Laboratories, the name I had had waiting in the wings since the spring of 1956. The old name had been purposely general so as not to reveal what we were up to. The new name was a bit misleading, promising future activity rather than describing current work. But that was precisely what I wanted the name to do.

The name change was an immediate hit with our staff. Not so at all levels of the government. Donald Quarles, by then the Deputy Secretary of Defense under Charles Wilson, telephoned me two days later, on Wednesday morning. He seemed a bit on edge as he informed me that he and the Secretary had just learned I had announced a new name for the group at Ramo–Wooldridge that was engaged in the ICBM program.

"You're a private company, so I can't tell you what to do, Si" were, as I recall, his words. "But I must inform you that the Secretary and I are very disturbed. You are the technical director of the most critical, highest-priority, largest program of the Department of Defense, so you must be seen as having your feet firmly on the ground. The Secretary and I have agreed that this showmanship of the Russians soon will be rated trivial, which it really is. Their caper will be forgotten in two weeks. We're afraid you might then look foolish for having reacted impulsively, taking off into space, just the way the media have. So I'm asking you to consider dropping that new name."

I replied that I certainly would consider it (as he had requested), but my unspoken thoughts focused on his statement that Sputnik would be downrated to trivial and forgotten in two weeks. When we hung up, I asked myself, "Why don't I stall for two weeks?" and it so happened that, instead of dying out, the response to Sputnik mushroomed incredibly. I left the new name in place and I never heard about the matter again from the Office of the Secretary of Defense. By the third week, I had begun planning to exploit the title Space Technology Laboratories.

Industry's role in the impending space drama seemed totally predictable. The companies in the gigantic industrial complex devoted to the ICBM program in October 1957 possessed the capability to produce the hardware for the ICBM, and with their engineering staffs and factory unions, they would push hard to win contracts to develop and manufacture new space hardware, and thus maintain business volume and jobs. They would, of course, receive strong support from their congressmen, who would eagerly vote funds to protect employment among their constituents.

The public's emotional response to the Soviet Union's challenge combined with the industrial-congressional partnership would be powerful forces in building a national space program quickly. But others would surely be heard from. Well before Sputnik, the U.S. military knew that communications, intelligence, reconnaissance, and the command and control of ground, sea, and air battles could be greatly improved through space technology. Military leaders could be counted on to accelerate their efforts immediately to get funding to put equipment in orbit, a project they had been itching to begin but on which they had had to bide their time.

Finally, one could be confident that, with the Russian Sputniks in orbit, prominent pure-research scientists in the universities, including those who had originated the IGY program, soon would propose to dramatically increase research in space science. Space had been recognized before Sputnik as an exciting new arena for exploring the fundamental laws of nature. Because the American ICBM program had been highly classified, it had seemed remote to scientists not associated with it and they had not clamored to have their instruments placed thousands or millions of miles from Earth. Sputnik's launch surely would cause them to come forth now with ideas interesting not only to the scientific fraternity but to the public and hence to the Congress. They would propose space probes to sense light, infrared, radio, X-ray, and other radiation coming from the outermost reaches of the universe, to study the planets Venus and Mars and the more distant objects of our solar system from close up, and to examine Earth from space.

Good business planning for the space era ahead had to include predicting how the government would move. In the Defense Department, the Air Force surely would take the initiative, since its ICBM hardware and facilities would give it a head start. But all the services and the intelligence agencies would have an interest in improved communication, navigation, weather prediction, and observations of potential enemies' industrial activities and battlefields, so it could be expected that the Air Force would not be handed a monopoly. Inter-agency rivalry would exist in space, as it already did on Earth and in its atmosphere.

The way the government had handled atomic energy years earlier suggested how it might organize for the space effort. At the end of WW II, the application of nuclear science had been solely military, the atom bomb. It was clear that the government would support further nuclear advances, but politics favored giving non-warlike applications of atomic physics a semblance of equal priority. So instead of placing all nuclear activity in the Department of

Defense, the Congress had created the Atomic Energy Commission. With this experience as a guide, it was reasonable to expect the government to set up a new agency for space-science research and civilian applications.

These considerations suggested in October 1957 that we should expect a large-scale space program, with roles for the military services and for the pure researchers in the universities, based on expansion of the nation's resources created by the ICBM program. The program would be managed partly by the Department of Defense and partly by a new civilian space agency. As I look back now, I realize that the predicting I did then should be labeled mundanely analytical, rather than boldly imaginative. That the U.S. would soon embark on a project to land a man on the moon was a possibility I considered in 1957–58 but thought too unlikely to be funded. It was not included on my serious planning list.

Armed with my predictions, I went before the board of directors of Thompson Products, the financial backer of the Ramo–Wooldridge Corporation, in January 1958, to recommend a free-enterprise risk investment. It was to build a complex in which we would accommodate not only our ICBM team but also special laboratory, fabrication, assembly, and test facilities for the development and production of spacecraft. Counting everything from the land to the buildings and equipment, I estimated that some $25 million would be required. (Inflation, compounded over the past thirty years, would make this the equivalent of a $200 million gamble today.)

The proposed complex would contain many innovative features especially designed for spacecraft. Key to success, our team knew well, would be the ability to deal with the one-shot nature of placing equipment in orbit. Everything would have to be perfected before the boost into space, because once the spacecraft was launched, it would be impossible to make it work well by remote control if essential units were poorly designed or unreliable. And it would have been absurdly uneconomic to launch another spacecraft especially designed to bring a failed spacecraft back to Earth for repair or redesign. At the risk of diminishing reliability by adding complexity, it would be sensible to equip a typical spacecraft with some limited ability to alter its orientation or trajectory in response to signals sent from Earth. Granted such exceptions as these to post-launch adjustments, the main rule for spacecraft engineering would be to attain a high degree of confidence in the performance and life of the spacecraft before it is lofted.

This meant that the fabrication process and facilities would need to be different from those of ordinary production plants. Ingenious ways would have to be employed to check out the design of components to make certain that they would operate properly together when in space. Each tiny semiconductor, solar cell, switch, wire, circuit, sensor, pipe, valve, motor, bearing, gear, nut, bolt, connector, spring, insulator, fastener, magnet, or coil would have to be kept track of as it was fabricated, assembled into a flyable component, and finally placed in the spacecraft and tied in with the surrounding components. It would have to be protected constantly, so that after it was completed and tested as ready, no harm could inadvertently come to it. Unusual cleanliness would have to be maintained. The air would have to be constantly filtered. Technicians would have to wear covers over their shoes, hair, and clothing. The highly clean areas would have to be equipped with pressurized, dirt-removing, access booths so that workers would not bring particles of dust to a working component that would later cause a malfunction in space.

Components would have to be shaken and subjected to temperature, pressure, vacuum, and other environmental conditions duplicating those the apparatus would sustain during the boost and in space. The entire spacecraft would have to be placed in a large chamber from which the air would be withdrawn to create the near-perfect vacuum experienced thousands of miles above Earth's atmosphere. In a fifty-foot-diameter vacuum-holding sphere, we would have to install a high-temperature source simulating the sun's radiation striking one side of the spacecraft. The sphere's inner surface would have to be black and made cold to simulate outer space. This would test the structure's ability to handle extreme temperature differences. Again, the spacecraft would have to be placed in an "electronically quiet" chamber, one radio shielded so fully that test signals could be directed at the capsule, or received from its transmitters, without the confusing presence of the extraneous signals and static always abounding on Earth.

The company's board of directors approved the plan to create this complex and we built TRW's Space Park on one hundred acres in Redondo Beach, California. No such facility was erected in the late 1950s and early 1960s anywhere else in the United States, all our potential competitors taking it for granted that they should be given a spacecraft contract before risking an investment in such a facility. It proved fortunate for my continued good standing with the board of the company that events followed the predictions on which our space-facility gamble was based. NASA was created as anticipated (in October 1958), and its first contract to industry to build a spacecraft, called Pioneer I, was let to TRW.* We were able to win that award over the competition because of the steps we had taken earlier.

Later, satellites for worldwide intercontinental commercial telephony and TV transmission and for military communications and intelligence were designed and built by TRW's Space Technology Laboratories, as was the satellite-based space-data network for NASA. The first spacecraft to reach the outer planets Jupiter and Saturn and then escape from the solar system (carrying observational instruments primarily, but also clues to inform other intelligent life in the universe of our existence here on Earth, should any of them happen onto that craft) was a TRW project. We constructed the first arms-control spacecraft, capable of sensing nuclear tests anywhere about the globe, and a microminiaturized laboratory that was landed on Mars to search for life there.

Not long after President Kennedy's inauguration, the key space event for the future was to land a man on the moon. Before the Apollo project was approved and funded by Congress in late 1961, the Congress held hearings in which the "experts" were questioned.

---

* After Ramo–Wooldridge and Thompson Products merged in October 1958 and TRW became the name of the combined company. Space Technology Laboratories, originally a Ramo–Wooldridge division of which I was president, was made a separate corporate subsidiary of TRW, with Louis Dunn and later Ruben Mettler as its president.

Some argued that the enormous funds for the proposed project (about 100 billion 1988 dollars) would be better spent on scientific research to observe the universe from distant unmanned spacecraft, or to gain a deeper understanding of living cells, or determine the inner makeup of the atom's nucleus, or seek a cure for cancer. Many scientists felt the lunar landings would be little more than a dead-end psychological stunt of very minor scientific value.

If we had wanted only to examine the moon scientifically, we surely could have done so more quickly and cheaply by sending instrument packages there, including a device to pick up moon rocks and return them to Earth automatically, if getting hold of such matter was considered important enough. It soon became clear, however, that those who did not favor the Apollo program underestimated the American public's zeal for winning a space race with the Soviet Union. To be the first nation to put humans into a spacecraft and transport them for a walk on the moon would satisfy the nation's emotional needs as no other project could.

Of all the testimony presented during the congressional hearings on the proposed Apollo program, mine may have been the most equivocal. Everyone else seemed to be solidly for or against the project, but I decided only to describe what I thought were the pluses and minuses of going ahead. The chairman, Congressman John W. McCormack, said after my presentation was finished: "Dr. Ramo, I can't tell whether you are for this project or not." His comment was a fair one. I had too many misgivings to be a genuine advocate and yet I did not want to come out against the program.

In the first place, I felt that the project, already begun in a preliminary way, was certain to receive full backing regardless of what I said. The influences in favor were far stronger than those opposed. President Kennedy, after the Bay of Pigs fiasco, was determined to show courageous leadership and bolster America's confidence, and probably his own as well. By initiating a program to place an American on the moon, he certainly found a popular way to accomplish that. (Kennedy announced his decision to seek funding for the Apollo in a message to Congress on May 25, 1961, five weeks after the Bay of Pigs landing on April 17, 1961. On April

12, 1961, five days before the Bay of Pigs, the Soviet Union had placed the first human in orbit, making it imperative that we set out to catch up and outdo them.) The aerospace industry wanted the contracts the program would generate, and their congressmen backed them up. The public, knowing little about the technical challenges and costs and the potentially negative impact on other programs (less glamorous ones would have to take a backseat in funding), was wildly enthusiastic about a journey to the moon. Most engineers felt neutral about Apollo, but not those in the aerospace industry; they recognized that only a fantastic challenge like a manned lunar landing would ensure strong public backing for space, so they were enthusiastic about the project. It seemed that the Congress surely would vote the funds by an overwhelming majority.

Any inclination I might have had to speak out against Apollo was constrained also because of my admiration for the head of NASA, James E. Webb, one of the most competent individuals I had ever known. (He had been a successful lawyer, a top industry executive, director of the Bureau of the Budget, and Under-Secretary of State, and was outstanding in all these posts, before taking on the NASA job in the Kennedy Administration.) When the Apollo program was being organized, Webb, in anticipation of congressional backing, asked me to help him select one of our top executives to join NASA to run their manned programs. This resulted in Dr. George Mueller's becoming associate administrator of NASA for manned space flight. It was impossible for me to be negative or even lukewarm in public about the Apollo project when one of my protégés was to take on the major responsibility for its success.

Why, if the Apollo was sure to fly anyway and I could not really argue against it, did I not take advantage of the invitation to testify before Congress to come out strongly for the program, grab a banner, and rush to the head of the parade? After all, TRW was a space pioneer and its revenues would be enhanced by the program. We were not an "airplane cockpit" company and would not seek to build the main Apollo vehicles, but we surely could expect to supply many sophisticated subsystems. Apollo would mean that less financing would be available for other civilian spacecraft, but it seemed a good guess that even if Apollo was not approved, that money would not necessarily be allocated to those projects. There was nothing in sight comparable with a manned lunar landing to elicit congressional and public support for space. The U.S. military space programs would be separate, rated critical, and independently funded, and TRW would win a good share of the contracts in any case. I knew that if I were a NASA official judging competitors for contract awards on the Apollo program, I would not rate a company's performance as likely to be superb if one of its top officials went about knocking the program as a mistake. So why should I not do what I could to help both NASA and TRW by being a strong supporter?

My hesitancy stemmed from what I saw as extreme dangers to the astronauts. Unlike the ICBM project, where we could tolerate accidents in flight tests, Apollo flight failures were certain to cause human fatalities. It would not be the same as the occasional crash of a test airplane, because the entire world would be watching the Apollo flights. I felt certain that the program would suffer from unintended risk-taking common in government programs. (Contractors become increasingly optimistic as they compete; they go overboard in promising lower costs, better performance, and shorter schedules, outdoing each other to win contracts.) After the inevitable cost overruns and time slippages, gambles would be taken by NASA and the contractors. Steps needed to ensure the highest reliability and safety would be skipped. Even if there was no initial overoptimism, delivering men to the moon would be a whale of a new engineering experience, so there were certain to be human errors. During the flights, some things would be bound to go wrong. After a certain number of fatalities, the public would demand that the program be halted; it would not be judged vital to national security. The nation would be saddened, humiliated, and angry. The space industry and its engineers would get the blame.

My uneasiness about the Apollo program did not readily disappear as it progressed. In 1965 I accepted the chairmanship of an evaluation committee set up by the Central Intelligence Agency periodically to examine intelligence data with the objective of charting Soviet progress in space in comparison with our own. It was assumed that an all-out race to the moon was taking place. We would convene every several weeks to study the latest evidence, and after each session I would meet with the director of the C.I.A. (Richard Helms at that time) to report on the relative standing.

We were continually confounded by indications that the Soviets were not racing us to the moon. They kept placing astronauts in orbit with great success, and they were ground-testing large rocket engines that could boost a manned capsule to the moon. But our information and logical conjectures suggested that they were intent on exploring the moon with instruments, not men, exactly in line with my own preferences for a U.S. lunar program. What if they should attain success in examining the moon scientifically by or-biting it with instruments and landing instruments on it, while we were incurring fatalities, trying to deposit astronauts there? The Russians would be undisputed, seasoned champions in space, and we would be seen as immature, bumbling losers. I feared the Soviet Union might be doing it "right," and we might be doing it "wrong."

Imagine my alarm, then, when our first and only fatal accident in the entire Apollo program occurred. On January 27, 1967, the first Apollo capsule intended to fly with astronauts on board ex-perienced an internal fire and explosion while still on the launching pad at Cape Canaveral. All three astronauts in the capsule perished. This disaster stopped manned flights for eighteen months while changes were made in the design of the spacecraft and additional safety precautions were taken. I saw that tragedy as proof that my hunch had been right and that the Apollo program was in terrible trouble from which it might not emerge. I regretted not having opposed the project on these grounds at the very beginning, even if I had been ignored or looked upon as a doomsayer, a traitor to the industry and the space fraternity, a nuisance to NASA—and had greatly impaired my company, TRW.

It was lucky for me that I refrained from parading my misgivings in 1961, quietly accepted the Apollo program, and did everything

I could to ensure its success. The first successful landing of a man on the moon occurred on July 20, 1969, a few months earlier than the "end of the decade" December 1969 date I thought had been set by President Kennedy in 1961 with unjustified optimism and bravado. To my amazement, no further fatal accidents occurred in the entire Apollo program.

The successful lunar touchdown replaced the American public's sense of inferiority brought on by Sputnik with a feeling of newly confirmed superiority. Apprehension turned into exhilaration. American astronauts planting the U.S. flag and walking on the moon caused all Americans to walk taller. The Soviets, with their sensible, conservative program, based on examining the moon with unmanned instrument packages, had awful luck. Everything went wrong, and finally, after failure upon failure, they abandoned the project.

Although the Apollo program included a total of six manned landings on the moon that were accomplished to near perfection, one very scary, life-threatening accident occurred, as a result of which I had a most peculiar personal experience. It was with Apollo 13 in April 1970. An explosion in the spacecraft occurred as it was approaching the moon; the damage was extensive, but the astronauts' capsule remained safe and sound. Destroyed was the rocket motor to be used for takeoff from the moon after the planned landing. (In the Apollo scheme, the three-man main capsule, after arriving at the moon, went into orbit around it. Then two astronauts separated from the main craft in a lunar-landing vehicle, the third astronaut continuing to orbit. The pair landed safely, performed their duties, then took off to join the main vehicle for their return to Earth.)

With the propulsion designed for departing the lunar region no longer operative, it was imperative that the three-man spacecraft have its trajectory altered so as to clear the moon and that the separation of the lunar-landing vehicle be aborted. The only way to influence the motion of the spacecraft was to apply a force to it, and the only functioning rocket motor available to provide a thrust was a very small one whose primary job was to act as a retrorocket to slow down the lunar-landing vehicle and arrange for its soft landing on the moon. This propulsion system was equipped with only a modest amount of fuel, but the rocket thrust was controllable in both strength and direction.

One of TRW's assignments on the Apollo program was to design and produce that lunar-landing rocket and its controls. By remarkable coincidence, another of TRW's responsibilities was the computerized control of the Apollo flights. Part of that latter task was to preprogram the computers at the control center in Houston so as to be ready to act quickly to try to save the astronauts should something go wrong in flight. One possibility prepared for was the loss of the moon takeoff rocket and the consequent need to employ the small, lunar-landing motor in an attempt to return to Earth. This is exactly what was required on the ill-fated Apollo 13. Immediately after the explosion, TRW's computer-programming engineers started a crash effort to apply the ready computer program to figure out when to fire the little rocket—with what strength of thrust, for how long a duration, in what direction, at what particular points in the flight path—to dodge the moon, escape its gravity, return to Earth's vicinity, slow down so as not to burn up in the atmosphere, and land in the ocean near where the Navy was prepared to lift the astronauts from the water—all this by precisely rationed use of the limited available fuel.

To everyone's relief, when the computations were completed, they showed that it was possible—if everything was done just right, with essentially no margin for error—to rescue the astronauts by a controlled rocket-thrust program. The appropriate signals were sent, the little rocket performed perfectly, the astronauts were saved, and TRW's team had the gratitude of the astronauts and their families and of the whole NASA community.

I happened to be in Italy on my way to the Milan airport for a flight to London when the explosion occurred. No bulletin could reach me about the drama that was starting to unfold, but millions around the world heard the news: would the astronauts, nearing the moon, be able to avoid a collision and get back to Earth alive? I had just arrived at the airport and sat down to wait for my flight, when I was accosted by a television news team. Somehow the Milan TV news people had learned that TRW was involved, and they knew that I was a principal executive of that company and in Milan because I had given a talk the day before at a professional convention which had been covered by the media.

I responded to the TV interviewer at the airport in all innocence and puzzlement. I knew absolutely nothing at that moment. (I had even been unaware that a lunar flight was in progress; what with several successful landings earlier, my mind was on other things.) He didn't believe me. I learned afterward that TV newscasts in Europe later that day showed the airport scene, with me protesting a lack of knowledge and the interviewer suggesting that I was trying to avoid being associated with a fatal accident for which my company, he hinted, was probably to blame. It was not until I arrived in London that I learned what had happened on Apollo 13. To this day, I believe America was remarkably fortunate to have lost only three astronauts in the entire manned lunar-landing program.

Because the first step on the moon was taken by an American, the act became a symbol of the United States' undisputed world leadership in technology. In the future, as the world looked back on the twentieth century, although several enormous technological achievements might compete for historical first place (such as nuclear energy, electronic computers, genetic engineering, or space conquest), the landing of a man on the moon surely would be rated in a class by itself. And it was the United States that did it. So it followed that the United States was in a class by itself.

The phenomenal first touchdown on the moon closed the 1960s for America with glory, but what was to follow in the 1970s? What did the achievement mean as to the society's future utilization of space technology? We were surely not going to colonize the moon immediately. It appeared not at all sensible to extract lunar materials for near-term use on Earth. Further manned voyages to the moon, it seemed to the nation's leading scientists, would not give us nearly as much new knowledge as could be obtained by cheaper, easier means.

U.S. researchers were more interested in sending instrumented spacecraft to the other planets, and during the 1960s we had begun to place telescopes and other instruments in orbit to observe the Earth and the rest of the universe from outer space. Without waiting for decades and spending hundreds of billions of dollars to land astronauts on Mars and bring them back to Earth with the scientific data they might gather there, an instrumented robot was landed on that planet. This mechanism scooped up Martian surface matter. Then a microminiaturized laboratory within the package, highly automated and under computer control, processed the matter, scrutinized it scientifically for signs of existing or past life, and transmitted the data back to Earth. The physical scientists had little interest in putting humans in space in the 1960s and 1970s, and their priorities remain unchanged today.

Television and telephony between continents by unmanned satellites were seen to be superior to the old means, and communication companies began to use this technology aggressively in the 1960s. The DoD never created a humans-in-space program, never having wished to divert funds from unmanned-spacecraft projects, which they deemed of higher priority to improve military communications, intelligence, and reconnaissance.

So, as the 1970s opened, the space age was booming, but with unmanned spacecraft. The Apollo flights lost the attention of the public after a half-dozen successful landings (the last in December 1972) had accomplished the program's psychological mission. It was disturbing that the very space activity—humans in space—that had so enhanced America's image as the world's leader in technology was in trouble. The lunar-landing program had failed to establish that man deserved a priority role in space. The projects proposed had neither focus nor realistic justification for major continuing support, and they failed to attract it. * NASA budgets drifted downward.

---

* Skylab, a manned space station, was placed in orbit in 1973, using Apollo booster hardware. It remained there for six years, until it lost orbital speed and descended in pieces in Australia. Almost all that time, the station was empty and unused. After astronauts set space-walk records, NASA ran out of salable ideas for missions and out of funds. (With the Shuttle program's severe schedule slippage, NASA also lacked means to service Skylab.)

Confusion about justifications and priorities for manned space efforts have adversely affected the overall U.S. space program ever since. If we wish to study physical phenomena in space, instruments will measure them more accurately and completely than humans can. If we want to learn how Earth appears from space or what Venus is like up close, manmade devices can pick up anything human eyes can, and more. The same is true of military projects. Even keeping a spacecraft on a desired trajectory is a function best suited to manufactured devices. Advances in technology have made possible ever more sophisticated automation of information—whether it be sensing, data processing, on-board control, navigation, or communication back to Earth—at lowered cost, with less weight and with increasingly high reliability. Such advances lessen the dependence on astronauts.

It is common sense, however, that automating everything is not always best. Equally, to rely totally on human hands and backs or brains and senses for every task, deliberately excluding all mechanical or electronic aids, is not the optimum extreme. The human species is produced by low-skilled labor and its annual maintenance cost is low, considering that the body offers a remarkable combination of sensing and motions, memory and reasoning. But mechanical devices can exert a much greater force and withstand a much more severe environment. A human being can multiply a one-digit number by another at the rate of only one per second. An electronic computer can multiply two multiple-digit numbers in a billionth of a second. It is reasonable to assume that each category, people and machines, will have its place in space as well as on the ground. Including a human being in a spacecraft, however, complicates the project enormously. The health, comfort, and safe return of an astronaut must be provided for, narrowing the range of permissible risk-taking, and adding weight, cost, and time to the exercise. A very good reason must exist for including humans in space vehicles.

Huge space projects are proposed from time to time (for example, arrays of several miles in length and breadth to gather solar energy, convert it to microwaves, and beam it to ground receivers to power a city) that would require many astronaut-mechanics working a long time in high orbit to assemble the vast number of pieces making up the structure—it would be nonsensical to try to construct grandiose systems in space with robots operated by remote control from Earth. But the idea of providing electric energy for Earth in this enormously costly and complex manner is nonsensical in the first place. So far, every imagined space installation that, because of its size and the need for a multiple assembly operation, would absolutely require putting humans in space to build it has exhibited doubtful near-term value. Certain interesting semiconductor, pharmaceutical, and other materials are producible only in a nearly gravity-free environment. It is not evident, however, that the value of the end products would be consistent with the anticipated high cost of manufacturing them in space, and those unusual materials do not appear to be vital to society. An unarguable need to place any living thing in space (man, monkey, bug, or plant) arises only if the objective is to learn how that organism will fare in a gravity-free environment. To gather such knowledge in a hurry is not now a compelling requirement for national security or commercial competition.

We must recognize, of course, that some of our countrymen have a powerful urge to see Americans land on Mars someday, and ahead of astronauts from the Soviet Union. Yes, alas, there are always the Russians. Their reasons for placing astronauts in orbit may be no more specific or readily convincing than ours, but they seem intent on maintaining a station there, permanently occupied by humans. Their steady manned space activities are seen by some around the world as proving that they lead in space technology generally, and the political negatives to us of that impression would seem to require that we carry on some sort of appropriate program using astronauts. Moreover, it would be dangerous to assume that no role will ever exist for human beings in space. We should recognize that we are not smart enough to anticipate all future developments and needs in either military or civilian fields, and so must insure against overlooking important possibilities. As the 1960s ended, it would have been wise had we implemented for the 1970s and 1980s a calmly conceived, but modest research program of long duration on human ability to cope with space.

America actually accepted a seven-year hiatus after the last Apollo flight before it again placed humans in orbit, this time on the space Shuttle. The idea to develop the Shuttle began to take shape in 1973 for a number of reasons. One was economic. With the anticipated increased requirement to loft payloads regularly, it was natural for NASA to think it might be cheaper to launch them with a system in which at least part of the boosting equipment would return to Earth to be used again and again. Also, a large booster would be capable of taking a number of payloads up at the same time, and it was thought this might lower launching costs. To opt for a recoverable launch system did not automatically call, however, for the Shuttle's being manned. Still, humans clearly have capabilities that match well the tasks to be performed aboard a large craft if it is to discharge a number of diverse payloads at varying times during a flight.

Another motivation for the Shuttle was merely to reinject human beings into the nation's space program and satisfy the insistent desire that space be accessible to humans. The Apollo program had been huge, and to carry it out a large group of contractors, government bureaucracies, and individual experts had become involved, as had communities and congressional representatives. They all were hurt, economically and emotionally, when the man-in-space program was halted. Also, NASA believed that only with astronauts in the act could it hope to regain its lost image as the glamour agency of government and once again attract generous funding.

When detailed estimates of costs and time for the Shuttle were available, however, the figures were so high, and the time for its development so long, that NASA's ability to win support was thrown into question. Important military satellites, commercial communications satellites, and spacecraft for scientific research, all unmanned, would require the steady availability of boosters for a long time. But the U.S. already had unmanned, expendable launch vehicles adequate for some of these projects, and the industry could readily design bigger ones capable of placing in space all military and civilian spacecraft planned for the next decade and beyond. The Shuttle was not the only launching alternative, or even the best one.

The government, after considering the pros and cons, and weighing the political pressures from industry, NASA, DoD, and the science fraternity, decided to abandon the development and production of nonrecoverable launch vehicles and put all future U.S. payloads on the Shuttle. This decision, eliminating rivals, naturally increased the estimate of total tonnage to be launched annually by the Shuttle, cutting the estimated cost for launching individual payloads. Then (regrettably), to gain funding support, NASA based all estimates of cost, time, and performance on the most optimistic of possibilities. Because of this extreme optimism, the Shuttle program and its difficulties started at almost the same time. With the technical problems badly underestimated and the time allowed to complete the necessary steps far too short, the Shuttle's progress quickly slipped behind schedule. Much more funding had to be committed, some of it obtained by slighting NASA's other projects. The estimate of total payload weight the Shuttle was capable of carrying had to be lowered drastically, and the cost per pound to orbit payloads soared. The time and effort required between launches to get the Shuttle set for the next flight went way beyond estimates. (The main engines, it was initially claimed, would make fifty trips without requiring overhaul. Regular takeoffs by the Shuttle on a weekly schedule were expected. The actual schedule, before the Challenger accident, turned out to require months between takeoffs.)

Overoptimism made it impossible for the Shuttle to be launched into orbit on the committed dates. This created huge problems and much embarrassment. Some commercial American satellite projects that originally had counted on the Shuttle shifted to the Ariane, a European nonrecoverable booster, which could meet the schedule and also offer a lower launching price. (The European booster was hardly a technological advance. Its design copied the terminated U.S. expendable boosters that would have filled the need.)

The jewel in NASA's crown for many years was the scientific research program which sent unmanned spacecraft out to photograph the distant planets and record radiation from outer space. The U.S. had been preeminent in the use of space for scientific research, but the Shuttle program was responsible for a steady impairment of that position. When the Shuttle ran into cost overrun problems and delays, some of the space research projects were canceled, and all of them were greatly postponed. Support for planetary research explorations sank in the mid-1980s to twenty-five percent of the average budgets of the prior decade. NASA's nonmanned space efforts today get less than twenty percent of the agency's budget. A typical example of program slippage has been the Galileo project begun in 1977 for detailed study of the planet Jupiter. It was originally to be launched on the Shuttle in 1982. Even before the Challenger accident, problems with the Shuttle caused four postponements. The delay, having passed seven years, now seems likely to grow to ten. In 1986, in order to participate in the international effort to study the passby of Halley's Comet, American scientists had to arrange for their instruments to fly on a Soviet spacecraft.

The Challenger disaster in January 1986, which killed all seven passengers, led to a cessation of all Shuttle flights. It is clear now that the decision to put all our launching eggs in the Shuttle basket has caused the U.S. to suffer a decade of seriously limited ability to orbit its military, commercial, and research spacecraft. Because of that mistake, some fifty American satellites have been scheduled on the Ariane booster from 1988 to 1990 and beyond, providing that foreign launcher with a backlog of over $2 billion of business. Western Union, originally scheduled to orbit its Westar satellite on an early Shuttle flight, signed a letter of intent to have China do the boosting. As this is being written, other American commercial satellite producers are engaging in discussions with the Russians to boost American payloads into orbit. A large space telescope, finished and ready, and designed for launching from the Shuttle, sits in mothballs and will do so for years.

These are strange occurrences. The U.S. man-in-space program, previously heroic and the shining symbol of our superiority, has humbled the nation. And what would have happened if the estimates on the Shuttle—the market, cost, reliability, time to complete, risk to human life, and performance—had been realistic? The program probably would not have been funded. Instead, something much better might have occurred. For one, a modest and independent research program on humans in space could have been initiated. An unfrenzied, long-term program would have been appropriate because time was not critical (then or now) either for national security or for commercial reasons. Then, to launch the truly necessary payloads, unmanned expendable boosters could have been employed. They would have been reliable at lower costs, on schedule, and with no risk of human fatalities. No American boosting business would have been shifted to foreign competitors.

It never made sense to risk lives to launch unmanned spacecraft. If one unmanned booster in ten fails, the program costs are merely ten percent higher than anticipated. If one manned booster in ten fails, the program must be halted, probably for years, while an attempt is made to decrease the failure rate to one in a hundred or less, a tremendous challenge.

NASA compounded the Shuttle program errors. When manned craft are labeled experimental, they are understood to be dangerous. Those risking their lives flying in them are properly admired as heroes; they are doing something important for the nation even if the activity has a fair probability of killing them. If tragedies occur, there is sorrow, but the show goes on. The Shuttle, instead, was presented as a system for placing payloads into orbit economically, reliably, and safely. This optimistic misrepresentation went so far that senators and schoolteachers were included in the flights, obviously for public-relations purposes, with no serious on-board missions. When the Shuttle launches resume this year or next, it will be clear to the public that another fatal accident might happen. If it does, the Shuttle program may be ended in one catastrophic blow to the U.S. space capability and position.

When the Challenger disaster occurred, the White House's response was crisis-dominated. An investigatory commission, headed by former Secretary of State William Rogers, was appointed to find out whether the tragedy was caused by mechanical failure or human error. The commission's task was not to determine why we chose from the outset to gamble the nation's role in space on a launching system requiring humans aboard on every flight, a risky means for lofting payloads. The commission's hearings focused on the Challenger's failed O-rings, not on examining the nation's decision-making process when the Shuttle program was initiated.

Few voices were heard in strong opposition to the Shuttle program back in the 1970s. Except for some academic scientists who feared (quite justifiably, it turned out) that the Shuttle would usurp too much of available space funding, thus hampering space research, everyone was for the program—industry, Congress, NASA, DoD, and the White House. I had the same misgivings I had felt earlier about the Apollo program, but now I had an additional reason to keep them to myself. How could I argue in 1973–74 that the Shuttle was being overoptimistically presented and that serious delays, cost overruns, and disastrous accidents were likely, when the lunar-landing program had turned out so well and I had been so far off in my pessimistic expectations for it? How could I have presumed to advise my friend and long-time associate, Jim Fletcher—head of NASA when the Shuttle decision was being made—that everyone else counseling him was wrong? I couldn't, I didn't, and it did not occur to me that I should. In hindsight, I wish I had.

Neither NASA nor the White House has yet seemed to recognize adequately the mistakes of the past. After some months, two billion dollars was found to buy a replacement for Challenger, but no crash effort was initiated, although it was clearly called for, to produce an expendable, unmanned launcher, capable of orbiting everything required for years ahead in military, commercial, and space science activities, all of which are unmanned. (Some still-available expendable boosters suitable for lofting low-weight payloads had been ordered by the Air Force before the accident, but not in any great hurry.) Admittedly, there are technical challenges in building a new, large, expendable booster quickly, but that is far easier than increasing the Shuttle's safety and reliability so that regular flights can be counted on. Indeed, the date when the Shuttle might fly again and the frequency with which it might be used to launch spacecraft were again optimistically estimated after the Challenger accident and have twice had to be substantially revised. Despite the efforts by many on the inside (and loud shouts from many of us on the outside) to get on with the new expendable booster program, it is jelling very slowly. NASA, DoD, and the White House seem to be moving on a slow, committee route.

Probably more than any other government agency, NASA is beset by crisis, confusion, and pressures from its constituencies; it must bargain with Congress and sell itself to the media to get what it is after. But does NASA have a long-range space program? In asking that question, we must note in fairness that, because space is a developing field, NASA's goals cannot realistically ever be expected to be complete and to remain constant. Whatever is scheduled for the years ahead will continually need to be reconsidered and updated. Since space is so heavily involved with the long-term economic, security, and scientific research interests of the nation, however, it is not easy to accept that our space-program planning has been and is intermittent, political, and short-range.

The United States does not have an agenda for space for the next two decades, one which lists priorities, objectives, projects, dates, and funding requirements, which has recognition and approval from and stature with both the government's executive branch and the Congress, which is visible to and respected by the industry and the science and technology fraternity, and which has the understanding and support of all these influential players. I know Jim Fletcher is not happy with this state of affairs, but he is only one man concerned with policy. More leadership needs to come from the White House. Other crises seem to have priority there.

NASA's announced premier future project is the manned space station, a complex of interconnected facilities to remain permanently in orbit, able to accommodate astronauts for long periods. Like the Shuttle, it qualifies in some ways as a reasonable building block in the eventual extensive occupation of space by humans. But exactly as happened earlier with the Shuttle, extremely optimistic estimates about costs, performance, and time required for implementation are being made. A funding of around $30 billion is being put forth now as sufficient (the figure was $7 billion when the program was first approved by the President in 1985); the technical difficulties, safety hazards, and schedule slips will doubtless raise the figure to $50 billion or more. And there is no way to benefit from this initial expenditure unless liberal annual funding continues indefinitely to cover work by the astronauts stationed there. That program is vague as to its nature and potential.

Merely assembling the space station is expected to involve some thirty to forty Shuttle trips to carry astronaut-mechanics back and forth and to loft the equipment in orbit. What with other important payloads that must be orbited during the same period, NASA will need a sensationally long streak of luck in Shuttle launchings—a fantasy, in view of the Shuttle's record to date.

Suppose the emphasis had shifted after the Challenger accident to expendable boosters. What might have been done with the existing Shuttle craft? Improved to be adequately safe, with no hurry or corner cutting, those vehicles could have been assigned to a conservative man-in-space research program. Only professionals fully knowledgeable about the risks inherent in experimental craft would be permitted to fly in the Shuttle. The flights would gradually give us the experience to provide a safe space environment for astronauts. The flights also would allow for initial experimenting with such ideas as the manufacture of unusual materials in space. Emphasizing the research aspect of the Shuttle would have meant accepting a delay in the erecting of a permanent manned station in orbit. However, a sounder manned-space-station program would probably have yielded useful results earlier in the end than will the presently planned, overly optimistic space-platform project, which is almost certain to be plagued by delays, cost overruns, and perhaps preventable fatalities.

Just before the Challenger accident, the President, acting not on a White House perception of the need but on a directive from the Congress, appointed a commission to recommend long-range space plans for the nation. The group envisaged possible projects as far as the first half of the next century. One recommendation was to initiate a program that would land astronauts on Mars sometime in the next quarter century. One conclusion reached by the commission was that the U.S. space program has been overcommitted and underfunded in the past. The commission report was completely overshadowed by the Challenger accident, which put into question almost anything the commission might have recommended. Months have given way to years now and still no hearings have been held and no other responses have been made to the commission's recommendations. Meanwhile, other groups (from Senator Spark Matsunaga, the first to suggest it, to various space-science enthusiasts) have proposed that manned exploration of Mars be undertaken as a joint effort with the Soviet Union.

If the U.S. government is going to call again on experienced individuals outside NASA to aid in planning for space projects, they should not be asked this time to suggest projects for the decades ahead. They should be asked instead to recommend ways in which the nation might plan and implement a steady, credible long-term space program. We do not need to rush desperately to open negotiations with the U.S.S.R. to organize a joint mission that would create a permanent colony on Mars. A cooperative venture of some sort with the Soviets might be a good idea at some point, but it should fit into a well-thought-out U.S. space program, and no such program exists today.

The Shuttle and the permanent manned space station are paradigms of what in recent decades has become the American government's approach to making decisions on large technological projects. Instead of drawing up well-reasoned objectives based on realistic performance, cost, and timing—and with a balance of near-term and long-term goals selected after considering alternatives that the same funding might make possible—we act in a frenzy. If a project is truly a major advance, too many unknowns exist to allow accurate forecasts of cost and usefulness. To be on the safe side, the worst would have to be assumed for every questionable figure; the result would keep the proposed project from being accepted and funded. The involved government agency, the industry seeking contracts, members of Congress whose constituencies stand to gain, and the participating scientists and engineers choose, instead, the route of high optimism. Realists are labeled pessimists and are excluded. The project is then funded, and shortly after the contracts are let, the difficulties begin. Trouble is hidden for a year or so, after which the project becomes a public embarrassment.

In our highly technological society, we should continually expect to select and implement huge science-technology programs in which the federal government is the principal force. These projects would be over and above what the technological industry, the universities, and the private sector carry on independently. In large-scale military, space, energy, biomedical, and environmental projects, the government will be the decider, sponsor, director, overseer, and often the customer. Such projects will typically involve tens of billions of dollars, several government agencies, and much negotiating with the Congress, and will affect the economic strength and security of the nation. It follows, then, that integration of policy and planning, the setting of priorities, allocation of resources, and final decisions must come from the White House. The President must have around him assistants capable of assembling the men and women whose expertise can support strong leadership. Science and technology policy-making in the White House has for far too long been highly inadequate. We must next discuss it.

FIVE

Rockefeller and Science in the White House

Early in 1975, shortly after Nelson Rockefeller became Vice President in the Ford Administration, a telephone call came in to me from the White House. The business day had just begun in Los Angeles. Mrs. Rice, my secretary, buzzed me and I stepped away from a meeting just getting underway. As though giving me an offhand message, she reported, straight-faced, that a White House operator was on the line inquiring if Dr. Ramo was available for Vice President Rockefeller. Mrs. Rice mischievously asked me, "Is Dr. Ramo available?" I immediately switched the receiver to the incoming call and said, "Hello. This is Simon Ramo speaking." I expected the operator to ask me to hold. Instead, a gravelly voice said, "Is that so—well, this is Nelson Rockefeller speaking. How are you, Si? The last time we talked, it was 1968—in California—at John McCone's home."

I had not expected such an opening, because my acquaintanceship with Nelson Rockefeller was superficial. I remembered well that he had been in Southern California and at the McCones'*

---

* John McCone, a prominent California industrialist and community leader, who had at various times been Under-Secretary of the Air Force, chairman of the Atomic Energy Commission, and director of the C.I.A., was then back in his San Marino home.

for a small dinner party in his honor in 1968 during his travels in a late-start attempt to challenge Richard Nixon for the Republican nomination. That occasion had been the only opportunity I had ever had to talk with Rockefeller. At his initiative, we had speculated briefly about how future advances in technology might change society. I had recalled being impressed with his interest in the subject. I had not seen him since, but cannot say I was amazed that he had that special skill many politicians develop of remembering people even after meeting them for a very short time.

He then went on to say something like: "I have a task, an important one, that President Ford has asked me to give attention to. I think it's one you're interested in and I hope you might help me with. You get to Washington occasionally, I understand. The next time you happen to be here, perhaps you could drop in on me and we might have lunch."

The next day, just happening to be in Washington, I had lunch with Nelson Rockefeller in his office.

"I have a question for you," he said after we finished a first course of jellied tomato consommé, during which we updated in a rambling way our earlier discussion about the effect of advancing technology on society. "What is the right role for the White House in science and technology?"

Ever since the Soviet Union's surprising Sputnik launch in 1957, shortly after which Eisenhower established the position of Special Assistant to the President for Science and Technology, a science and technology advisor had existed in the White House. This had been so, that is, until Richard Nixon's second term began in January 1973. The Office of Science and Technology (OST), as it came to be called, and the President's Science Advisory Committee (PSAC), which was an extension of that office, were regarded as nuisances by Nixon and his principal staff aides. They denigrated the office for four years and contemplated the pleasure of eliminating it. Dr. Lee DuBridge, one of the world's most prominent science statesmen, had left the presidency of the California Institute of Technology to accept Nixon's invitation to be his science advisor. He told me later that Nixon made only one direct request of him during his tenure. It was to prepare a one-page abstract of a book (only slightly related to science) that Nixon had heard about.

DuBridge resigned after two years and was replaced by Dr. Edward David of the Bell Laboratories. It was said by some scientists, aware of Nixon's scant interest in advice from their fraternity, that David had been selected because, being younger and less well known than DuBridge, he could be ignored more easily. It was just Nixon's luck that David turned out to be exceptionally smart and actively conscientious; the combination made him extremely hard to ignore.

The PSAC members, only part-time advisors, and individuals of high prestige in their fields, did not see themselves as part of the White House staff. They felt no need to be devoted to President Nixon's positions, although they preserved confidentiality and did not go public with the results of their deliberations. When Nixon pushed hard for an American Supersonic Transport (SST), for example, the PSAC splashed cold water on it, predicting the SST would have extremely negative impact on the environment (impairing the planet's protective ozone layer, generating intolerable noise at low altitude and on the ground, and setting off supersonic shock waves at high altitude). They also decried the bad economics of the SST, which they ascribed to a severe disparity between the likely low revenues and the equally likely high costs of development and operation. Nixon wanted the Congress to make the SST a government-sponsored program, but Congress, like the PSAC, saw it as not fit to be funded.

After his landslide victory in November 1972, Nixon abolished the OST and banished both science advisor David and the PSAC, thus cutting the link between the White House and the nation's leading science and technology professionals. Nixon was privileged to do that. He needed no approval from the Congress, because the OST had been created by executive order.

I had heard before our luncheon that Nelson Rockefeller, almost from the moment he arrived in the White House in December 1974—after Nixon resigned because of Watergate, and Gerald Ford was President—had expressed vehemently to Ford his concern that science and technology were missing from the President's staff. It was difficult for Rockefeller to imagine any important issue—national security, international commercial competitiveness, employment, inflation, productivity, energy, economic expansion—that did not involve science and technology in a significant way. As he made this point over a broiled veal chop, fresh green beans, and a little star-shaped mound of mashed turnips (I think that's what it was), I thought about the Rockefeller family's philanthropy, about Nelson's well-known interest when Governor of New York in the universities of that state, the many private universities and foundations that the family had launched or nurtured over the years, and the remarkable record of those organizations in science—the University of Chicago and Rockefeller University, for example. Sitting there looking at him and listening to his comments, I said to myself: This man has a natural appreciation for the benefits science can generate.

It is absolutely unforgivable in this highly technological society of ours, commented the Vice President, for the White House to neglect science and technology. Carrying out the government's science-and-technology programs should be the responsibility of the Defense Department, NASA, the National Science Foundation, and other operating units of the government—but only up to a point. Policy regarding such programs needs to be integrated "right here, around the President," he stated.

We began to discuss how varied the White House's role is in dealing with science and technology. The federal government's sponsorship of basic research in the universities, for instance, is very different from its mission in the development of energy alternatives, or space exploration, or computers and communications, or air transportation, or automobiles, or military weapons.

By the time the honeydew melon was put on the table, Rockefeller had told me that he had President Ford's backing to re-create an office of science and technology within the White House, but this time, as the Vice President put it, to "do it right." He explained that the new office was to be defined and implemented in full cooperation with the Congress, through legislation, so that no future President who might not comprehend the importance to the country of science and technology could easily abolish it.

Rockefeller said he hoped I would give substantial personal time to help him on this project. He also told me why he had called upon someone like me to assist him. Questions of pure science, he emphasized, were not for the White House to deal with, but setting policy on science and technology was a different matter. To set up an office to integrate policy, the Vice President felt he should seek aid from someone whose experience included putting science and technology to work. He believed a proper White House office should focus on the relationship of science and technology to the social, economic, security, and political problems the President must deal with.

I assumed that he had considered various names recommended to him for help and had then decided to try me out. I was to come back after thinking about his proposal and suggest to him how to tackle the task. He stressed that he wanted to move quickly. It occurred to me that maybe he was in a hurry to determine if I was going to be productive, so he could turn immediately to someone else if I was not.

I left the Vice President's office resolved to try as hard as I could to help him bring science wisdom back to the White House. My assisting him would be a perfect match of interests. For at least a decade, it had seemed that in every activity I had been involved in—TRW management, universities, government advice, national academy affairs—evidence would constantly turn up of great weakness in government formulation of policy on issues concerning science and technology. Too often, the government failed in its responsibility and hindered progress. My favorite "broad national interest" hobby had become pondering such science-technology policy issues as: How do we arrange for the United States to win international technology competitions? How can advances in science and technology be best applied to provide national security? What is the proper role of government in fostering basic scientific research and advances in technology when the nation is so peculiarly a hybrid of government power and free enterprise? How can we as a nation improve the way in which we examine alternatives, set priorities, and organize for action in science and technology? How can the United States exert world leadership for a successful transition to a future when, it is to be hoped, technology will be used to the fullest to benefit society?

For several years I had deliberately chosen my activities, aside from my main TRW responsibility, to involve myself in these questions. An invitation to deliver a university lecture or a graduation address, serve on a government advisory board, or present a paper or write an article or a book was accepted or not, depending on whether the event related to the science-society-government connection.

By the time I met with the Vice President, I had developed some strong convictions on the subject. One, for example, was that future U.S. world leadership in technology would hinge on greatly enhancing our technological entrepreneurship (to be discussed in a later chapter). Another was that America's success in attaining supremacy in science and technology and supporting social stability in the world could be furthered by vision and leadership in the White House. In addition to political, national-security, and economic matters, the White House staff and the President should play a major role in spurring science and technology and be vitally concerned with their social and economic impact. So I thought I had some idea of what to suggest for the new White House office Rockefeller was talking about. Now, unexpectedly, I was being given an opportunity to participate in creating that office. And with Nelson Rockefeller behind the idea, there might really be action!

But certain concerns kept my expectations from soaring too high. Over the years, I had also built up some negative biases. One was that the federal government was a totally inept bureaucracy, a permanent handicap to progress. Another was that its leading executives were ignorant about science and technology and overly disposed to ignore long-range considerations and focus on immediate crises. At the same time, I knew how difficult it was for government leaders to find time for long-range deliberations, and the situation was worse, not unique, when science and technology were involved. I had arrived at the White House with prejudices, but as I left the meeting, I decided to be optimistic. After all, here was Nelson Rockefeller attacking a science-society issue with great sincerity and sophistication. Moreover, by allowing my new hopes to push my biases into the background, I found it not difficult to recall that other leading officials on occasion had recognized the importance of science and technology.

Take Dr. Henry Kissinger, for example. Seeking to give attention to significant interdisciplinary issues, Kissinger, after becoming Secretary of State in the second Nixon term in early 1973, appointed an Advisory Committee to the Secretary of State for Science and Foreign Affairs. I was invited to serve on it. Before this committee were concerns such as nuclear-weapons proliferation and international control of fissile material; the prevention of the transfer of know-how for the design and building of nuclear bombs; the oceans' resources (the potential for mining the ocean bottoms and the forming of an international organization to hold rights to such resources); international space agreements (assignments of positioning slots for space satellites, radio-frequency allocations, and the rights and obligations of nations in scanning Earth for physical resources); the flow of computerized information (agreements for electronic data transfer across borders); environmental controls (the effects of fuel burning, chemical processing, and nuclear-waste disposal by individual nations on the soil, waters, and atmosphere of other nations).

Kissinger at one point pondered whether it is better for our advances in science and technology to be held totally to ourselves or to be made partially available to other nations in return for their cooperation in important international matters. He sent me to the Soviet Union in September 1973, to visit with their leading technical-operations managers. He had in mind tempting them with the possibility of transfers of some of our civilian technology if they were to adopt a cooperative stance on numerous contentious issues. *

---

* The formal invitation actually came to me through the National Science Foundation. Having been told that the mission was Kissinger's idea, but not being clear as to what I was expected to accomplish, I placed a call to Kissinger in Washington and was told he was out of the city. That night he and I accidentally found ourselves at the same dinner at a private home in Malibu, California, and I got my instructions "to leave the Soviet officials with the feeling that we take detente seriously and that, with growing detente, technology interchange may not be precluded."

But Kissinger did not really have time for foreign-policy questions involving science and technology. He had planned to attend our committee meetings, but he never made it even to one. No sooner had he established the committee than he had to contend with the 1973 Arab–Israeli war and the possibility of a U.S.–Soviet Union confrontation in the Near East. Then came Watergate. Though it did not involve Kissinger personally, it understandably distracted his attention from other problems.

Whether my mission to the Soviet Union was a success, I was not able to judge. I wrote a memorandum after I returned that essentially said the Russians were extremely anxious to lay their hands on our technology and might do some things in return that we would find advantageous, but it was clear that our industry, where that technology was to be found, would not share it without a proper quid pro quo. I never got to report directly to the Secretary on the trip.

The Advisory Committee to the Secretary of State for Science and Foreign Affairs carried on its activities in the absence of a White House science-and-technology office. No White House interest in the committee's recommendations was ever apparent. Such lack of communication surely limited the panel's usefulness.

Having attacked an array of issues that seemed to us to be extremely important, the committee was naturally concerned that there was no permanent high-level post in the State Department with a continuing responsibility for science-related matters. We proposed that there be an Assistant Secretary of State for Science and Foreign Affairs. A new position was actually created, but with the strange and complex title of Assistant Secretary of State for Oceans and International Environmental and Scientific Affairs. When it came time to make the appointment, the White House looked upon the office as providing the opportunity to solve a political-appointee problem. It happened that the energy crisis had forced the setting up of ERDA (the Energy Research and Development Administration); the AEC (Atomic Energy Commission) lost its name and independence and its functions were placed within ERDA. Dr. Dixy Lee Ray, the AEC chairman and a respected scientist, had hoped she would be chosen to head ERDA. When she was not, the White House had the brilliant idea that she and her admirers would be kept happy with a different prize. She was persuaded to become the first Assistant Secretary of State for Oceans and International Environmental and Scientific Affairs. She quickly found she was too far back on the waiting list to get in to see the Secretary and could not obtain approval for the staff and budget she felt necessary. So she resigned and later ran successfully for governor of the state of Washington. The office remained unfilled.

After Jimmy Carter became President in 1977, many months elapsed before an appointment was made, the low prestige of the office made evident by this neglect. In every new Administration, it seems, the key players lack background in technology; they tend, therefore, to be slow in making appointments to offices dealing with such matters. Typically, positions such as head of NASA, the White House science advisor, or assistant secretaries dealing with science or technology are filled months after other appointments are made. The eventual appointee was Patsy Takemoto Mink, who had been defeated the previous November for reelection as congresswoman from Hawaii. She had no background whatsoever in science or technology. The reason for her selection was to give the state of Hawaii representation in the Carter Administration. (She came from the one state totally surrounded by water; her appointment tied in well with the word "oceans" in the title.)

Kissinger's Advisory Committee on Science and Foreign Affairs may have served some useful purposes. On the whole, however, its creation was mainly significant as evidence that Henry Kissinger (despite the comment he would enjoy making whenever he ran into me that while he knew a little about political science he knew nothing of physical science) understood that science does have a place in long-range foreign-policy decisions.

I planned to report back to Rockefeller in two weeks. I could sound out numerous wise and informed people by telephone in that time, and I decided that this would be the last occasion when I would deliver digests to the Vice President of what others had suggested. When I next saw him, I suggested that he set up a task force to give him recommendations firsthand on how to bring science and technology considerations into decision-making at the White House. The group's members would range from top researchers at the universities to principal executives of leading technological corporations. A few pertinently experienced economists also would be included. President Ford, I proposed, should personally appoint the task force; that would indicate to the distinguished people we would want on the panel that the mission was important.

Among those nominated were: Murray Gell-Mann, Nobel laureate in physics at Cal Tech; Donald Kennedy, the head of biology at Stanford (now its president): Marina von Neumann Whitman (daughter of John von Neumann), a former member of the Council of Economic Advisors in the White House; Carl Djerassi, the inventor of the Pill; Edward Teller, professor at large, University of California; Edwin Land, the founder of Polaroid; Arthur Beuche, senior vice president for science and technology at General Electric; Lewis Branscomb, IBM's chief scientist; Frank Press, head of the Earth Sciences Department at M.I.T.; Ivan Bennett, M.D. and Provost, N.Y.U.; Norman Rasmussen, professor of nuclear engineering at M.I.T.; William Nierenberg, director of the Scripps Institute of Oceanography; William Baker, president of the Bell Laboratories; and others of unusual distinction who were ideally suited to this task. I proposed that Bill Baker be named co-chairman and that Hans Mark, then director of the NASA Ames Laboratory and today chancellor of the University of Texas, be my deputy.

Rockefeller and I agreed that our group would first list the most important national issues involving science and technology. With regard to each issue, a problem or an opportunity, we would state why the White House should participate actively instead of leaving the matter to the private sector or some existing government department. Then the task force would advise the White House how it might deal with the issue. After considering a substantial number of issues, we would be able to describe clearly the office the White House should create to handle such matters. Rockefeller could then discuss with the President and congressional leaders how to establish that office.

The members of the task force were chosen, President Ford signed the invitations to them, they all accepted, and we began our sessions. The Vice President attended every meeting except one we held on the West Coast. During our deliberations, which took place over several months in 1975–76, Rockefeller arranged two substantial meetings and one shorter one with President Ford. We reported what we were up to and obtained his enthusiastic support. We produced a report with several pages devoted to each of some seventy issues. This "Issues Book" described each item and then explained why it needed White House attention. Here are a few examples, to illustrate the variety of our concerns:

Nuclear Energy How crucial to the nation is nuclear-based electric power? Should priority go instead to greater use of coal? How do we integrate the nation's plans and controls for production, storage, and disposal of enriched uranium materials and nuclear waste? How much R&D funds should be spent on new nuclear techniques such as controlled thermonuclear fusion (the H-bomb principle applied to electric-power generation)?

Regulation of Genetic Engineering Microbiology developments are making possible the genetic engineering of useful new living matter. But previously untested life-forms might cause new diseases and should not be created freely. Setting balances between risks and gains cannot simply be left to the private sector or dealt with by a small, isolated agency of the federal bureaucracy. Congress usually reacts to a new danger by setting up still another new regulatory agency. How can the White House provide leadership here?

Technology Export Controls The Defense Department, anxious to deny the Soviet Union our advanced technology, always wants to ban the export to any foreign country of most U.S. technological products. U.S. companies badly want the sales revenues, and most such products are available from Japanese and European competitors, whose governments encourage exports. The Commerce, State, and Defense Departments have differing views, while the academic community argues that openness is important to science. Aside from classified information and equipment, what exports of U.S. technology should we ban? Who should police the bans? What is the proper balance between international commercial competitiveness and national security?

Space and Basic Research Space provides gains for the civilian life of the nation and its national security, but is also an arena for basic research into the laws of the universe. Plans for spacecraft to gather scientific data in outer space must be related to astrophysical and other programs of the National Science Foundation and to the Department of Energy's multibillion-dollar particle-accelerator projects because they all seek data on the fundamentals of radiation and matter. Space-research planning and priority therefore must be judged in the context of total available government funding for all physical scientific research and cannot be left to NASA alone.

Science and Math Education A future national crisis is building because of America's declining number of annual high-school graduates adequately trained in science and mathematics. Why has the problem arisen and how can it be solved? Can the decentralized school districts in the U.S. be expected to appreciate and act on the problem without federal-government articulation of it? What should be the federal-government role in seeking a solution and what agency should deal with it?

The seventy issues we pinpointed shared certain characteristics: all could have important impact on our political-economic-social well-being; many billions of dollars were involved; several independent agencies of the U.S. government played key roles, each agency with its own agenda; leadership was needed to set goals and priorities and assign to each program its proper share of the nation's limited resources; the White House was where the decisions should be made. One conclusion was obvious. Without informed scientific and technological advice, the President and the White House staff could not be expected to form wise policy.

One of the seventy issues, the impact on the nation of rapid advances in computers and communications (information technology), especially interested Nelson Rockefeller. He asked me to visit him for some extended brainstorming on this one topic.

He appreciated the fact that information is what makes the world spin, and he accepted the task force's conclusion that what we can do with information is being revolutionized by new technology. Information can be acquired and stored, processed, pondered, transmitted, and used a thousand—sometimes a million—times more rapidly, cheaply, and effectively than before. All pursuits—production, transportation, finance, research, education, government—will be radically altered by information technology, the key to instant availability of information.

I pictured for the Vice President two-way national networks connecting a hundred million electronic terminals in offices, factories, homes, schools, hospitals, airlines, and almost everywhere else, providing a giant surge in information over existing telephone, radio and TV broadcasting, cable TV, and computer networks. Financial transactions, manufacturing and distribution schedules, purchases, medical information, crime data, video business-conferencing signals—every conceivable kind of information moving instantly about the nation, tying its operations together.

Rockefeller asked me to guess how big the expenditures would be if the information technology already available in the mid-1970s was installed in America wherever a substantial economic return on investment would result. I said it would be well over a trillion dollars. The book value of assets of the nation's telephone system, I pointed out, is in the hundreds of billions of dollars.

"I see," he responded quickly, adding something like, "and that's only from connecting telephones together. If there are a hundred million computers in the future instead of just telephone receivers, and we connect the computers through a network, then it ought to cost ten times more—that's where you get the trillion figure."

Granted that the financial impact will be great, the social impact, Rockefeller commented, will be even greater. Since virtually all tasks will be accomplished more efficiently, many jobs will be eliminated even as new ones are created. The greater the economic gain to be realized, the greater will be the speed of implementation and the rougher the dislocations. The government, he pointed out, will then be expected by the public to try to manage the social upheaval.

Who, if not the government, we agreed, could be called on to protect privacy yet guarantee free access to the information networks that will enter virtually every home and workplace? Who else could prevent monopolies in the supply of information, installation of transmission systems, and equipment manufacture? Who else could set common standards so equipment can be compatible? Who but the government could police to prevent the deliberate input of misinformation? Who but the government could set the rules as private companies link their operating data to attain efficiency in production and distribution?

We were already seeing, I noted to Rockefeller, the beginnings of a network in which electronic terminals are used to transfer money from the buyer's to the seller's account. Only the government could deal with fraud as money is shifted electronically, and virtually instantaneously.

Rockefeller said that government could never cope with all these challenges. The technology will move too fast, and so will the applications if there are good returns on investment. The government, he predicted, will always lag far behind in setting policy and rules.

Then, he said essentially this: "This computer revolution is a permanent revolution. It will go on for years, decades, and longer. The government will probably do nothing more than just attack the evils the public will demand be eliminated. The government will periodically pass laws prohibiting some things, and it will argue forever about many more things without substantive action. We'll have to trust that the computer revolution will produce more benefits than harm."

Naturally, with our task force's book of seventy issues in mind, I asked him whether his pessimistic comments were intended to apply to all those issues. Rockefeller said I was wrong to think him pessimistic. Being realistic, recognizing that the government will do an inadequate job, does not mean, he said, that we shouldn't try to improve the government's performance, including that of the White House. Running a government is always a contest, he explained, among three alternatives: getting the right things done; getting something done, right or wrong; and doing nothing at all. We needed to keep fighting the battles, hoping to win as many as possible, to get the right things done. But we shouldn't ever expect to win enough battles to win the war.

A congressional bill was worked out by late 1975 and passed in 1976, authorizing the Office of Science and Technology Policy (OSTP). As Rockefeller and our task force had urged, the bill's wording gave the office's director, also to be known as the President's science advisor, a very high status, just below the cabinet secretaries and above the level of under-secretary. During Congress's deliberations, some members thought the legislation was still not adequate to guarantee strength of future science and technology. They proposed that the executive branch should have a Department of Science and Technology headed by a Secretary of Science and Technology. It was not totally clear how much of the government's science and technology functions the advocates of this approach would shift into the new department. After all, the scientific approach is an intellectual discipline that, like common sense or logic, should be present to some extent everywhere in government. It would be naïve to think that the responsibility for science and technology now based in various agencies—defense, health, agriculture, interior, transportation, energy, commerce, space, etc.— could be shifted to and consolidated in one department. This concern nevertheless led the Congress to add an item to the bill calling for a President's Committee on Science and Technology to carry out a two-year study and then recommend to the Congress the best means for the government to handle matters involving science and technology.

By the time the legislation cleared both houses of Congress, only a few months remained of the Ford Administration. President Ford asked me to become the science advisor and I declined. I am sure he and Rockefeller respected my reasons. Although TRW's business volume at that time was only about one-third government-contract-related, its projects were conspicuously important. I could dispose of my TRW shares, but I could hardly divest myself of my closest friends and protégés who would go on running TRW. So I would still be regarded as a TRW insider by some members of the government bureaucracy and the competitive industry, and possibly by a few of the senators considering my confirmation. The White House would hardly benefit if the appointee had such a handicap. I suggested that Dr. Guy Stever, a distinguished scientist-executive who was already in the government as the director of the National Science Foundation, be asked by the President to move to the White House as the first director of OSTP.* This was arranged.

I was then invited to be the chairman of the President's Committee on Science and Technology created by the OSTP bill. (The legislation did not contemplate the chairman's becoming a government employee.) I agreed, and the committee was formed and began its studies. When Carter became President, we committee members submitted our resignations, a customary act with a change of Administration, and the President chose not to continue the committee.

I felt that I came to know Nelson Rockefeller the executive well. I have had a bit of contact with Presidents and Vice Presidents, and I have been close to others in the science-and-technology fraternity who have dealt with White House principals. Rockefeller was very much above the average in his appreciation of the importance of science and technology. The rest could not hide their feelings that these were arcane fields. All Presidents, from Roosevelt to Reagan, apparently enjoyed being briefed about occasional new scientific discoveries or engineering achievements; when such projects were called to their attention, they would make a remark or wear an expression suggesting that they marveled at the accomplishment. But they preferred not to get deeply into problems of

---

* Dr. Stever, before his NSF position, had been a leading professor of engineering at M.I.T., the chief scientist of the U.S. Air Force, the president of Carnegie–Mellon University, and an experienced consultant to technological industry, so he was amply qualified for the OSTP position.

major scientific and technological importance.* (Jimmy Carter, who had a Naval Academy education, often confused by the media with a science education, displayed an interest in science and technology. He is described, however, as being as much in awe of leading scientists as other Presidents were.)

Nelson Rockefeller felt at home with scientists and engineers. He would ask questions, never concerned that he might display ignorance. Science-related issues did not lead him to depart from his natural tendency to be a strong activist. If someone merely mentioned a project that might bring benefits, he would immediately want to discuss whether it should be implemented. He believed that the private sector should be relied upon to the maximum. Equally, however, he assumed that anything with a substantial impact on the country's economy or security or the people's health and happiness should involve the government. He had an intense desire to come to grips with what the government role should be to achieve progress.

Rockefeller really liked people. It was no pose. He did not put scientists and engineers in a separate category. He liked them, too. He was as much at ease talking to them about their subjects as he was with business executives, politicians, lawyers, labor leaders, or university presidents.

When the Ford–Rockefeller Administration came to an end, with the Office of Science and Technology Policy established, I thought my relationship with Nelson Rockefeller was over. But there was to be one more adventure. Perhaps I should label it a near-adventure, or, more precisely, a near-miss. The plan was exciting. It was to be technological entrepreneurship on a scale beyond any new business venture in history—not amazing, considering that Rockefeller had conceived the project.

When he left office in January 1977, he continued to be fas-

---

* There might appear to be conspicuous exceptions, such as F.D.R.'s ordering the development of the atom bomb after reading the message delivered to him from Einstein recommending it and expressing the fear that the Nazis might do it first. But to F.D.R. that was a political decision. In view of the possible negative consequences of his not making the decision, he thought it worth the gamble; he needed no lengthy briefings about the underlying science.

cinated with putting science-and-technology breakthroughs to work. This drove him to do some inventing. He called on me early in 1978 to join him in his Rockefeller Center office in New York City, as he had done a few years before in the White House, and he described a radical idea. He visualized a new technological corporation that would not develop, manufacture, and sell technological products but would instead be the sponsor, financial backer, selector, and stimulator of the development of new technology. It would sponsor start-up technological companies anywhere in the world and also seek to create joint ventures with existing high-technology corporations. It would select the projects, assemble the teams, and provide the wherewithal from its very large pool of investment capital.

Nelson Rockefeller planned to be chairman of the new company. From the staff of the Rockefeller family investment activities, he selected an outstanding business executive, Arthur Taylor, whom he proposed for president and chief executive officer. He invited me to be the third member of the management team, to participate in deliberations about the science and technology involved and perhaps to divide my time between the new company and TRW, in which I was approaching the mandatory retirement age of sixty-five for officers. (He hoped TRW would take on contracts to help implement some of the projects.)

The source of capital—he had in mind no less a figure than $4 billion—was to be Saudi Arabia. That oil-rich nation was investing many billions of dollars in external financial assets during that period. Rockefeller had two coupled lines of thought that led him to believe the Saudis would be interested. First, he felt he could convince them that it made sense as a long-term investment for a very small fraction of the enormous funds (around $100 billion) coming into that country annually from crude-oil sales to be put at risk in bold high-technology ventures chosen by experts. Second, Rockefeller knew he had very considerable personal credibility with the Saudis. (Aside from his prestige and wide contacts, the family was associated with oil riches, so I assumed he suspected the Saudi leadership might feel a natural linkage.) His plan was for the parent company to be formed as an equal partnership between the Saudis and a newly founded American business entity; the financing would be in the form of a long-term loan from the Saudis to the joint venture. As the project prospered and matured from the investment stage to profitability, interest would be paid on the loan. When earnings rose above the interest payments, the net would be shared by the partners.

After some preliminary indirect communications, Rockefeller visited Saudi Arabia to open the discussion. Soon after, when King Khalid came briefly and secretly to the United States for medical treatment, he and Rockefeller met and did a handshake on the deal in New York City. This did not mean that all was settled and a sure thing. Far from it. Many of the basic objectives and most of the details of implementation had not even been taken up. But my hunch was that Nelson Rockefeller would succeed with the venture. I expected to play a major part in the selection of projects and the lining up of existing technological organizations or the launching of new ones to carry out those projects.

On Sunday, September 20, 1978, I was to fly to New York City to be available first thing Monday for a meeting with Rockefeller to work on details. I canceled my reservation in sadness when the news came on Saturday morning of his sudden and fatal heart attack the night before.

The timing of the launch of that exciting new company was particularly right from the standpoint of Rockefeller's freedom from political responsibilities and restrictions, his special stature and worldwide relationships, his strong interest in advancing technology, the availability of discretionary funds from the Saudis, Rockefeller's and my common experience which gave us confidence in each other, and my retirement as an officer of TRW. But, in the end, it was tragically wrong.

The effort expended in helping OSTP come into existence was not wasted, and by now OSTP has survived three (Ford, Carter, and Reagan) Administrations. I am very fearful, however, that a future President, and more particularly the influential people around him, may again downgrade the importance of science and technology on the White House agenda. This is not an unjustified concern; exactly that kind of downrating occurred at the start of both the Carter and the Reagan Administrations, as I shall relate.

When a new President is elected, he has only a few weeks to go through a major metamorphosis from candidate running for office to the executive occupying the White House. He wishes to assume his new duties from day one with his major appointees in place, so it has become the practice of the President-elect to appoint task forces to aid in the transition. Typically, prominent individuals knowledgeable, for example, about the budget, defense, health, energy, labor, and agriculture are asked to serve. (Also typical is the appointment to these task forces of some people of little competence who were exceptionally supportive in the election. Fortunately, such appointees usually do only a modest amount of harm.

Jimmy Carter created a number of such transition groups. When I saw them listed in the newspapers, I was disappointed to find no reference to science and technology. That Carter was not unmindful of the importance of science and technology was shown by his early appointment of Dr. Harold Brown as Secretary of Defense. Brown, a Ph.D. in physics, I knew to be a scientist-executive of the highest caliber. He had previously been the director of the famous Lawrence Livermore National Laboratory, the director of Research and Development for the Defense Department (now called Under-Secretary of Defense), the Secretary of the Air Force, and the president of the California Institute of Technology. He was the first and only physical scientist to be Secretary of Defense.

Having been an active trustee of Cal Tech during Brown's eight years as its president, I was well acquainted with him. Actually, I had come to know and admire him many years before that. I was one of those he telephoned immediately after being named Secretary, to ask for suggestions for filling various posts in the DoD. I did not burden Harold then with questions about where things stood in the appointing of someone to head the White House Science and Technology Office, which was not his responsibility. It was reasonable to assume that the new President would make that appointment shortly. As the weeks passed, however, I began to be concerned; and I was receiving telephone calls from leading scientists and engineers around the country who knew I had worked with Rockefeller in getting the new office created. They reported rumors that the White House doubted it was necessary to fill the OSTP position. "Here we go again," my callers said. "Another Nixon White House."

Months passed, and I was about to phone Harold Brown, thinking that appealing to him would be the most effective way to press for action, when I received a puzzling telephone call. With no advance notice, two individuals who said they were President Carter's "transition task force" for the Office of Science and Technology Policy announced they were in Los Angeles and wanted to come see me. I dropped everything, of course, glad that I happened to be in town. Within an hour, a pair of pleasant men in their twenties appeared, fresh from Georgia by way of Washington. They were anxious to interrogate me about the office that it was their job to study; they were supposed to make recommendations to keep or discontinue it.

When their questions began, I found myself bewildered and then realized that they had not read the congressional bill describing and establishing OSTP. They had no feel at all for what the office was about. They concentrated on the title Science Advisor to the President and seemed to assume the advisor would sit in the White House near an intercom console ready to answer authoritatively should he hear a buzz and then the voice of the President asking a scientific question like "What is the difference between an atom and a molecule?" It is not fanciful to suggest that they also imagined that this White House chief scientist, being a scientist, would wear a white coat and perhaps somewhere down in the bowels of the Executive Office Building he would have a laboratory. They wondered what he was supposed to do in it.

I began to suspect that the conversation could not proceed at a high level of sophistication. That hunch was confirmed when I learned neither of them had been exposed even to a college course in science. I tried to explain what the Office of Science and Technology Policy was intended to be when Congress wrote the legislation, only to discover that the word "policy" was rather a mystery to them. I gave them some history on the original job as established by President Eisenhower and abolished by President Nixon. I ended by urging them to regard OSTP as very important and to recommend that the appointment be made quickly. The moment they left, anxious to allay my fears, I put in a call to Secretary Harold Brown.

Harold, although occupied to the hilt with his critical DoD job, saw the danger of further delay in properly filling the post and promised to check into the matter. We agreed to talk again the next day to compare the candidates each of us would propose for the position, and his list and mine turned out to be virtually the same. High with both of us was Frank Press. Press had been a member of the task force President Ford had appointed to aid Nelson Rockefeller in establishing OSTP. He was one of the leading figures in earth sciences. He had been a prominent professor at Cal Tech, leaving there to head the Department of Earth Sciences at M.I.T. By now it was April, and to my pleasure Frank Press was invited by President Carter to head the OSTP and he accepted.

The science job in the Carter White House was, thus, finally filled with a competent person. It was not clear that anyone in the White House in April 1976 looked upon it as the key position it was intended to be, but that did not bother Press. He was so objective, intelligent, patient, and mature that his personal influence and the contributions made by his office grew steadily. He was active not only on the pure-research front but also in attacking America's slipping productivity. During his tenure, at least some of the President's staff gradually learned about advances in science and technology and their importance to many national issues. By the time Press finished his four years in office, OSTP was well on the way to becoming what those of us who had been so anxious to get it established thought it ought to be. After serving the Carter Administration with distinction, Frank Press was elected president of the National Academy of Sciences. He still leads this extraordinary organization of the nation's leading scientists. It is the most important body outside of government in influencing U.S. science policy.

When Ronald Reagan won the Presidency in November 1980, transition task forces were again appointed, and I was asked to chair the science-and-technology task force. I proposed that Arthur Beuche, General Electric's then senior vice president for science and technology, be made a co-chairman because we needed one on the East Coast who could be more readily available than I. We quickly assembled a group of highly regarded scientists and engineers from academe and industry across the nation and applied ourselves to the two main assigned tasks. One was to list the important science-related issues that we thought deserved early attention at the White House level. I met with Frank Press to get his advice. Although he had used the Issues Book put together by our earlier Ford–Rockefeller effort and had made considerable progress on most of the seventy items in it and on many other matters as well, we found we could still justify the relisting of many of these points* some five years later.

Our other chore was to suggest names for Presidential appointments for those posts in which a science-and-technology background should be a factor. Altogether, there were some twenty-five such positions. (Incidentally, we paid no attention to political affiliations as we compiled our lists.)

We tried and failed to do one other thing to help President-elect Reagan. We were mindful that many thoughtful citizens shared a concern about America's diminishing world stature in technology, so we thought it would be highly beneficial if President Reagan's writers injected an appropriate paragraph or two into his Inaugural Address. We wanted the President's words to demonstrate his appreciation of the fact that not only our national security but also our economic growth had become dependent on science and technology. We wanted him to promise leadership in attaining the greatest American scientific-and-technological strength.

Accordingly, we wrote a page that we thought might be useful

---

* Two, for example, were nuclear-reactor safety and waste disposal, and the growing drop in quality of public-school education in science and math. Another was the role of humans in space. Still another was the low rate of America's increase in productivity. All four of these issues remain unresolved in 1988.

to the President's speech drafters and we sent it to the President through channels. Our task force reported to the President by way of Edwin Meese. Meese's initial responsibilities included many things, of which integrating information and advice from all transition task forces was but one. There were two layers between us and Meese, so to avoid dependence on this multistep communication route, I deposited one copy each with two mutual friends who I knew were seeing Ronald Reagan often and could be counted on to hand it to him. I know the President-elect received both copies of the missive because when he spotted me at a dinner party in the California desert during the holidays at the end of December 1980 he pointed to his inside pocket, smiled, and said, "I've received all ten copies." I thus knew that he was aware that I had made a special effort to get the words to him and, more important, that he was not anxious to hear a sales pitch from me that evening.

Some sentences very similar to what we set down were used by the President in his State of the Union address two years later. But we struck out at inauguration time. Those around the President most influential in setting priorities did not rate science and technology highly. I reached that conclusion, not because of our failure to get our paragraphs into the speech, because other items I could not presume to rate might well have deserved priority. But in the weeks since Reagan's inauguration it became apparent that the Office of Science and Technology Policy was considered a minor post, one maybe not even worth filling. Like Jimmy Carter's insiders, Ronald Reagan's inner circle included no one with real experience who recognized that science and technology could enhance the nation's strength and well-being.

Having said this, though, I feel it important also to say that the Reagan Administration's inability to recognize the need for competence in science and technology within the White House staff was manifested in a substantially different way from the initial neglect in the Carter Administration. After giving proper priority to the cabinet positions and others conspicuous to the general public, the White House personnel office got around to what they saw as the lesser jobs. The OSTP post, in the mind of the White

House's recruiting staff, was far from the position described in the bill passed by Congress. I remember one conversation with Pendleton James, head of the personnel office, in which he found my claim unbelievable (he had never read the law setting up OSTP) that its director was designated in the bill to be on a level with deputy secretaries* of the cabinet and above under-secretaries.

I doubt that more than one of the key figures in the initial Reagan White House staff (Martin Anderson, an economist with an MIT engineering degree as well) had ever heard of the Office of Science and Technology Policy. The first impression of most was that the President's science advisor would largely advise a low echelon of OMB (Office of Management and Budget) on the small part of the overall budget that is allocated to pure research and would be little more than a lobbyist pushing for increased federal grants to universities. There was no appreciation of the fact that in many crucial areas of national security, world trade, employment, energy supply, tax policies, environmental protection, antitrust, health, education, and so on, advancing science and technology play a significant role in creating the issues, providing possibilities for resolving them, or offering unforeseen new opportunities worth grasping. The principal White House staff hadn't the slightest suspicion that they might possibly lack this appreciation, and doubtless would have resented being told so. Their only substantial experience was in practical politics, public relations, economics, law, budgeting, or academic political science.

I began vigorously to urge that the OSTP post be filled quickly. I went to everyone, from my good friend and sometime tennis partner, William French Smith, the new Attorney General, to Reagan's "kitchen cabinet" of close personal friends, to press for action. With Art Beuche at the top of our task force's list, I particularly pushed the recommendation that he be offered the job. Finally, he was called by Meese and invited to accept, but he declined, since he felt by then that the low rating of the position

---

* Only three departments, Treasury, State, and Defense, have deputy secretaries; the rest have only under-secretaries and assistant secretaries. Hence, the head of OSTP had been set at an exceedingly high level by Congress.

by the White House had been well established. Pen James and I both thought that would be reversed if President Reagan himself telephoned Beuche and asked him to accept. The call was arranged. Beuche told the President he would consider the invitation, but then called back in a day to say no again.

Interest in filling the job then sagged, and weeks passed before the personnel office got around to it again. This time they merely sounded out candidates by telephone. One after another of the nationally prominent people our task force had suggested for the position were called by a personnel-office underling and asked whether they would accept an invitation to head OSTP if they were offered it. They all replied in the negative. In each instance, they felt insulted at being interrogated so superficially as to their interest by a lowly placed subordinate. After a question or two to that assistant, who revealed a lack of understanding of the office, each candidate decided that the post must be rated in the White House as even less important than he had already come to believe.

After this exercise had been completed, I received a call from Pen James, who in effect said, "We've asked seven people to take the job, Si, and they've all turned us down. What do we do now?"

"Well, Pen," I was disappointed enough to reply testily, "the part in the play has been cut down to a walk-on and yet you've been trying to get Katharine Hepburn."

By this time I had given up hope that we might persuade Reagan's principal aides to reevaluate the OSTP. It seemed that the important thing was to save it by getting some capable person to fill the office who would accept the job despite the evident need to be patient for one or two years. I recommended to Pen James that he set out to find a capable scientist or engineer, but one less prominent and younger than the individuals the task force had listed. I decided to retire from the name-suggesting game, but gave James a list of people to call for help. Ultimately, the post was offered to George Keyworth, who accepted it. Dr. Keyworth held a highly responsible position at the Los Alamos National Laboratories, renowned for its nuclear-weapons development, but he was not one of the best-known names in science and technology and had not previously been involved in major government decision-making. His selection disappointed some of our leading scientists and engineers. The placing of someone at the head of OSTP who was not of conspicuously high national stature confirmed their feelings that the importance of the science advisor to the President had been diminished by the Reagan Administration. A few felt compelled to call to tell me that I had not done well in chairing the Reagan transition task force.

Keyworth disconcerted some academic scientists early in his tenure at the White House by pointing out clearly that priorities would have to be set for the allocation of available research funds. The federal budget for basic science support would be generous, he promised,* but the available funding would fail to cover all the projects that researchers in each and every field wanted to pursue. They knew that was the case, but they resented his saying it and regarded that kind of talk as disloyal to the science fraternity, defecting to the enemy, the budgeteers in the White House. They felt the role of the chief scientist was to represent them; they were inclined to measure Keyworth's performance by how much backing they received. I thought Keyworth's comments totally in order and was not at all disappointed by his taking a realistic and frank stand.

Keyworth was a key performer on the occasion of President Reagan's announcement of the Strategic Defense Initiative (SDI, or Star Wars) on March 23, 1983. Along with some others, I had been urgently requested by telephone the afternoon before to take an early plane from California and be at the White House for dinner the next day for some undisclosed purpose. The President, it was already known, was going on national television that evening to defend his defense budget, which was expected to have difficulty in Congress. Assembled in the White House at 5:00 p.m. the next day were some twenty of us outsiders and a similar number of insiders of cabinet or near-cabinet level. At 5:30 p.m. the President's close friend, Judge William Clark, at that time National Security Advisor, invited us to be seated. The President came in, read the

---

* Indeed, Keyworth carried on determined battles against David Stockman's OMB, and led a successful drive that substantially increased the budget for university research.

several paragraphs from his address disclosing the SDI plan, and left. Clark next informed us that we would view the full address on television while having dinner and that after dinner the President would rejoin us. Before dinner we had cocktails, and before that, a free-for-all discussion.

Judge Clark absented himself from the platform when the discussion was about to begin and turned the duties over to his deputy, Robert McFarlane, who was assisted by George Keyworth. The insiders made no comments, but the outsiders most certainly did. Every criticism or question about SDI that arose in the weeks, months, and years that followed emerged that evening: Could the President's expressed hope, making ICBMs "impotent and obsolete," ever be achieved? Have there been great secret scientific breakthroughs that could make defense really effective? If not, why the big announcement, since it was already known that a U.S. anti-missile research program had been in progress for years? Won't an implemented SDI cost a trillion dollars? Won't it be readily defeated at small cost by the Russians? Won't it cause the Soviet Union also to create a huge anti-ICBM program? Won't a defense system violate the ABM treaty? Won't SDI be destabilizing, causing the Soviet Union to escalate its offense capability?

A very clear concern of the audience was the wording in the President's announcement which seemed to suggest that the President might actually believe it possible to create a perfect shield, an impenetrable cover that would totally defend the nation from ICBMs, provide complete safety for our population, and eliminate the need to maintain a retaliatory capability as a deterrent to a nuclear strike.*

Keyworth and McFarlane could say little to allay the fears expressed by a number of those present, and the comments of the visitors during the discussion were much more critical than supportive. As we stood around for cocktails before going to the dining room, George Shultz asked me whether I thought it possible even

---

* I am positive that no one present who had a science background believed this to be possible in the forseeable future against a determined large-scale ICBM attack.

in principle to knock out Russian ICBMs with lasers. I said it certainly was possible in principle, because it would not violate any laws of physics. (Indeed, I told him, TRW had been under contract for some time to carry on R&D on high-powered lasers.) The practical question, I emphasized to the Secretary, was whether a system could ever be developed to destroy enemy ICBMs at acceptable cost, with useful kill performance, realistic operational reliability, and adequate invulnerability against Soviet counteractions.

Then Shultz asked the correct "what if" question: What if all those conditions I had just cited were met by a successful R&D program? Would such a laser system then stop a Russian ICBM attack? I replied, only partly kidding, that if I were the Russians I would carry a mirror with each ICBM.

"Shine your powerful laser beam on my missile to burn it up and you'll get the beam reflected right back at you with the speed of light, and your laser will burn up."

"Could they do that?" Shultz asked.

"Why not? If you can find my reentry vehicle as it zooms through space and hold your light beam on it, then give me credit for being able to point a mirror at your big laser as it sits up there relatively still in the sky."

"So we're back to the usual offense-defense contest, a never-ending one," he replied, quite correctly.

We agreed that neither of us knew, and doubted if anyone else in the Soviet Union or the United States knew at the time, how in the future the contest of offense vs. defense might actually develop. If this was so, a research program on ICBM defense was justified, but we could say little more than that.

At dinner we were seated at tables of eight, with a television screen at each table, and I found myself between Ed Meese and George Shultz. I asked Meese how the SDI announcement had been kept from the media. "We've all been led to believe that every secret in the White House gets leaked," I said, exaggerating only slightly. "Here you've invited a group of us who hold top-secret clearances. We read the papers and watch the TV news, and yet the announcement of the President came as a big surprise to us. Why did secrecy work so well this time?"

"Because," Meese said, "only six people knew about it, including the secretary who typed it."

Hearing this, I naturally turned to my other dinner partner, the Secretary of State, hardly one to be kept in the dark as the plan for the implementation of the SDI program was being conceived, and asked him when he had been informed that the President was going to make the announcement. He told me it was at four that very afternoon, an hour before the meeting began.

I wanted very much, but did not think it proper, to press Meese and Shultz as to exactly what their answers meant. Did Meese mean that only six people had participated in phrasing the President's paragraphs for delivery that evening? Or did Meese mean that only those few knew that the President had decided to dramatically speed up the development of defenses against ICBMs, a program that had been going on modestly for many years? I was aware before I arrived at the meeting that recommendations to enhance the ICBM defense program had been made recently by various groups—by the DoD, the nuclear-weapons laboratories of the DoE, the Office of Science and Technology Policy in the White House, the National Security Council staff, the Joint Chiefs of Staff, and a number of industrial contractors and individual scientists. It was also my understanding that the Joint Chiefs had been studying these proposals and were working on a report to go to the President. Sometime after the White House meeting, Richard De Lauer, then Under-Secretary of Defense, told me that he had read the Joint Chiefs' report two days before the President's announcement. The report included a recommendation to enlarge the missile-defense program. Also, De Lauer said he had been in the loop to inform Secretary Weinberger by classified cable a day before the President made the SDI announcement; Weinberger had been in Europe for several days.

From everything I learned that evening and since, I retain the impression that everyone—presumably with the exception of those six individuals, whoever they might have been (Reagan, Meese,

Clark, McFarlane, Keyworth, a stenographer?)—was taken by surprise by the announcement. This included the Joint Chiefs and Secretaries Shultz and Weinberger. They and a number of others merely knew that missile-defense efforts were to be enhanced soon. The President apparently had rather suddenly decided to include those paragraphs about the SDI in this particular address. The announcement gave the SDI program a status and emphasis almost equivalent to a major defense-policy change, and such a change had not been thoroughly prepared for by the White House staff.

After President Reagan announced the SDI, Keyworth became its chief White House booster and its defender against critics in the science fraternity and elsewhere. Because of the immediate and extensive controversy the project aroused, Keyworth was soon no longer handicapped by going unnoticed. But at the end of 1985, with a number of major contributions to his credit, Keyworth quit. I met with him just before he resigned from his office. It happened to be for the purpose of tapping his ideas on strengthening the SDI management team, a task I was then engaged in at the request of Secretary Weinberger. During that discussion, Keyworth mentioned some of the difficulties he faced as science advisor. I don't believe he had ever had the support anyone in the job would need to discharge the responsibilities properly.

James Baker, Chief of Staff in Reagan's first term (1981–85) decided very early, according to Keyworth, that Keyworth's concerns did not merit his personal attention. For all practical purposes, Keyworth reported to the President through Ed Meese. Science and technology were not Meese's strong suit, but when Meese left to become Attorney General, it was even harder for Keyworth to get attention. Yet he led a successful drive in the White House for added funding for the National Science Foundation so it could broaden its scope. Keyworth also pressed DoD and NASA during that period to create a crash effort to produce expendable boosters and not depend entirely on the troubled Shuttle to put important payloads into orbit, this before the Challenger accident. Had he succeeded, years of delay might have been avoided in launching satellites important to national security.

Keyworth's temporary successor was John McTague, who had been Keyworth's deputy. In June 1986, after six months as the acting science advisor, McTague left the White House to become vice president for research at the Ford Motor Company, a nationally prestigious R&D position that surely would not have been offered McTague were he not regarded as a highly qualified technical executive. Hearing that Don Regan had consulted me about candidates to succeed to the science-advisor post, McTague asked me in February 1986 to drop by the next time I was in Washington. I think McTague, like Keyworth, had in mind that it would be well for me to know some of the handicaps he faced in that office. I learned that he had never met Don Regan, his nominal boss, let alone the President, which meant that both were busy with matters they rated as more important than holding discussions with the science advisor.

When a major government office is vacated with ample notice, the appointment of a successor is usually announced almost immediately because an important post cannot be left unattended. That did not occur when Keyworth left in December 1985. Months went by without action. This was taken by the nation's scientists and engineers as additional confirmation that the White House had little interest in the position. But I know firsthand that the actual situation was different, more complex.

It was in the fall of 1985 when Keyworth let it be known in the White House that he would leave at year's end. In late December 1985, I saw Don Regan, who had now been the President's Chief of Staff for a year, at the usual year-end holiday dinner parties in the area of Palm Springs given for the President and Mrs. Reagan by their closest personal friends, to which some others of us were regularly invited. Having been told that I had been involved in setting up OSTP, Regan asked me for a reaction to the thought that the OSTP position need not be filled. He pointed out that it clearly had not been an important factor in White House decision-making and said he had had no reason to take an interest in the office's functions. I found this disturbing, of course, and argued with considerable fervor against abolishing the post. (At one of the dinners, on successive nights, Regan and I were at the same table with a very tolerant lady seated between us.)

Regan then invited me to continue the discussion in his White House office the next week, where I told him much of the history and rationale concerning the OSTP. I was elated when Regan stated with great firmness at the end of our meeting that he now understood the Office of Science and Technology Policy very differently. He pronounced himself grateful to me, and I think he meant it. He described the head of OSTP as needing to be a "heavyweight," a broad individual nationally distinguished in not one but two careers, science or engineering, and executive leadership.

"I'll have him attend all my staff meetings and encourage him to get into anything and everything," he said.

He pressed me for names of top-drawer individuals, and he invited some of them to the White House for preliminary discussions. He said some of the right things to them, I'm certain. He quickly perceived the differences between these exceptional people and those of lesser stature and talent (pressed on him as candidates for the post by senators, representatives, political contributors, and the White House personnel office), and he seemed to have lost all interest in having anyone in the job who would not be outstanding. But, alas, the prime prospects ended up saying no. Why? One reason was that Regan did not succeed in convincing these candidates that he really understood the OSTP position. Another was that Regan quite naturally arranged for them to talk with other staff members in the White House during their exploratory visits, and the low regard for the Office of Science and Technology Policy by the staff unfortunately became evident.

One candidate, for example, described to me his short meeting with Admiral John Poindexter, the President's National Security Advisor. Poindexter condescendingly allowed that he might occasionally "assign" a science matter, if one should turn up at the National Security Council, to the science advisor, but implied that he expected to be too busy to spend any time with him. Of course, every candidate to head OSTP who possessed suitable credentials for that position was well aware that about half of all important science-and-technology policy in the White House would involve serious national-security issues. Thus, a single meeting with Poindexter had the effect of lessening the importance of the job by half in the candidate's mind.

I know that Don Regan was very disappointed not to have an eminent individual in the OSTP job early in 1986. He had no intention of giving up. But in January 1986 the Challenger disaster occurred, and the repercussions affected in an unpredictable way the OSTP opening. James Beggs, who had been the head of NASA, happened to have as his deputy Dr. William Graham. Graham had been pressed on Beggs by the White House, and Beggs had resisted the appointment, believing that Graham's executive experience was too limited ("He has directed previously no more than a small study team"). In the middle of this standoff, the Challenger accident happened. Then, less than a month later, Beggs was suddenly indicted* as part of the government's action against General Dynamics Corporation, where Beggs had earlier been a senior corporate officer. He had to resign as head of NASA, and Graham became NASA's acting head.

This sequence of events made it necessary for Regan to find a new top administrator for NASA in a hurry, Graham being seen immediately as not a viable candidate. Regan spoke to me twice about individuals being considered in the White House for the NASA post. Since he never mentioned the OSTP opening in those conversations at all, I felt it would be out of order for me to question him about it. The new NASA director, Dr. James Fletcher (NASA's director in the seventies), was selected, and he decided not to keep Graham as his deputy. Unless a new job was found for Graham right away, still another highly placed Administration appointee would have been ousted with embarrassment. So Regan put aside his determination to elevate the OSTP, and Graham was given that job.

It was three months after the public announcement of Graham as the President's choice for science advisor before the White House

---

* In June 1987, the government dismissed all charges against Beggs for lack of evidence of any wrongdoing.

even got around to sending the formal papers on him to the Senate so confirmation proceedings could begin (though Graham had already been investigated and cleared for his previous NASA post, and the data were readily available). The Senate and anyone else interested saw how low the post was being rated by the White House. Finally, in September 1986, nine months after Keyworth had departed the OSTP post, Graham was called before the Senate confirmation committee. Only two senators showed up. The official vote in committee, a few weeks later, was favorable, ten to three, but it was the first time any nay votes had been cast on a science-advisor nominee in the entire twenty-five years that confirmation had been required. The rejection votes were regarded as protests against the White House's lack of recognition of the importance of the OSTP.

I assumed that the OSTP would now suffer a further reduction in stature and that its impact on White House decision-making would be negligible for the remainder of the President's term. The director would simply be a minor figure, among other staff members reporting to Donald Regan. The new director of OSTP would talk directly with Regan most infrequently, if at all, and with the President never. If Graham tried very hard, he might accomplish some useful lower-level coordinating of science matters and might influence here and there those among the White House staff who prepare details of R&D budgets. Graham also might provide a modicum of useful support for some positions taken on science-related issues or projects by the National Science Foundation, NASA, the Department of Defense, the Department of Energy, and other agencies. The nation's leading scientists, engineers, and executives in academe, industry, and government would not look to the OSTP, however, for leadership as they set their priorities.

Of course, Graham's abilities were unknown to almost everyone, certainly to me, when he was appointed to the job. I considered it possible that he might turn out to possess great talent for it—he had both Cal Tech and Stanford degrees, so I knew he was sound technically—but it would take time for him to demonstrate that. I asked myself accordingly whether there was anything I could conceivably do to help him, and decided I should risk being presumptuous by making one additional recommendation to Don Regan. It was that a President's Council of Science and Technology Advisors be established. Without altering the OSTP structure or Graham's position, the President, I suggested, should appoint, say, three distinguished individuals to constitute this new council. They should be people of international stature in science or engineering and with broad experience in relating science and technology to social, economic, and political issues. They should have reputations for breadth of intellect and interests and considerable knowledge of government. The advisors would be only part-time government consultants. * It would be essential that the council meet with the President regularly, but it would mainly assist Graham by proposing and recruiting ad hoc task forces of experts to provide detailed advice on specific issues. Its existence would raise Graham's prestige; he would be more likely to be listened to when he spoke.

Don Regan seemed much taken with the concept of the council; this might be a way to bring into certain higher-level White House deliberations precisely the kind of individuals he had failed to persuade to be the President's science advisor. He immediately asked Bill Graham to consider the idea. Graham then called and he and I had a good discussion about the council on his first trip to California following the announcement of his appointment. He had not yet been confirmed by the Senate. He regarded the proposal as serious but was hesitant to try to move on it before he was actually confirmed, which was quite understandable.

As luck would have it, by the time he had been confirmed and could get settled into his new job, the Iran–contra mess surfaced, and it quickly dominated Don Regan's schedule. I had become confident that Regan's interest in enhancing the science-and-technology presence in the White House was so serious that he

---

* The OSTP has always had prestigious consultants and advisory committees or councils, but they have been counselors to the head of OSTP, perceived as a medium- or low-level advisory office, rather than to the President, a very big difference. These individuals have helped the OSTP in its efforts, but I was seeking a tenfold strengthening of their visibility and influence.

would have taken the council idea to the President and would have succeeded in getting it approved. If the Iran arms-hostage dealing and the shifting of arms-sale funds to the contras had remained covert for a few more months, the council might have been in place in early 1987, helping Regan and Graham with numerous science-related issues that needed attention in the White House. But it was not to be.

These on-and-off exposures I had with various Administrations as they engaged in making appointments to science-based government positions have provided me with rather limited satisfactions over the years. But some of the disappointment I felt was offset by favorable results on other fronts. Getting any specific office filled is, after all, a short-range problem. I became especially determined to promote sensible action on longer-range issues. To take one example, I felt strongly that the government was simply not doing its part to lay a proper foundation for a stronger American future in science and technology. Little effort was being made to stem the deteriorating quality of elementary- and high-school education in science and math. At our larger universities, the science facilities and equipment available for graduate study and research were generally first-class. But the undergraduate laboratories in virtually all those universities and the many four-year colleges of the nation were becoming dilapidated and out of date. Pitifully small funds were made available to modernize them. The United States was certain to have an ever-decreasing fraction of the world's engineers and scientists, yet we were essentially ignoring the fact that we could double our supply by bringing women and minorities into the technical professions.

By the start of the 1980s, a substantial group of us in academe, industry, and government had determined that it was imperative to try to create a stronger pool of talent in science and technology. We began aggressively to use the media, wrote articles and gave speeches, visited with congressmen, employed the platforms of the National Academies of Science and Engineering, and lobbied professional societies and groups of business leaders for their support. The situation had become so serious that we could wait no longer to implement broad programs. Keyworth pushed as hard as he could, and in the end rather effectively, from his OSTP post in the White House. We all took a particularly strong interest in the National Science Foundation (NSF).

The NSF is the principal federally supported sponsor of basic university research in the physical sciences. (DoD and NASA provide added support, and the National Institutes of Health are the prime funders of biomedical research.) NSF's charter also requires it to foster education in science and math from kindergarten to the Ph.D. and to support education in engineering. NSF is charged as well to accelerate the entry of women and minorities into science and engineering. For decades, the foundation had almost totally neglected most such activities and had essentially limited itself to funding graduate and postdoctoral physical-science research in the universities. The National Science Board (NSB), the group responsible for overseeing the NSF and setting its operating policies, had consisted almost entirely of leading academic researchers.

In 1984 Dr. Roland Schmitt, a distinguished scientist and the senior vice president of General Electric for science and technology, became the new chairman of the NSB. He combined forces with Keyworth to head a successful drive by those of us seeking an expansion of NSF activities to recruit Dr. Erich Bloch from IBM (he was one of their top engineering executives) to be the new director at NSF. Bloch and Schmitt then quickly began to lay out a future NSF program to reverse a clear trend by improving the nation's strength in science and technology. It was in this connection that I became a member of the National Science Board (a Presidential appointment, requiring Senate confirmation) and the chairman of its new Committee on Education and Human Resources dealing particularly with the expanded NSF roles.

Every month during 1985–86, I journeyed to Washington to attend the NSB meetings, and each time I stole away from the scheduled lunches and dinners and spent those hours visiting with senators and representatives whose committee assignments made them key to favorable congressional treatment of our goal. This was to be no less than a bold doubling of the NSF budget over five years, from a bit over $1.5 billion to more than $3 billion (by a more than fifteen percent steady increase each year).

In December 1986, Erich Bloch called and told me an Administration decision to achieve that doubling had been made informally after a presentation he had made in the White House which had been attended by the key budget planners, most of the cabinet, and the President. Bloch thought the decision was too good to be true and wanted me to plug it again in the desert during the coming holidays when he knew I would see the President. So I tried to reinforce the decision on New Year's Eve, December 31, 1986, by congratulating the President on his backing of the plan, speaking of it as though it was firm. I was delighted that he did not declare the congratulations to be premature or misinformed.

The NSF program, if the plan survives, * will include researching means to improve science and math education from kindergarten through the undergraduate college years; modernizing facilities and equipment in our colleges and universities; setting up a wave of new scholarships and fellowships to encourage women and minorities to enter science; improving engineering education and research in American universities in cooperation with industry.

These NSF programs constitute the aggressive leadership and stimulation that only the federal government can provide. The NSF funding and its efforts will be triggers and stimulants; if all goes as planned, they will be matched and expanded many times over across the nation by local school districts, the states, the universities, and industry.

In the past, however, numerous wrong steps, and the right ones greatly delayed or not taken at all, have hurt America's standing as a technological nation. In the next chapter, let us look at the decline of our world leadership in technology, to see how far it has gone, to try to understand why and ask if the decline is reversible.

---

* Alas, it has been cut somewhat because of the budget-deficit crisis.

SIX

The Decline of U.S. Technology Leadership

As the 1960s ended, the public's love affair with advances in technology seemed to pass its peak. During the 1970s, thinking people in the United States and abroad began to suspect that the romance of technology with society was not moving toward a smooth, wholly blissful marriage. I don't mean to suggest that on January 1, 1970, the benefits of advances in technology suddenly were reassessed. (After all, throughout history some have decried the consequences of technology advance. The complaints may have started with the invention of the wheel, because that breakthrough surely was followed by serious mishaps stemming from the unaccustomed speed that wheels made possible.) Rather, we have been much more likely to wonder in the 1970–80s than in the 1950–60s whether the negative aspects of the society's becoming highly technological might not outweigh the benefits.

Coincidentally, worldwide belief in America's preeminence in technology attained its zenith in the early 1970s, and a new image of the United States as a fading leader in technology began to emerge. The evidence of America's preeminence in science and technology as the 1960s closed went well beyond our spectacular lunar landings. Our universities and electronics industry, by their rapid advance of semiconductor and computer science and technology, had laid the groundwork for a revolution that would transcend the industrial revolution of the previous two centuries. This time, man's brains and senses would be extended by technology, and the advantages to society seemed to promise greater benefits than machinery did when it so dramatically enhanced human muscle power in the nineteenth century. In microbiology, American scientists were the principal pioneers in reaching a higher level of understanding of the living cell; unprecedented advances in diagnosis and cure of disease seemed just ahead. American airplanes brought us into the jet age and dominated the skies over the non-Communist world. America was developing and constructing nuclear plants for generating electricity at a rate the rest of the world could not hope to match, seeming to ensure us plentiful electric power in the future.

In the late 1960s and early 1970s, technological corporations in the United States were wooed avidly by other countries. Foreign governments competed to offer incentives to our companies to set up operations in their countries to provide employment based on our more advanced high technology. France's Jean Jacques Servan-Schreiber wrote his widely read, convincing book, *The American Challenge*, in 1968, in which he predicted long-term industrial domination by America, owing to its commanding lead in technology and in management know-how. We Americans could take justifiable pride in the way we had helped Western Europe and Japan rebuild after World War II by generously sharing our resources with them. By the end of the 1960s, it was evident that their economic strength had not only been restored but was reaching new heights, but we worried little about having created competitors. We seemed headed for such higher technological plateaus that they always would have to play catch-up. By the mid-1970s, however, it had become obvious that we were being outdone by Japan and Western Europe in many technological fields and that the prime position of the United States in technology could no longer go unchallenged.

The detente with the Soviet Union at the end of the 1960s petered out in the 1970s, during which time the Soviet Union built a strategic-missile arsenal surpassing ours. An energy crisis occurred in 1973, and we simply could not get ourselves organized to handle it. High levels of environmental pollution, unforeseen hazards in our nuclear power plants, and newly recognized severe dangers from burning fossil fuel and the disposal of dangerous nuclear and chemical waste presented us with fearsome threats. We were unable to respond effectively to this environmental bad news. We could not seem to devise ways to balance risks, costs, and bans.

The United States was on the whole the foremost technological nation in 1970, yet, when the 1980s opened, a look back disclosed a decade of steady loss of position. Our established approaches to reaching national goals, setting policies and priorities, and organizing for needed action had been exposed as woefully inadequate. The evidence of the serious imbalance, the mismatch, between rapidly accelerating technology and lagging social progress became overwhelming. We were increasingly able to destroy civilization but unable to prevent such destruction.

In NATO, our strategy by the 1970s to counter a possible Soviet Union attack on Western Europe was not to mount a defense strong enough to resist successfully. Instead, we accepted their superiority in conventional forces. We said that should the Russians cross into Western Europe and appear to be winning, we would employ nuclear weapons. Such a plan might have deterred the Soviets when we alone had nuclear weapons. But was it believable in 1980, when we could expect immediate, strong nuclear retaliation? In the late 1970s, I had occasion to spend a week talking with the generals and ambassadors of NATO countries and the principal executives of technological companies serving the organization. Virtually all of them told me they thought the announced NATO plan to avert defeat by being the first to use nuclear weapons was not credible, although, of course, they would not dream of saying so publicly.

The Vietnam War, in a different way, presented solid proof of the lack of realism concerning advanced technology and political-military problem-solving. It never made sense for the United States even to consider bombing North Vietnam with nuclear weapons to end that war (although some superhawks in America would periodically propose that course). Scientists, engineers, and military experts continually were brought together and asked to study how more sophisticated technology might be employed to aid the U.S. in Vietnam; it was hoped that superior means would be devised to find, intercept, and destroy our enemies, who were fighting a guerrilla war. I participated in some of these efforts. They always proved discouraging. Too long a period of R&D was needed for anything worth attempting, and the potential benefits were too few and too speculative. We were no better prepared to cope with jungle warfare in Vietnam than we were able to deal with the country politically.

Was this malaise about the weakening U.S. technology position a personal one? Am I simply describing my own shift from optimism in the 1950s and 1960s to pessimism in the 1970s and 1980s, as youthful boldness and confidence gave way to middle-aged conservativeness and grouchy criticism? To answer these questions, let me relate what TRW and I were up to during those decades.

In the 1950–60s, TRW's success was a microcosm of U.S. success. The nation's growing stature in technology was reflected in TRW's performance. TRW became a multibillion-dollar corporation, with activities in Western Europe, Japan, South America, and elsewhere; roughly a third of our revenues came from operations outside the United States. We succeeded in creating a balance between commercial products sold to industry worldwide and U.S. government work in space and defense. We enjoyed an advantageous position in electronics and other high technology (stemming from the original Ramo–Wooldridge Corporation) and in precision-made mechanical components (an extension of the original Thompson Products activities). One in a hundred of all living physicists worked at TRW. We had our share of investments that were disappointing, but the average returns on investment and rates of revenue growth most often exceeded the performances of our competitors.

With TRW partaking of the overall American success in technology, I personally seemed to do well. When Ramo–Wooldridge and Thompson Products merged to form TRW in 1958, I had the privilege of designing my own position in the new entity. I had

had years of exceedingly high-pressure organization building and operating management responsibility at Hughes and in the directing of the ICBM program at Ramo–Wooldridge, and I was anxious now to devote my time to goals, priorities, and strategy and leave the daily monitoring of operations to others.* I thought the big challenge for the large technological corporation we had become would be to match our advancing technology to the needs of society. Though TRW was one of the top twenty-five of the world's technological companies, it would have the resources to take on only a portion of all that might interest us.

To succeed, I knew I would need to understand a larger array of matters than I had ever dealt with before. I would have to be able to think innovatively on an international scale and comprehend economic and social forces and political dynamics more deeply, because they would have as much to do with determining advances in technology as the technology breakthroughs themselves. Fortunately, I seemed again to be in the right place at the right time. It was easy for me to learn what I needed to know because industry, government, the financial world, and academe had realized that it was imperative to comprehend the impact of ever-advancing technology.

President Nixon's cabinet members, for example, decided that they needed advisory councils dealing with social-economic-political-technological issues. The United States Chamber of Commerce, the American Management Association, the Industrial Conference Board, and the societies of security analysts, bank economists, and many other professional groups set up committees and conferences to anticipate the influence of technological change on their activities. The organizers of these meetings realized, of course, that a scientist or engineer should be present, and they were not thinking about a Nobel laureate, a pure researcher. They wanted

---

* The first chief operating officer, the company's president, under John David Wright as TRW's founding chairman, was my original partner, Dean Wooldridge. He was followed by Horace Shepard and then Ruben Mettler, mentioned earlier. I was vice chairman and chairman of the policy committee (later chairman of the executive committee).

someone whose professional life had been spent putting science and technology to work. So I received far more invitations than I could accept.

I joined some corporate boards. I was invited to leading universities often, nominally to lecture on technology-business-government interactions, and I was particularly interested in meeting and talking with faculty and students. To enhance TRW's international growth, I traveled abroad and met with bankers, government officials, industry leaders, and the media. Ten percent of my time went to advisory activities in the Departments of Defense, State, Commerce, and Energy, and in NASA, the C.I.A., and the White House. I came to know well prominent politicians, industry leaders, economists, educators, publishers, bankers (and occasional virtuoso musicians), all, it is safe to say, with backgrounds very different from mine.

By the middle 1970s, these outside activities, carried on to help match TRW's potential with the world's opportunities, had forced me to realize how great were the shortcomings of the technological society and how science and technology could by no means solve all problems. I became increasingly concerned with the evidence of America's slippage from a position of technological preeminence. I was puzzled by the confusion between the roles of government and of the private sector in the United States. Even as I was becoming more expert at playing the game of free enterprise, I was having increasing difficulty understanding how the goals of TRW (and other companies) should relate to the goals of the nation— or perhaps I should say, how to cope with the lack of such goals.

My own frame of mind could be described, first in the 1950–60s, and then the 1970–80s, by two contrasting analogies. In the 1960s, I was a daring surfer. I rode high on powerful waves, moving at great speed yet maintaining my stability, exhilarated by the challenge, excited by the knowledge that the dynamic movement carrying me with it was dangerous, but progressing confidently in the right direction. By the middle 1970s, I had begun to feel more like a busy sailor steering a boat that, for all I knew, might not be strong enough to take being buffeted about by rough seas. Nonetheless, I was determined to maintain a steady course even without a reliable compass. Let me cite an example.

During the 1960s and 1970s, we were much engaged at TRW in expanding our international operations. With the entire world becoming technological, it was essential that we operate in the global market. The company had a lead in several kinds of high technology which we needed to exploit to the maximum. Japan offered a special opportunity. We found we could make attractive business arrangements in Japan for their use of our technology. We realized that by employing our know-how the Japanese would advance the date when their competitive power became highly significant. On the other hand, they were willing to pay well for our expertise. We could readily pit the pros against the cons and structure agreements that would provide us with long-term benefits. For instance, TRW might acquire a part interest in a Japanese company in return for furnishing our technology, and, in addition, might receive royalty payments on all sales based on that technology. As part owners of Japanese industry, our shareholders would gain as these companies prospered. If we disdained such deals, the Japanese would develop equivalent technology a little later by themselves or make similar arrangements with our competitors.

We were sure we knew how to achieve the most profitable relationships. But I wondered what was good for the country. Should we hold back on these negotiations because of some overriding reason that we might not be aware of? What were the government's policies?

I took such questions to appropriate cabinet members and other executives in the Nixon Administration. I told them about our plans for multinational expansion. I claimed we knew how to run TRW, but confessed to not knowing the implications for our national interest. I pressed these government officials for guidance. Alas, in response I would get pontification and equivocal doubletalk. I recall only one exception, Peter Peterson. (Peterson was assistant to President Nixon for International Economic Affairs and later Secretary of Commerce. I served on Peterson's advisory committee.) Peterson was immediately helpful, but also very frank to admit that real government policy, long-range, positive, and carefully worked out, was lacking. The only choice was to steer TRW by our own guidelines.

Let us shift now from this personal commentary to a more orderly recital of how great the U.S. slip from technological superiority really has become, how penalizing the loss of preeminence is to the nation, and what if anything we might do about it.

Virtually every country on earth is convinced that its wealth, economic growth, social progress, and national security is vitally dependent on a vigorous development of technology.* Consequently, nations are making all-out efforts to enhance their technology. There is an intense struggle for technological superiority. By winning contests, a nation can be more the master of its fate while also enjoying the fruits of technology. To lose too often can be catastrophic.

The foreign competition that has developed in the last several decades is very important to America because we do not have the alternative of becoming a nontechnological nation. Even our exports of raw foodstuffs depend on our technological strengths; without our machinery and chemicals, we could not produce for export. The world's economic health depends on each nation's making optimum use of its human and natural resources, trading portions of its output to other nations, and receiving in return what others are best able to provide. Unfortunately, in recent decades the United States has lost its position as global champion in technology and has become an average performer, winning some contests, but losing more.

We used to lead the world in annual gains in productivity (output per worker hour). During the last decade we reached the bottom of the list of all industrialized nations in this growth rate,

---

* In a major speech carried on Moscow television in March 1985, immediately after assuming leadership, Mikhail Gorbachev stated: "The party views the acceleration of scientific and technical progress as the main direction of its economic strategy, as the main lever for the intensification of the national economy and for raising its efficiency, and hence for the solution of all other economic and social issues."

the key to higher living standards. During the 1970s, productivity in U.S. manufacturing industries increased by around thirty percent, a strong contrast with the increase of about sixty percent in both France and West Germany and over a hundred percent in Japan. Because of their rapid improvement, a half-dozen nations will pass us in absolute productivity by 1990. * We now rank tenth in GNP per person, behind every major non-Communist industrial country except the United Kingdom and Italy.

To maintain technological strength relative to the rest of the world, the United States should steadily expand its efforts in R&D. Unfortunately, when military funding is subtracted, the fraction of our GNP invested in research and development has netted out to a decrease over the last twenty years, while the ratio has increased substantially in Japan and Western Europe.

University research, largely funded by government, is vital to the strength of our future technology. The government's funding of basic research in the universities, when properly adjusted for inflation, fell off badly in the 1970s when it should have been rising substantially, as it did in other high-tech countries. Increases were made in the 1980s, but we lost time. During the past two decades, our government's bureaucratic behavior has caused administrative costs within universities to balloon, a large fraction of each research grant going not for the intended research but rather for lawyers, accountants, and experts on government regulations. Further, the United States is the only major nation that insists on funding R&D on a fragmented basis and requires year-to-year recontracting of grants. In early summer, university scientists will not yet know whether the next academic year's research programs will continue to be supported; the university will be uncertain whether to fire or hire assistants, who usually are Ph.D. candidates.

The percentage of scientists and engineers in the U.S. labor force has been declining for some twenty years, while they have doubled in both Japan and Germany. During the 1970s, the number of Ph.D.s in physics employed in America dropped ten percent

---

* By the mid-1980s, Japan's productivity had exceeded the U.S.'s by twenty-five percent in motor vehicles, ten percent in steel, and twenty percent in electrical machinery.

even as the world became increasingly dependent on the work of physicists.

American-based companies have been losing out in world markets and even here at home in consumer electronics, cameras, automobiles, machinery that produces consumer goods (like sewing machines and tools), and in heavy machinery. The U.S. share of world trade for all high-technology products has dropped from thirty percent in the 1960s to less than twenty percent in the 1980s. In manufactured products, we still enjoyed a trade surplus of $17 billion in 1980, but by 1985 that figure had become a $100 billion deficit and has been growing ever since. One-seventh of all our manufacturing jobs depend on exports. Loss of export volume is now a major cause of unemployment in the United States.

Periodically, studies are made of important technological breakthroughs. U.S. inventions and developments completely dominated such lists in midcentury. In the past several years, however, fewer than half the listed items have been of U.S. origin. Twenty years ago, the U.S. Patent Office's grants to foreigners were barely noticeable. Today foreign inventors are obtaining almost half the American patents; patenting by U.S. inventors actually declined about twenty-five percent during the 1970s.

All indicators suggest that in the future this nation will be superior in far fewer of the significant technologies. Consider that the typical American grade-school student spends a total of one hour a day on math and science; this figure is exceeded two or more times in Japan and Europe. Half of our mathematics teachers in our nation's high schools are not certified and teach the subject with temporary certificates. Only about one hundred thousand U.S. high-school students take calculus, and usually for only part of a year. Five million high-school students in the Soviet Union have a full two years of calculus. Thousands of American freshmen engineering students are now assigned to remedial classes in mathematics before they can start to study calculus, which they should have done in high school.

More than half of U.S. high-school graduates have not had even one year of science. Only one competent science teacher is available to teach science for every two high schools. Of the twenty-five thousand high schools in the U.S. today, only seven thousand even offer a physics course. (In 1970, most did.) None of this surprises those who know that both mathematics and science high-school teachers declined by about seventy percent during the 1970s. In a typical year in the 1980s, there were ten times as many who abandoned math-teaching jobs than were graduated from college with majors in math education. We are badly undereducating in science and math, but the problem is much broader. Around a third of America's high-school students become dropouts, and over ten percent of our total population over age eighteen is functionally illiterate.

Of every thousand college graduates America now turns out, only seven are engineers. Among the Japanese, the figure is forty. The Soviet Union now graduates five times as many engineers a year as we do. The number of Ph.D.s in science and engineering produced annually is a key indicator of future technological strength. In an increasingly technological society, this number should rise steadily. But Americans earned five percent fewer such doctorates in 1986 than in 1980 (which was down ten percent from the peak in the early 1970s). Meanwhile, doctorates from American universities granted to foreign citizens rose forty percent in 1980–86. Since 1981, foreigners have received more than half of the engineering Ph.D.s. In 1986, foreigners received thirty percent of all science and engineering doctorates awarded in America. It used to be that most foreign-born Ph.D.s educated in our universities became U.S. citizens. Now more are returning home to take part in the boom in technological work. Between the 1970s and the 1980s, U.S. corporations with operations in foreign countries almost doubled the amount of R&D they conducted there.

The number of scientists and engineers graduating from U.S. colleges and universities has not grown fast enough to keep up with our industry's needs. In some segments of our technological industry, a shortage of engineers and scientists is all that keeps them from growing faster. It was estimated in 1985 that seventeen thousand entry-level openings in industry for engineers could not be filled. There are at least two thousand unfilled engineering teaching positions in American universities. The personnel needs of American industry are expanding rapidly in certain fields, such as computers, while our universities are becoming short of professors and graduates in precisely these most promising professions. The situation will surely become worse.

For many years, the government actually decreased its grants for university engineering programs instead of increasing them to train more engineers. (This trend is, fortunately, now being reversed, but we have far to go.) The government in the past has viewed the training of engineers as industry's concern. In both Japan and Germany, universities, industry, and government cooperate closely to expand engineering education. But American industrial leadership, with the exception of a few companies in a few fields at a few universities, is busy fighting foreign competition and has shown little interest in this longer-range need. U.S. corporate financial support of universities has risen slightly in the past few years, it is true, but from a level far too low. As a percentage of pretax income, when properly corrected for inflation, this support actually dropped during the 1970s. For years I have been involved with a few others in campaigns urging American technological corporations to donate a mere two percent of their R&D budgets, or one percent of their earnings before taxes, to help improve the nation's engineering schools. But only a small fraction of American companies have seen fit to bring their contributions to these extremely modest levels.

Without major increases in government and industry support of science, math, and engineering education in our schools and universities, the United States in future decades will descend to mediocrity as a technological society.

The threats to American eminence in technology are made worse by a number of economic-political factors. One is our large government budget deficit, a consequence of which until just recently has been the dollar's high exchange rate against the currency of other industrialized nations. This meant for years that foreign products were automatically priced lower here and ours higher abroad, causing our technological industry to lose revenues needed to finance R&D. Another is our record in capital investment. It has been estimated that half the productivity increases in the United States in the last twenty-five years have been the direct result of advances in manufacturing technology. But U.S. capital-investment trends today do not suggest that we shall see a rapid growth in such innovation. The total funds we have been putting behind each worker to improve manufacturing performance is below that of our principal international competitors.

Our inflation and high real interest rates over two decades have accentuated this difference. Japanese interest rates have averaged half of ours, making investments in their industry more attractive. In the middle 1960s, we ranked first in the world in capital investment per capita. By the middle 1970s, we had slipped to sixth place. When the investment in nondefense manufacturing plants is pulled out of the total, our nonmilitary investment over the last two decades averaged out at below three percent of GNP, a ratio lower than that of any other industrialized nation.

The average age of a factory in the United States is twenty years, while in Japan and West Germany it is ten; their factories incorporate more advanced manufacturing technology. In the 1950–60s, production techniques pioneered in the United States were looked up to worldwide as the way to raise productivity; foreign manufacturers used to copy us. Today, robotry and computer-controlled manufacturing are symbolic of technologically up-to-date production, and Japan is the acknowledged leader. Major American firms are taking out licenses in Japanese technology.

The structure of rewards to U.S. managers of industry fails to encourage long-term risk-taking, and this holds back investments in new technologies. The American pattern is to rate the performance of business management by a simple score: earnings for the period just ended, compared with the same period the year before. Operating managers usually receive base salaries plus bonuses set by the level and growth of reported earnings. Unfortunately, projects in advanced technology usually take longer to mature—from the very beginning, through the loss-certain development and start-up phases, to a profit period—than the average length of time an operating executive remains in his job. (A recent study has shown that the average period during which a chief executive officer of a public company or the general manager of a corporate division occupies his post is less than six years.) A typical manager hence has a bias against long-term projects, whose high start-up costs will hurt his earnings record, financial remuneration, and prestige, and where the successes, should they eventually occur, will add only to the standing and income of his successors.

The competitive situation is made more serious for the United States because of the scope of our military R&D. Since it is concentrated on the most difficult of technical projects, it usurps a disproportionate fraction, around half, of the country's technological resources. The mere comparing of dollars of expenditures on military and civilian R&D doesn't tell us how great the effect really is. Designing a military computer may not call for a smarter computer engineer than designing a civilian computer, but creating complex computer networks to provide command-control-communications intelligence for the Armed Forces soaks up huge numbers of hardware and software engineers. Designing a modern battle tank requires more engineering effort than a commercial truck. The new Stealth bomber, by the time it enters the Air Force's inventory, will have used far more engineer years than would have been necessary to develop the most advanced passenger plane for the commercial airlines.

Since the United States considers itself the chief protector of the non-Communist world, our technological resources are severely strained as we try to accommodate both our huge military-weapons R&D programs and civilian products that would be competitive throughout the world. As a fraction of gross national product allocated to the military arena, Western Europe spends twenty-five percent of equivalent U.S. expenditures, and Japan's contribution is trivial. *

---

* The U.S. uses over forty percent of its defense budget, nearly $140 billion, to support NATO, more than the Europeans spend. Japan is a "free rider"; our nuclear umbrella protects them at no cost to them whatever.

In the decades just ahead, we probably will still garner more points in the world technology olympics than any other country, because of our large population, broadly developed infrastructure, and considerable natural resources. The pertinent competition to consider, however, is not from any single nation but from the total of them all. It seems safe to predict that America will have a decreasing fraction of the world's engineers and that other nations on the average will back up their engineers with resources comparable to those we can make available. The expected distribution of the globe's effectively employed engineers is such that by the year 2000 four out of five future technological breakthroughs and major refinements are likely to originate outside the United States. Many Americans have worried that our advanced technology has been transferred too generously to other nations and feel that we must curb such transfers; this fear implies, of course, that we are generally ahead of others. The realistic challenge in the future may not be how to keep our leading technology from foreign countries but rather how to acquire theirs. *

How could this have happened? How could the U.S. have changed so quickly from being preeminent in technology to being a country with diminished future prospects? Is our system, from goal setting to implementation, which has never been perfect, no longer suited to the nature of an ever more technological society? Does our free-enterprise system lack strength or applicability? Could the government do more to improve the competitive position of the United States? Are Americans too poorly informed, and thus fail to demand changes they should realize are needed?

There is plenty of blame to go around. Parents? The parents of American schoolchildren have spent billions of dollars to buy their children computer games (useful, aside from entertainment, only for developing quick eye-hand coordination, not for learning either

---

* In 1987, the National Academy of Engineering examined thirty-four aspects of frontier engineering (such as robotry, artificial intelligence, nuclear-plant safety, high-speed rail transportation, and combustion technology) and found Japan superior or at least equal to the United States in twenty-five, Germany in twenty-two, United Kingdom in twenty, France in fifteen, and Sweden in twelve.

mathematics or computer science), but they have steadily voted down taxes to provide more funds to pay math and science teachers adequately in their children's schools. The federal government? In 1981, the new Administration suggested that the Department of Education should be abolished. Industry? In the 1980s, the largest American technological corporations conspicuously lowered their interest in striving for major technology advances and instead gave priority to spending their funds to acquire nontechnological companies. We must be aware as we allocate blame that every sector of the nation must play a part if the performance of the United States is to be improved.

Let us consider specific steps to reverse the present trend, and ask who among the nation's decision-makers and implementers should take them. These actions fall into two categories, the "easy" and the "difficult." The easy actions require no change in the Constitution, the American culture, or the general pattern of our lives. They will come about if only we recognize the problems and choose our priorities carefully. The second, difficult category involves steps that can be taken only if the majority of citizens come to a greater understanding of the shortcomings of the way we now operate. The hard decisions will involve making substantial changes in the way we do things. But we must not for that reason regard this category as hopeless and throw up our hands. Too much is at stake. We should pin down what ought to be done and probe how to start doing it. Let us look first at examples in the easy category.

The free market should automatically correct some of our shortcomings, given enough time, and nothing could be easier than just to let that happen. If America has too few Ph.D.s in engineering, or too few math teachers for the elementary grades, or computer scientists, then salaries will rise in those fields. The news of the opportunities will get around and young people and their parents will work, push, and sacrifice to prepare to fill the openings. Technological corporations, finding they are losing out to foreign competitors, will eventually halt or decrease dividends and increase their R&D budgets in order to improve their products and manufacturing technology and seek to win back the markets they have lost. If there are too few college graduates in the most important fields, industry ultimately will find ways to help the universities to produce more needed graduates.

Will such good trends really materialize and grow? Self-corrections surely will play a part in bucking the growing negatives. By themselves, however, they will be highly inadequate. It may take only a decade for the free market to produce more computer scientists, but five decades may pass before the free market causes us to pay math teachers in high school enough to ensure that we will have such teachers.

In our country, when we face an important problem that requires an attack by government, serious action is taken only after most citizens have clearly perceived the problem. For strong public pressure to form, the situation must first become so bad that it is widely seen as intolerable. Hence, the pragmatic American formula for progress is that things have to get much worse before they can get better. Facetious as it may sound, we can justify being optimistic about our eventual success with step 2, leading to a superior technological U.S. society, because we are now moving ahead so rapidly on step 1. Take education in math as one example.

Our inferiority in the teaching of math to our youngsters has finally started to hit the front pages. The problem has finally become that bad. Parents are learning for the first time from newspaper headlines that, in standard (identical) exams given to children in most non-Communist nations, United States elementary and high-school students scored last among the industrialized nations and only slightly ahead of the average of the underdeveloped countries.* These astounding results are not merely news reports. They are the subject of serious editorial commentary.

While the media were parading these results, I found occasion, as a member of the National Science Board, to bring up the subject frequently with senators and representatives in Washington. I learned

---

* In these exams, the same in each country, the average twelfth-grade math student in Japan outperformed ninety-five percent of comparable U.S. twelfth-graders. Only one of the top one hundred scorers among fifth-grade students from typical U.S. schools (Chicago and Minneapolis) and similar schools in China (Beijing) and Japan (Sendai) was an American.

that they, too, were becoming aware of our outrageously low math scores, and they expressed amazement that such educational inferiority could have developed without our taking notice and engaging in action. They pledged themselves to look favorably on appropriate federal-government activity in an attempt to change the situation. They expressed hope that the Administration would present Congress with aggressive proposals.

This new congressional attitude, and the sense of growing public appreciation of the problem on which that attitude is based, has enabled the National Science Foundation to get approval from the Administration for innovative programs in primary and secondary education. Funding from the Congress has followed. New programs costing tens of millions of dollars per year are now slated to rise quickly to the $100 million level. This shows that, on certain aspects of the educational problem, things are so unacceptable that we must move; step 1 is giving way now to step 2.

In California, in the spring of 1987, Governor Deukmejian found himself with an unexpected $700 million surplus in the state treasury. Seeking to add to his popularity, he proposed to refund the money to the taxpayers (a mere $75 each). But the legislature, the media, and the parents screamed in protest and demanded that the money be used instead to improve elementary and secondary education in the state. The governor found himself embarrassed and badly out of touch, having failed to appreciate the growing political force behind improving education. That force is not, of course, based on a public sense that we need only more science and math education. The broader view is building that the quality of American education is below an acceptable standard in language, history, civics, geography—the broad spectrum of requirements for citizenship and for participation in the good life.

As public awareness of the situation grows, parents will change their priorities and insist on changes in the resources allocated to education, even if that means increases in school taxes and in teachers' salaries to compete with industry's higher salaries. Eventually, this is bound to lead more university students to consider teaching as a profession.

Industry is awakening as well. An excellent example of that is the effort of David Packard, chairman of Hewlett–Packard, who has led White House-sponsored studies of shortcomings in our university education. Those studies have influenced the projects and budgets of the National Research Foundation and caused the formation of joint government and industry programs to substantially improve facilities and instrumentation for undergraduate college education. Packard's associate, John Young, president of Hewlett–Packard, and Robert Anderson, chairman of Rockwell International, are two other industry leaders who, in heading Presidential commissions and councils on productivity, innovation, and international competitiveness, have helped to pinpoint our problems and to suggest opportunities for improvement.

The two most influential organizations representing the leadership of the largest corporations in America are the Business Roundtable and the Business Council. For decades, those who have chaired these organizations have been the heads of the biggest companies in sales and assets, and their chief interests have been to lobby in Washington on tax and other economic-political issues important to big business. In recent years my close associate, Ruben Mettler, chairman of TRW Inc. (a large company, but a tenth the size of the biggest), was made the chairman of the Business Roundtable, 1982–84, and then of the Business Council, 1985–86. (The council meets three times a year with cabinet-level government officials, and the President is often in attendance.) This is the first time that an individual with a Ph.D. (and knowledge of the growing lag in American primary, secondary, and university education and the consequences of this lag) has assumed positions of such importance in influencing the thinking of corporate leadership. Rube has participated in the so-called Business–Higher Education Forum, made up of the heads of America's largest universities and of its largest corporations; the objective of the forum is to improve university education.

To minimize the involvement of the federal government in selecting the content of education in the primary and secondary schools may be, in the main, sound. As the crisis builds, however,

American voters will realize that education deserves more attention and will insist that the federal government play an important role. Opportunities do exist to further the urgent national need to improve education with the capabilities that only the federal government possesses. For example, our high schools require laboratories for science teaching, but laboratories are so difficult and expensive to create and operate that they are disappearing, an intolerable situation for a technological nation. Moreover, most high-school laboratories are out of date. Modern facilities and experiments are badly needed, but to develop them is out of the question if local school districts act separately. Fortunately, the principles of physics and chemistry are the same in New England, Kansas, and California. A national program spurred by federal-government contracts with competitive industry, using teams of engineers and science teachers, could conceive innovative, up-to-date laboratory experiments that would teach the fundamentals with cleverly designed and very economical, standardized apparatus and facilities. The hardware and software then could be mass-produced and purchased by the school districts at reasonable prices.

Funding and administering elementary and high-school education is almost entirely the job of state, county, and city school districts. But there is not only a role for the federal government; there is also an important role for the President of the United States. I can best illustrate this by describing an occasion in which I appeared on a program dealing with high-school education that was opened by a public address by President Reagan.

It was an all-day session held at a high school in the greater Los Angeles area (Whittier) early in 1984. The President was giving speeches around the country on issues presumably considered by his political advisors to be of potential importance in the election that fall. Word of the sad decline of American education and of growing voter discontent apparently had reached the White House. Editorials in newspapers, commentary on TV, and statements made by members of Congress, the National Academies of Science and Engineering, and national leaders in education were beginning to point to the apparent low interest of the Administration in education. In response, Presidential advisors who suggest priorities decided that it was time for the education issue to be addressed.

The theme the Department of Education in Washington had chosen years before, an echo of the President's early occasional comments on education, was that the federal government really had no part to play in primary and secondary education. The argument was frequently repeated that we cannot cure every problem by throwing money at it, and especially not federal money thrown at school districts. When the President's advisors and speech writers heard about the remarkable performance of a large high school in California, they thought they had come upon an example worth highlighting. Whittier High School, almost entirely made up of minority students, had outstanding success in getting them into college. The White House put the President on the program as the keynote speaker at a conference to be held at this school.

In his address, the President congratulated the host high school for its unusual accomplishments. He went on to say that its record demonstrated that determination and hard work, not more money from the federal government, are the keys to outstanding education.

The speaker who followed after the President left was a state-education official. He pointed out that this high school had been used as a testing ground for an experiment paid for by California state funds. A team of outstanding teachers had been assembled at that school with the unusual assignment of picking the exceptional students and drilling them for months to prepare them to take college-entrance exams and otherwise improve their chances of getting into college. That scheme had worked. There was an enormous increase in the number of students aspiring to go on to college and getting into the college of their choice, usually on a scholarship. Unfortunately, the administrator went on to disclose, this unique program had just been terminated. There was no longer money for it in the new, reduced high-school budget. The special team of teachers, he said sadly, was gone from the high school.

This event illustrated what not to do at the White House in scheduling the President of the United States to talk about improving education. Imagine where we might be in 1988 if, starting at the beginning of his first term in 1981, the President's program had steadily urged parents to drive their school districts hard, favor appropriate increases in taxes to provide higher pay for teachers, and do all the other sensible things that would follow if they understood the problem. If only the President's prestige and skills in communication had been employed to inform the nation how badly we compare with competitive nations in the education of our children for a technological society. If only the President had helped Americans to relate quality of education to our future standard of living, national security, and general domestic tranquillity. It would not have been impossible—in fact, it would have been easy—for President Reagan's talents to be applied to emphasize the crying need for concern about education.

The government's inadequate response to rapid technological advance is not a monopoly of the executive branch. Congress has not acted on the easy-to-change shortcomings of our laws that affect the nation's competitiveness. Take our antitrust laws, as one example. Congress has for years contemplated revising our basic antitrust legislation but is still nowhere near ready to act. We are still living under antiquated antitrust laws that originated some hundred years ago and that are now a handicap to increased technological strength and competitiveness.

In the 1970s, for instance, the U.S. government took both AT&T and IBM to court, accusing them of being monopolies in their two supposedly different sectors, AT&T in communications and IBM in computers. Anyone even slightly sophisticated in the computer-communications field knew that it had become impossible to separate the field into two separate parts. AT&T and IBM, both applying developing technology to serve their customers, had no choice but to cover a broadening array of computer-communications services. Hence, each of these two mammoth companies was clearly and rapidly becoming the other's competitor. Several congressional committees and a number of agencies of the executive branch (such as the Defense and Commerce Departments and the Federal Communications Commission) were very slowly recognizing the inevitable—and, in fact, the already existing—merging of communications and computers into one field of information technology.

Thus, important parts of the government realized that AT&T and IBM were competitors, while another part of government was simultaneously trying to break them up by categorizing each as a monopoly. After a decade of pursuing monopoly ghosts at monstrous expense, the government dropped the antitrust case against IBM, but forced the split of AT&T. Whether this was good for America or the world was never an issue before the court. The court action, with its highly significant consequences, was solely in response to laws designed for a rather isolated country in a technologically adolescent age, not a mature technological nation operating in a highly interactive world economy. Lacking updated legislation, Judge Harold Greene, a distinguished jurist but an individual without a single day's industrial-management experience, was forced to take on the unprecedented job of reorganizing the largest and most complex of U.S. corporations.

During the prosecution of the court action against AT&T, the Deputy Secretary of Defense, Frank Carlucci, wrote to the Department of Justice that "because the AT&T network is the most important communications net we have to serve our strategic systems . . . severe problems will confront the Department of Defense if this network is broken up. Accordingly, it is the position of the Secretary of Defense that the pending suit against AT&T be dismissed." But neither the Attorney General nor the court could ignore the law on the books, not even when abiding by it might be detrimental to national security. The proper steps would have been for the President to have pressed Congress to pass appropriate new legislation and for Congress to have done so promptly.

In view of the importance of international competition for the welfare of the United States, at least one change in antitrust law would appear to be long overdue and easy to implement. U.S.-based companies should not be categorized as monopolies but should be free of antitrust restrictions and allowed to combine forces when the real competitors are foreign-based, particularly those subsidized by their governments. For the Congress to so update antitrust legislation is relatively straightforward; it does not require a constitutional amendment. Easy steps like these will be taken as public understanding builds that inaction is hurting the nation.

Let us move now to a discussion of the "hard" category, to those problems that are much more difficult to eliminate and where appropriate action would seem to require major changes in the way we see and do things. We can get into this subject quickly by comparing ourselves with Japan, a nation that does things quite differently and surely has been very successful.

Japan's economic growth has paralleled the steady loss by U.S. technological industry of domestic and international markets, so many American industrial and political leaders are unable to think calmly about Japan. This prime competitor is castigated for its market policies at home, and seen as handicapping the entry of American products into Japan. Such criticism goes hand in hand with proposals that the United States severely restrict imports from Japan. Now, it may be that more American-manufactured products could be sold in Japan, thus easing the large trade imbalance between our two countries, if the Japanese would eliminate all barriers to sale of U.S. products there. But would a magical disappearance of every hindrance enable General Motors to sell many Chevrolets in Japan in competition with cars specifically designed for Japanese needs and preferences, lower-priced autos that millions of Americans have also chosen over U.S.-made models? Would American steel makers—whose older plants require substantially more labor hours and energy to produce a ton of steel and which operate with a higher labor pay rate—win many orders from Japanese steel users if there were open competitions? If American electronic consumer products (like tape recorders, radios, handheld computers, television sets, and the like) could be offered freely to Japan's consumers, they would have to be produced in Asia to be cost-competitive.

So there must be factors beyond their import barriers that have led to Japan's success. Why not simply copy Japan? Let us imagine how we would do it.

First, we would have to create a political environment so stable that a strong majority consensus would be reached on every key issue, as commonly happens in Japan. We also would have to arrange for the same political party to be in power simultaneously in the Senate, the House of Representatives, and the White House over a period of many years. (So far, this doesn't sound easy to do.) When the Japanese decide to try for world superiority in any technological arena, it is natural for them to arrange full cooperation among private companies, the government, banks, and labor. In the United States, the relationships of these entities are essentially adversarial. The Japanese have a key which they use skillfully to unlock the doors to world trade in technology. We in the United States, often drunk with conceit about our permanent superiority, have had difficulty sobering up enough to get our key in the door.

The Japanese understand the concept of national interest and they share it. We argue inconclusively about what it is. They can establish a cooperative plan based on agreed-upon objectives and stick to it for years. For this approach to be applied in the United States, we would have to invent a way to set national goals and priorities.

Let us go even further in fantasizing about how to copy Japan. Suppose that the U.S. government were to cut expenditures and were to tax soundly, thus eliminating our huge budget deficits. Having accomplished this, we would then enjoy low real interest rates and low inflation, factors that have been of tremendous value to the Japanese for almost half a century in building their technological industry. Imagine also that the public in the United States, like the Japanese, were to embrace the concept of saving, instead of overspending (by both consumers and government) and over-borrowing (again, by both) to fund the spending. For decades, Japan has averaged a twenty-five percent ratio of savings to the GNP, whereas the U.S. figure is less than five percent.

Finally, while dreaming, let us persuade Western Europe and Japan that it is now their turn to take on the main burden of defending the free world against potential military action by the Soviet Union.

If all these steps could be taken—a scenario we can play out only in our minds, the equivalent of hallucinating—we would then have the foundation for matching Japan in international competition. Aping the Japanese is frequently mentioned in industrial, academic, and government circles and in the business press, but the idea, I submit, is unrelated to reality.

We are more likely to find ourselves so angry at the Japanese and others because of their trade success that we will move to embrace protectionism. We might then save jobs for Americans in industries that are being bested by cheaper or better products from the outside, but we would be denying to most other Americans the low cost and high quality of those same products. (Why else do we now buy them?) If we lacked imported components and materials, many products assembled in America would be higher in price, and fewer would be sold in the U.S. and abroad, which might lead to their not being manufactured at all. Our unemployment rate might be temporarily lower in some protected industries, but it would surely be higher generally. Other nations would reciprocate, raising their trade barriers. World trade would be reduced, and world recession would threaten us. We would experience a decreasing standard of living.

Every country has social and economic difficulties and a citizenry that looks to the government to improve things. Since the international movement of assets is bound to affect conditions within each nation, it is impossible for governments to keep their hands off this flow. Accordingly, the protectionist approach to international trade will be active forever. We are unlikely, however, to see a world ahead totally in the grip of protectionism, because the very different one-world, free-market approach to trade offers powerful economic benefits. In this approach, raw materials, manufactured products, services, money, technology, management, and even labor cross borders without constraint. Each nation offers what it can to others at free-market prices. It chooses what it pleases from what other nations present to the unfettered world marketplace. When each entity concentrates on what it is most suited to do, those fortunate to possess superior resources, skills, and developed infrastructure will admittedly enjoy advantages. But if the output of any nation, richly endowed or not, is available to others, then they all will fare better economically. It is, thus, difficult for governments to put free-trade mechanisms entirely aside, and that is without doubt a permanent situation. International commerce will continue to exist as a hybrid of free trade and protectionism.

If neither emulating Japan nor barring foreign products with high tariffs will be helpful to the United States, how can we improve our chances in world trade? Among other things, we have to improve policy-making. The pattern of our democracy causes our government to handle most problems with short-term political expediency, rather than long-range policies. The government formulates few policies of significance because political constituents' priorities and demands are so diverse. Surely, rational deliberations should include choosing goals, examining alternatives, setting priorities, and evolving strategy for their implementation. In America, speeches about long-range objectives are little more than the mumbo-jumbo of political leaders at election time: cut the size of government, decrease taxes, make America militarily stronger, eliminate poverty, broaden opportunity. These phrases are paralleled by a steady stream of subgoals, which, whether vague or specific, are short-lived, such as: cut next year's deficit by X dollars, freeze government salaries for one year, lower (or raise) speed limits on our highways.

In the United States, private capital at risk (the foundation for free enterprise) has regularly gone into technology to create an enormous flow of products that has changed not only America but the entire world. If this was sufficient, government policy should simply be to create a supporting infrastructure and a sound economic environment, and then stay out of the way. Free enterprise cannot fully sponsor and control new technology, however. The government's leverage on private decision-making concerning science and technology is very powerful and is here to stay.

Consider, for example, that about half of all U.S. research and development is directly funded by the government. It pays for most of the pure research in our universities. It specifies and buys all military-weapons systems and most spacecraft. It sponsors advanced atomic-energy research. The government affects the operations of technological industry: it grants patents, interprets antitrust laws, determines fair-trade practices, prices utilities' services, allocates radio-broadcast privileges; it regulates to protect our safety, our health, and the environment; and it exacts taxes and offers tax incentives that greatly affect returns on investments in technology and hence on the rate of such investments.

In America there is a lot more to policy, of course, than what stems from government activity, whether the government's policy contribution is deliberate or the result of benign neglect or confusion. Myriad policy-related actions go on all the time in private as well as government sectors; together they create the hodgepodge that really ends up being the U.S. national policy. Take the activities of multinational corporations.

Multinational companies operate so as to meet their clear objectives of maximizing return on investment. Unless it is illegal, they will move their funds, technology, management know-how, production, equipment, materials, and employees from one nation to another to achieve those objectives. A multinational corporation's management has no responsibility to ensure increasing employment for the citizens of any country where it operates. An American-based multinational corporation may be headed by an American who is patriotic and wants to see a healthy, growing American economy. But it is not his job to act or to use his company's assets to realize such a goal.

If the product of an American multinational can be manufactured for the domestic U.S. market or the world at large at lowest cost in a foreign country, the top management will arrange that, or it will lose out to competitors who will, and the management that failed to take such action can expect to be replaced. If there is a shortage of Ph.D.s in science and engineering in the United States but not in Western Europe, then American-based multinational corporations will establish research-and-development operations in Western Europe. It is not a primary concern of U.S. multinationals how American-originated technology fares in the competitive international arena.

American multinational corporations need American government support in order to compete with multinational corporations chartered in other countries. The American government needs the aid of powerful and innovative American multinational corporations to achieve national objectives. Thus, it is often important for the corporations and the government to join forces. The concept of the United States government as merely monitoring, regulating, and punishing illegal actions by American corporations, rather than as a partner in ensuring the health and vigor of those corporations, is clearly out of date in an international, competitive, technological world.

The corporations that have been most vigorous in pressing for United States government support have mainly been companies that want to hold on to their American market through high tariffs on competitive imports. There have been few attempts by government and private industry to establish cooperative government-industry policies and strategies with the object of attaining the greatest possible satisfactions for the average American. In an increasingly technological society, we will need substantially more imaginative cooperation between the private and the public sector. Such cooperation has never been the American way, and that will have to change.

Consider energy, which involves both the private sector and the government on an international scale. As in national security, communication, and transportation, cooperation between the government and private corporations is vital to ensure an adequate supply of energy for the nation. That we have not had such cooperation is evident in the way we handled the energy problem over the last two decades.

In April 1973, George Shultz, our present Secretary of State, occupied an office down the hall from President Nixon's. Shultz, in effect, held two jobs at that time. He was Secretary of the Treasury, and his main office, I suppose it would be correct to say, was in the Treasury Department. He was also Nixon's principal assistant on economic affairs and other matters. It was in this second role that in April 1973 Shultz invited William O. Baker, then president of the Bell Telephone Laboratories, and me to meet with him.

The Secretary started the meeting by noting the disparity between the increasing demand for oil in America and the shrinking domestic supply. The severe instability of the Near East might halt the export of oil from there at any time; in that event, the threat to both our economy and our national security was obvious. (The Arab–Israeli war broke out six months later, on Yom Kippur.) He raised two questions: Could science and new technologies alleviate the coming oil shortage by providing new sources of energy? Could the use of energy in production, transportation, heating, and elsewhere be reduced substantially through new technology?

The two of us, the Secretary commented, were running large research-and-development operations in private industry, and that was why he had called on us. Could not the private sector, he asked, handle any future energy problem without government intervention? The technological industry should be able to create new energy alternatives and devise ways to use energy more efficiently. Industry, not the government, has the experts. But would private industry really do it? Shultz expressed the concern that if an energy problem developed, the public might demand federal intervention. Then a new government energy research-and-development agency would be established, just as earlier, when the Soviet Union launched Sputnik, the government responded by setting up NASA. Maybe a new agency was required for space, he said. But, he asked, must the government also take the initiative for R&D in energy? A strong and increasing demand for energy is out there waiting to be filled. Shouldn't that translate into attractive corporate returns for those willing to invest in energy technology?

I was no oilman, but I had been active in having TRW build a profitable, growing business (hundreds of millions of dollars annually) in submersible oil-well pumps and other equipment and services for the oil industry and I was seeing a great many oil-company executives. Although they would often refer to possible oil shortages, they had not predicted that they were imminent.

There was little evidence that these companies were desperately searching for alternatives to oil or developing new processes to conserve energy in production and transportation. The automobile industry was carrying on substantial R&D activities, but in early 1973 they had not initiated crash programs to redesign their autos for a time soon to come when sales might hinge on cars that consumed much less fuel.

Private industry would deal with the energy problem if the profits were attractive. So I predicted to Shultz that potential financial returns on investment would be weighed by the industry against perceived risks. This was, I knew, an obvious point to the Secretary, who holds a doctorate in economics from M.I.T. and a few years before had headed the distinguished business school at the University of Chicago, but a not-so-obvious parallel issue had to be discussed. It was that the private sector in the energy field would expect the government to interfere in every aspect, to the detriment of the energy producers. The government would, for instance, influence adversely the critical relationship between return and risk by imposing price controls. This conviction would deter private investment. If Near East oil supplies were interrupted, development of alternative energy sources and methods for more effective utilization of energy might begin to have support, but as Bill Baker quickly pointed out, it would take years to advance from R&D to practical implementations. So, oil prices would rise quickly and the public would react with demands that the government set price ceilings.

Accordingly, should we realistically expect industry to risk huge amounts of capital to develop alternatives to petroleum? Liquid fuel could be produced from coal and shale, but only at much higher costs than existing crude oil. Of course, if supplies were cut off and petroleum prices moved far higher, then at some point it would be possible to produce liquid fuel from shale or coal at a competitive price. But the expected selling price would always be the dominant factor in determining private investment, and the government would surely fix the price. It would be set too low, because the government would be more responsive to the voter-consumer's idea of a suitable price than industry's criterion of a good return on investment to match the high risk. Moreover, the production of liquid fuel from shale or coal would surely create massive pollution. Private companies would know that the payback on their investment would depend on government-set environmental regulations. Those regulations would not necessarily be the right ones for industry, but those most politically popular—not the same thing at all.

If I was helpful to George Shultz, it was by insisting that the energy shortage he was predicting would not be solved by science and engineering advances alone or by the free-enterprise system acting on its own. Should a crisis arise, heavy involvement by the government would be inevitable. That would include the government's having to sponsor R&D on energy alternatives. The government might as well plan on this, I suggested, without enthusiasm. I guessed that George Shultz might already have reached this conclusion and to get confirmation was the principal reason he had asked Baker and me to meet with him.

Several months after the Shultz meeting, I found myself back in the White House as a member of a newly established White House Energy Research and Development Council. One could not ask for a better example of how government actions involving science and technology are likely to develop when planning and strategy are not begun early and carried on regularly in a deliberate, calm fashion, and cooperatively with the private sector. The council was asked by President Nixon to consider how the government might employ science and technology to help solve what by then was a full-blown energy crisis. Shultz's predictions had been accurate on every count. The first meeting of the council was called just after the outbreak of the Arab–Israeli war (October 1973), which was followed quickly by the imposition of an oil embargo by the Arabs and the start of a steep rise in the price of oil.

After the crisis hit, Nixon appointed a special assistant for energy, whom the media immediately mislabeled an "energy czar." He was John Love, the former governor of Colorado. The first session of the new R&D council was slated to open with President Nixon's swearing us in; however, the agenda had to be continually rearranged because President Nixon, we were told, had to give priority to some major emergency. (It turned out to be Spiro Agnew's removal as Vice President.) The day ended with Governor Love doing the swearing in.

The second meeting of the council was held a few weeks later, just after Governor Love resigned as the White House's energy coordinator and was replaced by William Simon, who was also Deputy Secretary of the Treasury under George Shultz. When the third meeting of the council took place, the principal government energy executive was Frank Zarb, who had replaced Bill Simon, who had replaced George Shultz, who had resigned as Secretary of the Treasury. At the following meeting, our link to the White House became John Sawhill, who had replaced Frank Zarb, who had left the government.

At this meeting, the council recommended the creation of a new agency (just as George Shultz feared would happen), to be called the Energy Research and Development Administration (ERDA). When Nixon resigned, ERDA had been created but was not yet fully established; the nation had only an ad hoc program on energy. No formal or even semiformal group of government and industry leaders was set up to plan an integrated short- and long-term solution to the energy problem. The question of the relation of the federal government to the private sector in energy R&D was receiving scant attention. There was much confusion as to whether the highest priority was to be fixing prices on crude oil and retail gasoline, or reducing the use of fuel (for instance, imposing severe automobile mileage standards on the manufacturers), or controlling damaging emanations from the burning of coal for the generation of electricity, or creating government subsidies to help develop fuel from shale, or speeding up the generation of nuclear-based electric power, or accelerating the development of solar energy, or inventing ways to conserve energy in industry, transportation, and the home, or setting up a government-held oil reserve. The government made disconnected hit-or-miss attacks on all these pieces of the overall problem.

George Shultz obviously had seen and understood the problem

ahead of time. But the system's inadequacies, and George Shultz's departure from government, precluded his taking hold, pulling the energy issue's many facets together, arranging for cooperation between government and the private sector, and getting the right things done in a timely way.

Little happened on energy policy during the short Ford Administration; things got neither worse nor better. The confusion increased in the Carter Administration despite its creating an Energy Department and an independent multibillion-dollar Synthetic Fuels Corporation, the latter soon dissolved by the Reagan Administration. The objectives of the entire government energy effort, from Nixon to Ford to Carter to Reagan, were unclear at all times (setting aside the silly political sloganeering, like "energy independence," which lasted a few weeks). What was clear was that there was a crisis, as evidenced by high gasoline prices and lines at the gas stations.

Heavy government involvement with energy has been perceived by the public as imperative ever since, but nothing faintly like a long-term energy policy or strategy exists to this day. Comes another major disruption of oil supply from the Near East and we can expect an energy crisis and chaos all over again.

To explore how to enhance the U.S. potential in technology and thus increase our chances of being secure, internationally competitive, and enjoying steadily improved living standards, two other important matters must be considered. The next chapter presents some possibilities for a much improved national-security picture, one in which resources devoted to the military can be reduced with safety, leaving more resources available for purely peaceful purposes. The final chapter suggests how technological entrepreneurship can be made to thrive in America to give us a unique advantage over other countries by advancing our technology and the exploitation of its benefits. Both chapters will continue a recital of needed changes in the American way of operating.

SEVEN

Prediction, Optimism, and Future National Defense

So far, I have dealt with events of the past and present, although with a few notions about the world ahead. The rest of the book will be concerned primarily with the future. I shall make predictions. None will be wild dreams. They will be logical extensions of present trends and past patterns, with a full portion of pure hunch thrown in. Before engaging in predictions, however, I feel compelled to defend the practice, because it is not a universally respected one. To be frank, predicting has a terrible reputation. If you engage in trying to look far ahead and still wish to be admired by your peers, you had better be careful how you describe what you are up to. You may admit to guessing at things to come if you smile while doing so, but do not claim to prophesy or you will be categorized with the nuts who foretell when the world will end.

Engineers and scientists would tell us that if we could predict discoveries and breakthroughs, then by definition they would not be discoveries and breakthroughs. Economists renounce all predicting, especially when done by other economists, who do it all the time. Chief executives of corporations habitually hold their own visions in high esteem and greet their planning department's forecasts with pronounced skepticism. Politicians, when deciding what positions to take, give priority to polls telling what voters want. Team up some foremost philosophers and successful pragmatists, and direct them to contact us after they have evolved an intellectual discipline for predicting the future, and we shall never hear from them again. No university offers a course in principles of prediction.

Trying to predict the future with great accuracy is not defensible. But if we are active and competent in some field, we are bound to be aware of important trends in it. We should regularly list possible developments, estimating for each the probability of its occurrence and its importance should it occur. Then, for those happenings deemed both probable and significant, we should ask ourselves what we can do early to enhance the positive and suppress the negative consequences. (We need, of course, to avoid falling in love with our predictions and committing all our resources on the rash assumption that our list will prove totally correct.)

To be sure, we shall find later that some of our predictions missed totally or did not describe accurately some occurrences that we were correct to include. But if we performed the exercise conscientiously, I submit we would very likely be ahead of where we would have been had we completely disavowed prediction. My own experience with prediction certainly bears this out. My gamble in leaving General Electric and joining Hughes to build a new military-technology organization in 1946 rested firmly on predictions. Detailed in an earlier chapter, they were: The Soviet Union would soon possess the A-bomb. The United States would create a colossal, high-tech air-defense system. Established industry would give first priority to civilian products neglected during the Depression and the war. The aircraft companies would be unprepared for electronics and systems engineering, both critical to success. This added up to an exciting opportunity for a new company.

But my predicting of the basis for the buildup of Hughes Aircraft unfortunately did not score one hundred percent. I had called certain events right on the button, but had failed properly to consider Howard Hughes himself, which came close to sinking the whole enterprise.

Like most others, I was taken by surprise by the Russian jump on us in developing the ICBM. I shouldn't have been. When the ICBM's significance to national security became evident, I realized that, far from being unforeseeable, the ICBM era could and should have been anticipated the moment the H-bomb was developed. If experts had been engaged in a thorough effort to predict technological advances in the atom bomb and in guided rockets, they could have plotted an enormous improvement for bomb yield-to-weight ratio, guidance accuracy, rocket-engine performance, structural strength, and every other aspect of missilery. Furthermore, as the 1950s began, it was observable that the development of air-defense systems against manned bombers was moving very rapidly. Both American and Soviet priorities should accordingly have been expected to shift to seeking better ways to deliver nuclear weapons.

Just such predictions, I learned later, had been made in 1951 by a small group of military planners (including Bernard Schriever), whose projections had been given essentially no attention. In the Defense Department, despite its constant dallying with projections, the concept of prediction lacked stature and predictions had little influence.

I had concluded from the Hughes and the ICBM experiences that one can get awfully busy with crisis activity and fail to take time to recognize the obvious next steps. The very fact that, while preoccupied with designing systems to defend against manned bombers, I had missed seeing the coming of the ICBM era caused me to be intensely interested in prediction as a worthwhile, even mandatory, side activity during the early stages of the ICBM program. And there was a real payoff. TRW was well prepared to participate when the space age was born and enjoyed a head start in becoming a leading space contractor. Still, I missed correctly anticipating the date of that birth by three years, an error exposed by the surprising Russian Sputnik in 1957.

Perhaps my most accurate prediction in the military-technology field came about because of the initiative of the then Secretary of Defense, Robert McNamara, and his deputy for R&D, John Foster. Throughout his management of the Defense Department during the Kennedy and Johnson Administrations, McNamara was controversial. He was a dynamic activist and it was never his approach to try to satisfy all possible critics before moving rapidly ahead in accordance with his best judgments. We have not had a Secretary of Defense more dissatisfied, however, with the way daily crises precluded long-range planning.

In 1967, McNamara invited me to his Pentagon office to visit with him and Foster, who had suggested me for a task they had in mind. Bob McNamara felt that high technology, which was essential to the Defense Department, was often not properly harnessed. He argued that we should have foreseen many years earlier the military problems we were encountering in Vietnam and should have figured out well ahead how technology might be applied to help solve them. Claiming: "I don't want some future Secretary of Defense asking who was that stupid, shortsighted Secretary of Defense back in the sixties," McNamara said he wanted to look far ahead and make an early start on promising technology turned up by concerted thinking about the future.

I was asked to chair a task force to look at the future relationship of technology and military power. The group was organized immediately and we drew up two lists. The first was of coming world crises that might endanger U.S. security and in which the U.S. should have available the option to employ military force. To create this list, the task force sought the judgments of the most able political and military experts. The second list was of technologies likely to emerge to provide significant future capabilities. Here we leaned heavily on members of our task force, who had been selected because of their outstanding records in pressing forward the frontiers of science and technology, and we added to their speculations those of prominent scientists and engineers in specialized fields.

After compiling the two lists, we looked for relations between them. Might any potentially troublesome military situation be handled better if we were to have available and to apply properly any of the listed potential advances in technology?

One day some fifteen years later, John Foster and I, out of curiosity, looked back at our predictions. It was evident that the task force had pointed to a number of trends and possibilities years ahead of when their importance actually became evident. This was not because we were magically prescient. We had simply focused our professional experience on a look ahead. Our list included such possibilities as enhancement of nuclear strategic weaponry by improved warhead yields and terminal accuracies; defense against ICBMs; nuclear blackmail by terrorist nations; technical sabotage in the U.S.; warfare in space; lasers and particle beams; electronic warfare, with military information increasingly computer-based, and with the contest to outdo the enemy in coding, intercepting, jamming and counterjamming making a battlefield out of the radio spectrum; reemergence of chemical and bacteriological warfare based on scientific breakthroughs; control of land or ocean battles or of the air over them by smart robotic missiles.

More important, however, than our scorecard in predicting future developments was the conclusion Foster and I reached that McNamara had been right in his feeling that DoD must anticipate potential military needs earlier and move more quickly to generate advances in science and technology that might meet them. The possibilities our task force had cited were not immediately showered with attention as McNamara had hoped. I think they would have been considered further had McNamara not left the DoD to head the World Bank at about the time in 1968 that our exercise was completed.

In the pages ahead, I shall present what might appear to be an overly optimistic picture of the possibilities of enhancing American security with fewer assigned technological resources. If we handle new military technology better, as I believe we can, we will also increase the technological resources available for civilian developments. If we could simultaneously boost technological entrepreneurship, the subject of the next chapter, the United States could regain preeminence in technology.

Let us first consider the most dangerous military field, nuclear warfare. For years the leaders of the two superpowers have regularly proclaimed that strategic nuclear weapons have no purpose other than to deter the other side from using theirs. These statements, if we take them at face value, imply that the weapons will never be employed. The United States and the Soviet Union have each spent trillions of today's dollars—on everything from research on the first atom bomb to the creation and maintenance of manned bombers, ICBMs, and missile-carrying submarines—for offensive capabilities that will not be used. If past practice continues, the superpowers each will spend another trillion by the century's end to ensure continued mutual deterrence.

But neither country can afford this level of expenditure. We have our $200 billion deficit; they, their near-zero economic growth. We need to apply more of our finite resources toward attaining technological competitiveness in world markets; the Soviet Union needs to develop its largely undeveloped resources. We need to maintain our standard of living; they need to raise theirs. These powerful economic forces alone are bound to drive, and are driving, both nations to favor large-scale reductions in their strategic forces.

If the Soviet Union were to possess a single megaton weapon that it could drop on New York City or Washington or Los Angeles, and we had a similar single bomb that we could explode over Moscow or Leningrad or Kiev, each threat should be enough to discourage the other superpower from committing the first cata-strophic act. But we each possess not one or hundreds, or even thousands, but tens of thousands of nuclear bombs and more, on land and in the sea and air. Despite these enormous inventories, I believe that neither the U.S. nor the Soviet Union will launch a nuclear strike against the other, because the leaderships know it would fail. Success would require that the blow virtually eliminate the stricken nation's capability to retaliate and also that the nuclear fallout not seriously injure the aggressor. Neither is possible.

Even if a Soviet attack could destroy ninety-nine percent of our one thousand land-based ICBMs, the Russian blitz planners would know that the ten remaining missiles could knock out ten of their principal cities. Each U.S. Poseidon submarine carries 160 nuclear warheads. Should one submarine survive and target its missiles on Soviet industry, they could destroy half of it and much of the surrounding population. So ruinous are strategic nuclear bombs, and so huge today's retaliatory forces, that a small deviation from perfection in an offensive strike makes the consequent expected retaliation unacceptable.

But no competent weapons engineer, American or Russian, would expect anywhere near perfection for so complex an operation, which obviously cannot be rehearsed and debugged. Think of the timing problem. Launching a single missile from a silo or a submarine at a precisely scheduled moment is a challenge, but achievable. But imagine coordinating a thousand launchings thousands of miles apart at sea and on land so that all the offensive warheads would arrive simultaneously. If U.S.S.R. warheads were to reach U.S. targets over a period of, say, thirty minutes, might we not release all our unhit missiles immediately after the first U.S.S.R. strike? Most of their bombs would land on empty silos, our retaliatory missiles being on their way to blast the Soviet Union. How could they exploit surprise anyway, with our satellites watching their approaching missiles? If they knocked out our "eyes" first, would not that signal an imminent attack and trigger retaliation? How could they possibly risk assuming that we would not respond?

Now, I must acknowledge that not every U.S. citizen, whether sophisticated in weaponry and U.S.–Soviet relations or not, accepts this version of the strategic-nuclear-weapons situation. Some predict that the U.S.S.R., out of evil intent, or having misread U.S. intentions, will one day initiate an all-out nuclear strike regardless of the consequences to them. Others believe that the U.S.S.R. already has, or will attain, such superiority in strategic weapons that in a monumental surprise attack they could obliterate nearly all our retaliatory force. They could then accept our weak retort and control the world.

If, indeed, the Soviet Union should decide on such an act, how would they structure it to give it a maximum chance of success?

We can predict that they would knock out our warning radars and satellites in the first wave. Simultaneously, they would detonate thousands of synchronized megaton-range nuclear bombs in the atmosphere over the United States. This would create an air over-pressure sufficient to eliminate all airplanes then in the sky, including those in our retaliatory system, such as manned bombers and airborne command centers. They might even employ saboteurs equipped with ground-to-air missiles, smuggled in and set up clandestinely, to knock out the airplane-based communication between the White House and our military commanders and our land- and sea-based missiles. High-altitude nuclear blasts would be set off to create electromagnetic pulses (EMPs) to black out our radio communications. Our submarines' home bases, of course, would also be hit.

Some of these first blows would be by nuclear bomb-carrying missiles launched from Soviet submarines near our coasts so that the advance-warning time would be less than five minutes. These activities would be time-coordinated with actions by Soviet agents on land who would destroy ground radio and TV transmitters, telephone relay stations and switching centers, and other vulnerable segments of the national communications systems, both military and civilian.

The Soviet Union's ICBMs assigned to take out our land-based ICBMs would be scheduled to land at precisely the same moment. Their strike planners would, of course, realize that our satellite and ground-based warning systems, before their early destruction, might observe the Soviet ICBMs as they were launched as well as their antisatellite weapons closing in on our satellites. Our military command and our President might thus learn of the imminent strike, and our retaliatory system might be alerted. However, by impairing our communications systems a mere few minutes later, the Russians would hope to keep our ICBM bases from receiving launch orders.

By exploding thousands of large nuclear warheads in every ocean region where our missile-carrying submarines might be, they could chance not knowing the precise whereabouts of our submarines. At the same time, by repeated nuclear blasts, the Soviets would destroy our ability to communicate with the submarines still operative and eliminate our ability to direct their commanders to launch retaliatory missiles.

To prevent the United States from managing a serious retaliatory blow at any later time, the Soviet Union would target the

U.S. infrastructure—communications, transportation and electric-power systems, dams and water-distributing networks, fuel stockpiles and pipelines, centers of military forces and command, and, of course, the White House, Congress, state capitals, and other important centers of government. They would hit our population as hard as they could, from the large cities to the rural areas; this would halt all substantive activities and throw the country into total confusion and panic. They could not afford to risk failure. Even if the aim was not to annihilate our population, a hundred million or more Americans would be vaporized, burned, or crushed to death or blinded or made critically ill by radiation. The firestorms in the cities and the secondary explosions from fuel and chemical storage facilities would add chaos to destruction. Most of the population who remained alive, lacking unadulterated food and water, medical help, shelter, transportation, and leadership, would be helpless.

The all-out nuclear attack I am picturing would be beyond any act in history in the scope of its preparation and implementation. Tens of thousands of specialists and an equal number of computers, communication links, satellites, missiles, and other equipment would have to work together with precision in second-to-second timing. Could such an attack be engineered? Would it succeed?

Any experienced systems engineer knows that for an operation this complex to work halfway perfectly, many complete run-throughs would be necessary. Obviously, no full-scale rehearsal is possible. But to achieve reliability, system parts would have to be tested, debugged, adjusted, and refined, again and again. Communications practice would fill the airwaves, and such exercises would be picked up by American monitoring facilities. We could not be unaware that preparations for an attack might be underway.

In each of the rehearsal exercises, as well as in the actual strike, some things surely would go wrong. The loading, pumping, containing, and controlling of liquid rocket fuels and their accompanying oxidizers are very touchy processes. Holds during countdown are normal. Getting one large missile off its launching pad within an hour of the intended moment is not a sure thing. Releasing a thousand large rockets, some from land, others from the ocean, separated geographically by several thousand miles, each within minutes of each other, is a monumental task. And all without a single full-scale tryout? To engineers with experience in such matters, that is preposterous. A valve might freeze in the pumping systems fueling a missile before takeoff, a pipe or joint might burst, during countdown a transistor or a switch might fail in some monitoring console, a circuit board might develop a short circuit and overheat, a gyroscope here or there might stick, or an essential monitoring instrument might malfunction. Human error might intrude in the setting of target locations, in launch timings, or in the coordination of signals for the vast number of interlocking steps. An order might be misunderstood or another not get through. And finally, one aspect of human behavior would be crucial: partial rehearsals would take place with everyone calm, knowing that an error could be corrected; but the actual attack would require cool, synchronized actions by thousands, with everyone under a doomsday pressure greater than any team of humans has ever experienced.

We can say with absolute certainty that the imagined U.S.S.R.'s knockout attempt would not come off perfectly, and they could not expect that it would. What deviation from perfection would the Soviet Union tolerate and still consider the raid a success? They certainly would have to score over ninety percent against our ICBM force of a thousand Minutemen. (As we indicated, even a ninety-nine-percent elimination of this force would not render the U.S.S.R. completely safe from retaliation.) The one hundred surviving missiles, launched at Soviet resources within a thousand miles of Moscow, even if only half worked perfectly, might easily destroy ninety percent of the infrastructure important for the Soviet Union to operate as a nation. A third of the population might be killed instantly, and an equal number put out of action.

The odds for success of the proposed attack, as calculated by the gambling experts in the Kremlin, would drop rapidly as they contemplated our submarine-based nuclear-missile force. These vessels, a substantial group on station at all times, carry thousands of warheads. Even if the Russians were to destroy half our submarines—and it is a very big ocean and no information we have suggests that the Soviet Union has attained a breakthrough permitting it to find our quiet subs with confidence—a thousand targets in the Soviet Union still could be destroyed in retaliation. (Even a single submarine, as we said, could produce unacceptable destruction.) Perhaps the Soviet Union could make it difficult or impossible for our damaged command structure to get signals through to our submarines to direct them to retaliate. But could the Soviets count on our having made no prior delegation of authority to our submarine commanders to fire missiles in the event of a communication blackout? What if these commanders were to launch their missiles at the Soviet Union, in accordance with prior directives, precisely because their instruments showed massive radioactivity and they had failed to receive the expected regular communications from the mainland within a specified period of time.

Part of our manned bomber forces is always in the air and would be on its way to the Soviet Union when the strike came. Perhaps most of these airplanes would be shot down when they crossed the U.S.S.R. borders, but would the Soviets not expect the planes to launch cruise missiles from a distance? If only a small fraction of these were to land on their targets, the damage would go far beyond what the Soviet Union's strike planners could possibly consider tolerable.

To complete this list of unacceptable risks, consider that even the best-engineered raid intended to be confined to America alone, when of the scale we have described, would produce deadly fallout, a substantial portion of it in the Soviet Union. Even if we do not retaliate at all, might not their own strike do them in later?

The Soviet Union has created bomb shelters to which they might send their officials before commencing their strike. But when these temporarily protected individuals emerge from their holes into the dangerously radioactive environment, they would lack means of communicating with the shreds of the nation that remained. A major portion of their population would be dead and most of the survivors would be unable to function. The Soviet military forces would be fragmented and immobile along radioactive roads.

It is to our mutual credit that so far we have had no opportunity to gather definitive data after an actual full-scale nuclear attack by the Soviet Union and a counterattack by the United States. Even using all of today's knowledge about the effects of nuclear-bomb blasts and the reliability of the engineering apparatus and personnel involved, no one can say with absolute certainty how it would all come out. I cannot prove my prediction that the Soviet Union's strike would fail. It is very probable, however, that their thrust would be at best a mixed success. That would equate to virtual suicide for them, and there is no way their leadership would be blind to that possibility.

I submit that this justifies the prediction that neither superpower will attempt a knockout nuclear blow at the other. I made the case by supposing the Soviet Union to be the first striker. Obviously, I could have written the argument with the United States as the aggressor, and granted many (unimportant) differences in detail, the conclusion would be the same. I think it is useless, even silly, to ask which nation is more likely to take the risk of trying to knock out the other; with neither's leadership insane, neither will do it. It is therefore in the interests of both nations to reduce their offense capability and simultaneously reduce annual expenditures.

This prediction leads to others. But one possibility should be dismissed immediately, even though it was touched on confusedly in the Reykjavik summit meeting of 1986. It is that the United States and the Soviet Union might agree at an early date on the elimination of *all* nuclear ballistic missiles. No President could persuade Congress and the U.S. citizenry to believe, even in the remote eventuality that he himself did, that the Soviet Union would not hide such weapons. Verification systems surely can be designed and installed that would preclude either country's secreting a thousand ICBMs. But the U.S.S.R. could hide ten or twenty, and probably many more, from any conceivably practical verification system. Surprising as it may seem to some Americans, the Soviet Union will expect us also to cheat. In practice, then, the lowest number of nuclear strategic weapons we could realistically both agree to keep in the near future will not be zero; it will be a figure somewhat higher than the number we each estimate the other might successfully conceal.

We might find ourselves comfortable with an agreed-upon verification system capable of keeping the level of large nuclear warheads at thousands rather than the present tens of thousands, with a related decrease in the number of delivery vehicles. A huge quantity of bombs would remain, but disarming down to ten percent of present forces would be a fabulous early accomplishment. Total elimination of nuclear weapons may be the subject of a worldwide, future international agreement, but that will not happen soon.

Meanwhile, even as we engage in these speculations, new technology is broadening the range of possibilities. It is now possible to design a defense system capable of destroying a significant fraction of incoming ICBMs before they arrive at their targets. * Of course, if we wish to shield our total population and resources from a large-scale attack, then a defense system would have to be perfect. If the U.S.S.R. sends five thousand bombs and our defense system eliminates ninety percent of them, that still lets five hundred survive, enough to completely destroy the U.S. several times over. As with offense, perfection unfortunately is impossible. A defense effort that seeks perfection would readily cost the trillion dollars we have already expended on offense.

But suppose the perceived uselessness of strategic nuclear war and the high costs of maintaining our present massive arsenals finally succeed in driving the superpowers to a pact to cut back greatly on offensive forces. As the scale of the offense is reduced—with an effective verification system in place to ensure that the offense adheres near to the set level—the cost of defending effectively

---

* In fact, against a small ICBM strike—one, ten, or twenty bomb-carrying reentry vehicles— a virtually impenetrable defense is technically straightforward and economically feasible. Using ground-based interceptor rockets (no kill weapons in space), a one-site installation could destroy incoming bombs headed for any Eastern U.S. targets; three could defend the entire country. The U.S.S.R. already has such a system in place (as permitted by the ABM treaty) to defend all its territory west of the Urals. We have no such defense. Should a crisis in relations arise tomorrow and the Soviets threaten or carry out a single ICBM blow at Washington, the President would have but two alternatives: give in to Soviet demands or start an all-out, civilization-destroying nuclear war. He could not reply in kind, directing a single ICBM at Moscow, because it would be shot down.

against it goes down rapidly, and it becomes more credible that the defense will be effective. If we take seriously the probability of substantial arms reduction, with real verification means installed, then a balancing of investments in offense and defense begins to be sensible. Also, it then turns out that the past and present vigorous controversy about the Strategic Defense Initiative (SDI) is way off target. The debates about the SDI are centered on the wrong time and a wrong role assumed for it.

Both critics and backers of SDI as a defense against an ICBM nuclear attack have tended to take for granted that the present strategic-weapons inventories of the superpowers are permanent. Opponents of an SDI see it costing a trillion dollars, too complicated to work at all, easily put out of commission by cheap counterstrokes by the U.S.S.R., and certainly nowhere near being an impervious shield. The system, its detractors point out, would have to find, follow, and destroy thousands of warheads, after it has first distinguished them from tens of thousands of decoys—all automatically, in minutes, when the system itself is under nuclear attack.

What if the Soviet Union and the United States actually do decide that they can still fear, scare, distrust, and deter each other with far fewer strategic nuclear offensive weapons? Assume, moreover, that each persisted in installing a system to verify adherence to that nuclear-arms reduction pact. What if, for example, only a tenth of the present U.S. and Soviet strategic missiles remain. No experienced weapons-system engineer would deny then that the balance between offense and defense is radically changed. Although a defense system would still be expensive, it would be possible to track and interfere with a greatly reduced offensive. I am involved in advisory activities to the DoD and several industrial corporations on strategic offense and defense matters, so I am up to date on detailed progress on our SDI program. I believe that today's technology does not permit us to design an effective defense system against an all-out Soviet attack using their present inventory of weapons, a force not yet affected by arms-reduction pacts. The system we could put in place might be able to destroy half their incoming missiles, but the other half would destroy our country, even as our retaliation would ruin theirs. Further research could improve that performance. However, without waiting for new, spectacular developments, if their offense is cut down to one-tenth by agreement, then I am confident that we can create a defense that could shoot down ninety percent of their incoming missiles.* Then the number landing on U.S. targets would be one-tenth of one-tenth, or one-hundredth, of their present force. (The U.S.S.R. leadership would then have to be a hundred times more insane to launch the strike.)

One way to judge the effectiveness of a defense system is to compare its cost with that of keeping the offense as effective as it was before the defense was implemented. If, for instance, a defense system is installed that can shoot down fifty percent of incoming missiles, then the attacker can presumably simply double the number of offensive missiles. If that doubling can be had at a small fraction of the cost of installing the defense system, then that defense system would not make economic sense. The number of offensive missiles getting through would be the same as before both sides took their steps.

This reasoning applies, however, only when no hard limits have been placed on the size of the offensive system. If there is an agreed-upon and verified ceiling on the offense, these economic trade-off criteria become irrelevant. By agreement, the offense cannot be increased to counter the defense, regardless of what fraction a defense system shoots down at whatever cost. Moreover, the cost of the defense does not have to be measured against the cost of the offense. The defense might be decided upon as worthwhile insurance as long as it is affordable, even if that cost should be greater than the cost of maintaining the allowed, limited offense. This means that we can expect no agreements about offense without an

---

* No ICBM attack could be successful against a well-designed defense system without including decoys in the attack. The decoys, to be effective, must be numerous and not too light; the reentry vehicles would have to be lightened by at least half the bomb weight to allow for the weight of the decoys. Accordingly, the mere existence on one side of a significant defense system, since it would force the other side to accommodate decoys in its offense system, would reduce the potency of an offense system strictly limited by pact to around one half, the equivalent of shooting down half the incoming missiles.

accompanying agreement about defense. Neither superpower could be expected to agree to drastically cut and limit offensive forces if only the other has an effective defense. The U.S.S.R. has proposed that neither of us install a defense system (although they already have a partial installation). That is one possible approach. I believe there are other and better approaches.

In fact, what emerges as astoundingly attractive is something President Reagan happened to mention in the second debate with Walter Mondale in 1984 (Mondale taking it as evidence that the President had lost his marbles); namely, that the United States might share missile-defense technology with the U.S.S.R. If we and they should decide to reduce nuclear inventories, our cooperating to implement an effective (although not perfect) shield against offensive ICBMs is no longer absurd. It is consistent with a common interest in arms control that both nations should install defense systems. With greatly reduced and fixed offenses, effective defenses would dispel the idea that either superpower might seriously plan a knockout nuclear strike. Both countries would have a high level of security, against an accidental launch as well, or an isolated attack by a terrorist nation, or a threat by either superpower to deliver a limited strike against the other.

Of course, we and the Soviet Union will agree to limit strategic weapons to low levels only if we can and do implement valid verification systems; the cheating issue will remain, however, and influence the extent of practical arms reduction. If a defense system is put in place by both sides, cheating will matter less because the defense system will act as a counter to attacking missiles, including those above the agreed-upon ceilings. The more likely it is that a surprise strike, even one enhanced somewhat by cheating, can be defended against successfully, the less attractive it will be to launch such a first strike. It will be less attractive to engage in cheating to help make an attack successful if launching an attack is unattractive in the first place. The less important cheating is, the more comfortable each nation can be about reducing and limiting its offense to ever lower levels. The more the offense is reduced, the more effective the defense will be. We find ourselves with a happy cycle of reinforcing moves that could gradually make ICBMs "impotent and obsolete"—albeit not in the way it was implied when the SDI program was first announced.

If we accept as realistic, rather than optimistic, the possibility that strategic nuclear arms will be reduced very greatly (say, by ninety percent) during the next decade, then looking ahead even further is irresistible. Might a true zero option on nuclear arms be expected in the future? Once we learn to live comfortably with verified, substantially lower strategic-nuclear-weapons inventories, and install defense systems for added security, then why not go all the way and outlaw nuclear offensive arms entirely?

A natural first reaction to predicting future total elimination of nuclear weapons is to view it as profoundly idealistic, because verification can never be perfect and, therefore, cheating can never be totally eliminated. But quite the opposite may come to be true. When each superpower is permitted a small quantity of ICBMs, adherence to the agreed limitation is more difficult to verify than when the number of ICBMs is committed to be absolutely zero. Consider: if we should spot a single Soviet Union ICBM, we will not know whether it is one of the permissible number or not. On the other hand, if ICBMs are totally outlawed, and we see one, then that they are cheating is obvious and certain.

Similar considerations apply to the bombs themselves and to the production, moving, and storing of fissile bomb material. What this adds up to is that in most important respects it is easier to verify and minimize cheating under a zero option. With the zero option, defense systems become more practical than ever. The zero option, with extensive verification and defense systems in place, essentially reduces to zero the probability that either superpower will attempt a nuclear strike.

We should even predict that by the year 2000 it might be agreed by all nations that any planned launches into space of communications satellites, research craft, or any other kind of vehicle must be announced in advance. The announcement would be followed by an international inspection team moving in to confirm that no bombs are on board and only then permit the launching. Anything unannounced and unapproved seen rising through the atmosphere would be assumed to be a dangerous weapon and would be shot down by the defense system with no danger to people on earth.

There is another danger, however—the threat of blackmail and suicide attacks by terrorist groups that may come into possession of nuclear bombs. Several hundred nuclear reactors generating electrical energy are operating today in some thirty countries. Incidental to the process is the creation of plutonium within the reactor's fuel rods; that plutonium can be extracted from the spent rods by available technology. Enough plutonium is now being automatically created by existing electric-power nuclear reactors to produce high-yield bombs at the rate of one per day. Those without nuclear bombs can buy the know-how, materials, and equipment needed to produce them, if not openly, then through clandestine means. A possible horrible threat of nuclear terrorism can be eliminated, I would argue, only by highly cooperative and aggressive leadership by the two superpowers. The United States and the Soviet Union, working together, could carry enough weight to influence any government's plans for nuclear weapons, including, in time, China, France, India, South Africa, Pakistan, Israel, Egypt, and even Libya. The thought of living with a nuclear threat from terrorist/dictator-controlled entities should be enough in itself to drive the two top nations to joint nuclear-arms reduction and control.

The foregoing predictions depend critically on having adequate arms-reduction verification systems in place. Although we know none can be perfect and some cheating has to be assumed, such systems can be developed. Because the evidence has been so weak for so long that we are moving toward large-scale nuclear arms reductions, little effort has been expended to develop verification techniques. They will begin to surface, I feel sure, in the very near future.

One example, an important partial answer to the verification challenge, suggests itself if we ask how the nuclear-weapon nations will handle the disposal problem if they substantially reduce the stockpiles of nuclear warheads. What should be done with the plutonium, or U-235, taken from inside the bombs as they become surplus? Do we simply allow this dangerous fissile matter to pile up? Do we bury it in the sea or launch it into outer space? I believe the answer is to convert this material into reactor fuel, which can be done by economical, state-of-the-art techniques. The fuel produced would be used to generate peacetime electric power. A tremendous amount of electrical energy was consumed in creating that bomb-grade material; we can get most of this energy back. Calculations based upon published estimates of warhead stockpiles indicate that enough fuel is contained in them to generate electric power for years at all the world's nuclear power plants.

Despite official secrecy, both the Soviets and the Americans know that each is capable of estimating with great accuracy the bomb stockpile of the other. The existing inventories of fissile material of the two nations are quite comparable. Suppose that both were to agree to bring a given weight of these elements—say, ninety percent of the estimated totals—to a jointly operated facility where it would be inspected and fed into a reprocessing operation that would turn it into electric-power reactor fuel. (Each nation could deliver one percent per day for ninety days, halting delivery if the other failed to comply.) With elegant simplicity, then, both nuclear-arms reduction and verification would be inherent and immediate.

Each superpower would assume, of course, that the other might hold back and hide some bomb matter or pursue a secret program of replacement. But with most of the present inventory given up to the conversion facility, an exceedingly high rate of production of fissile matter would be needed to replace it quickly. If one side were to cheat in so big a way, the scale of its operations would be disclosed readily. A slow, clandestine, determined effort to replace fissile materials doubtless could be carried out by the Soviet Union without our detecting it. This illustrates that there can be no final, perfect answer to the danger of nuclear war. We cannot by arms-reduction agreements halt all activities and advances in military technology, and it is unrealistic to expect negotiations to eliminate forever novel weapons based on future discoveries in nuclear physics. The potential for developing the unpredictable will exist, and so will the continuing need for enlarging and revising the terms of arms control. What we have described, however, would vastly lower the dangers and costs of nuclear-weapons systems.

If we accept the prediction that large-scale nuclear-arms reduction will occur in the 1990s, how should that influence our plans for other aspects of national security?

Take, for instance, the NATO pact, which unites the efforts of those Western European and North American countries that share an interest in the defense of Western Europe. This pact has brought a contingent of some 350,000 Americans to Europe. The presence of these troops has been both symbol and guarantor of American commitment to European defense. The NATO military forces have nuclear arms, but the steady buildup of Soviet armed forces in Europe suggests that their invading armies would have more soldiers, tanks, airplanes, and conventional arms than the NATO forces opposing them. (A recent DoD report to the Senate stated that the Warsaw Pact armies possess roughly a three-to-one advantage in overall firepower across the entire front.) Even relying only on conventional military defense, NATO forces might inflict substantial casualties against attacking Warsaw Pact armies, and this possibility has been considered a significant deterrent to a Soviet attack. The heart of deterrence, however, has been NATO's announcement that it will employ nuclear weapons, if necessary, to stop a Soviet invasion.

Unfortunately, the foregoing is a strategy that has been questionable ever since the U.S.S.R. developed a nuclear capability comparable with ours. The realistic supposition is that nuclear weapons will not be used first by NATO forces, because that would bring quick nuclear retaliation by the Soviet Union, turning Europe into a nuclear battleground and destroying it, population and all. A new approach is needed for the defense of Western Europe, one that assumes that nuclear weapons will not be employed by either side and that the Soviet Union (its first-strike nuclear option deterred by our inevitable retaliation) will use only conventional forces should it decide to invade Western Europe.

What should NATO's approach be?

A sensible answer must first take into account the relative strengths of the opposing sides. The NATO nations of Western Europe, even assuming no American or Canadian participation, are well able to mount a conventional force to match the Soviet Union's. Western Europe exceeds the U.S.S.R. and other Warsaw Pact countries in overall scientific, engineering, and industrial strength, having more than half again their combined GNP. European NATO nations have a population (366 million in 1980) that makes it statistically possible to field just as many soldiers as the Warsaw group (375 million in 1980), especially if one assumes a reasonable assignment of Soviet forces to guard the Chinese borders. The Soviet Union probably has more natural resources than Western Europe, Canada, and the U.S. combined, but they are mainly undeveloped. In the next few decades, Western Europe alone, if it wished, could arrange to place more resources from the world as a whole behind its military effort than could the U.S.S.R.

The NATO nations find it difficult to combine their military forces into a highly coordinated defense body. But the Warsaw Pact nations are not exactly devoted to each other. Of the fifty-eight Warsaw Pact divisions, fifteen are Polish. In an invasion of Western Europe, they surely would display limited enthusiasm to die for the Russians. Ten divisions are Czech, and experts consider them to be the least likely of Warsaw Pact forces to be loyal and effective.

One might reasonably conclude that Western Europe, if it chose, could effect at the least a standoff to any conventional attack. If this is a valid assumption, NATO would constitute a strong deterrent to the Soviets because a stalemate, a drawn-out war decided eventually by each side's production rates, would be tantamount to their losing. But the present situation is different. If the plan for NATO to employ nuclear weapons is credible as the real counter to a Russian invasion, 350,000 American troops in Europe are too many. On the other hand, if nuclear weapons are ruled out and we assume NATO must fight the huge Soviet armies with conventional forces, then these American units plus the present standing Western Europe armies add up to too few. But Western European nations are not interested in greatly expanding their conventional forces. To expect NATO to create a conventional military force as large as the available Soviet forces and sustain the high maintenance costs is unrealistic.

A more innovative approach is possible. If NATO strategy is altered to assume that no nuclear bombs will be employed, then the right role for the United States to assure Western Europe's security is not to provide larger American armies. It is, instead, to develop appropriate new weapons systems. Putting our advanced technology to work would give the Allies an edge in a nonnuclear war. In computers and communications systems, microminiaturized semiconductor chips, and robotry, we and the European NATO countries are far ahead of the U.S.S.R., and there is every reason to believe we will outdistance them further in the future, especially with Japan on our side. New information technology makes possible radically superior command, control, intelligence, and reconnaissance, and hence highly focused military action. With better battle information, our commanders at every level would be better able to direct our military efforts. Superior electronic tools would enable us to block Russian communications and prevent them from hampering ours. Coding, jamming, intercepting signals, processing incoming data in real time, making quick analyses of alternatives—all typical capabilities of electronic brainpower—would mean that NATO forces would be more effectively positioned and employed, while the Warsaw group's armies would be befuddled. Our forces would have the effectiveness of much larger ones.

The NATO nations' much greater technical capability also makes possible the design and manufacture of intelligent robotic weaponry of great power. Soviet tanks now outnumber NATO's by a factor of more than four. However, defenders who do not intend to become attackers have less need for tanks. Tanks to resist tanks as a concept of warfare are rapidly becoming obsolete. Smart, lightweight, mass-produced, accurate guided missiles that hunt and close in on large fixed or moving metal targets on the ground or ocean or in the skies are the reason for the obsolescence. Missiles launched from hand-held missile launchers or from aircraft or helicopters, or artillery using laser, microwave, or infrared beams for guidance, can disrupt a tank assault. Advanced homing electronics can enable an artillery piece to launch a smart bomb that can hit a moving tank at ten miles. Vast numbers of ground-to-air, ground-to-ground, and air-to-ground projectiles can be launched from a distance in safety, because technology permits us to "fire and forget" these target-seeking warheads.

One antitank missile system of this kind has been described in public literature. When massed enemy armor is detected, a large carrier missile is launched. Over the target area, it spews out a load of small missiles, each capable of sensing and homing in on a tank. One such carrier missile could take out an entire company of tanks twenty-five miles away. The Soviet Union could perhaps equally perform the R&D needed for such weaponry but would be hard-pressed to produce the substantial numbers required.

The use of the air could be denied to the U.S.S.R. by great numbers of surface-to-air guided missiles we could readily produce, while the allied terrain could be made impenetrable by "smart" electronic mines, set off should the enemy enter an area but rendered harmless to our forces by broadcast of coded instruction signals.

Another technological wonder illustrates that, with sufficient innovation, mass-produced weapons can be cheap, simple, and effective. Extremely thin fiber-optics cable, less than a human hair in diameter, can carry TV signals. A missile with a miniature TV camera in its nose can be launched to fly up and over nearby terrain (trees, hills, etc.) and look down for ground targets out of sight of the launch point. A ten-mile-long fiber-optics cable unwinding from a small reel as the missile flies connects the missile and the gunner. On his TV screen, the gunner sees what the missile sees. Using a steering joystick, he selects a target and sends signals back up the cable to direct the missile to strike that target.

These sophisticated weapons require the engineering and high-volume production of precision electronic and mechanical equipment. Such technology is exactly where America, Western Europe, and Japan are very strong and where the Soviet Union is particularly weak. The Soviet Union's backwardness in mass production of this kind of apparatus would put them at a distinct disadvantage if they contemplated an invasion.

What we are describing here is not to be confused with merely adding complexity to conventional weapons systems. In the past it has happened too often, almost regularly, that in their zeal to attain every conceivable improvement in performance, the U.S. military services have loaded many speculative features onto basic weapons, making them so expensive and unreliable as to defeat their purposes. On the contrary, like computers, which are getting smaller, cheaper, smarter, and more reliable each year, * the electronically controlled weapons I am referring to will be more economical and dependable when mass-produced. The sophisticated functions of which they are capable are inherent in the miniaturized semiconductor circuitry on chips, the product of major breakthroughs in the techniques of electronic fabrication. We are over a decade ahead of the U.S.S.R. in microchips. A robotic smart missile has no more complexity, and no greater number of precision mechanical parts or microcircuits, than a typical American personal computer plus the power-steering system of an automobile and a small rocket motor. We can produce such weapons by the millions. The Russians can't come close.

Military experts point out that there are only four routes to invade Western Europe from the east. None is easily traversed because of canals, bogs, concentrated urban sprawl, and even some narrow, winding mountain passages. Maneuvering the Warsaw Pact forces is more difficult than mounting a defense, because attacking armies must exploit surprise while concentrating their forces to form spearheads. They would need to seize opportunities of the moment, shift forces and tactics quickly; yet, with their command communications hampered by superior NATO electronic warfare capabil-

---

* A present microcomputer, compared with early electronic digital computers of the 1950s, costs less to produce by a thousand times, is a thousand times faster, uses one-thousandth of the space and power, and is a thousand times more reliable (it will run a thousand times longer without a failure).

ity, the Russians' numerically larger but less maneuverable forces would make counterattacks by NATO's automatic, smart weapons all the more effective.

The prediction we arrive at is that well-chosen, advanced, non-nuclear, low-priced, mass-produced military technology is the answer to deterring a Soviet nonnuclear invasion of Western Europe. This approach will be far superior to trying (and, doubtless, failing) to match them in conventional tanks and airplanes and men in uniform.

This prediction carries with it certain important corollary predictions and suggests actions to be taken. What would be the U.S.S.R.'s reaction to our announcing a crash R&D program to uplift NATO's defenses through advanced technology and mass production? I predict that they would be alarmed and would protest precisely as they did when President Reagan made his SDI announcement in March 1983. They knew before that date that we had been carrying on an R&D program on defense against an ICBM attack; indeed, they had been doing the same on a larger scale. But they issued no complaints until the President's SDI announcement. That apparently signaled to them that we were embarking on a new, all-out, large-scale advance in technology that threatened to upset the status quo. After several decades of all-out effort, they had created a mammoth ICBM capability that more than matched ours. If we chose to implement a major defense against those ICBMs, they would have to respond by doing the same. They would need to alter their offense substantially to counter our defense. They would quickly have to reduce the effectiveness of their ICBM bomb payloads so as to carry sophisticated decoys. They would have to build new booster rockets to achieve a much more rapid acceleration (by a quick burn entirely in the atmosphere) so our sensing devices in space could not pick up the rocket's exhaust so easily. They would have to add to their offense a capability to destroy our defense system.

They knew they could not equal us in an R&D race to develop sophisticated defenses against ICBMs because it was a contest in two fields in which they are decidedly inferior: computer microchips and mass production of precision electromechanical hardware. So they sought to stop the American SDI program. At first, their stand was that no further arms-reduction discussions could take place unless we abandoned the SDI project. When we stood firm, they decided to meet with us after all, but said that no agreements would result unless we limited our SDI program to "research inside a laboratory." Then they decided to take the initiative to propose nuclear-offense reduction.

If the President were to announce a superproject to raise NATO defense technology to new heights, the further prediction can be made that the Soviet Union would soon press for a pact to lower the size of offensive military forces on both sides of the border between the two Germanys. As with strategic weaponry, the more offensive forces in Europe are reduced, the more credible and cheaper defense becomes. The more effective the defense, the lower the threat of an attack.

Reducing the threat of war will make for increased civilian trade between the East and the West. This is very important, because the new defense technology—dominated by computers, microchips, and robotry—is very close to what is needed for substantial advances in productivity in the manufacture of consumer goods and industrial products and the creation of new products. The economic growth and higher living standards this new technology provides will very likely decrease international tension and lower expenditures for offensive military capabilities.

This suggests that we should predict for Western Europe, as we did in the case of strategic nuclear weaponry, an era in which military forces will emphasize defense rather than offense. Local warfare will persist in the underdeveloped areas of Asia, Africa, and South America, but mainly we should expect increasing international trade, including trade of technological products and technological information between East and West.

Without a solution to the nuclear-weapons threat, the future looks bleak indeed. But a way out is surfacing and I suggest that we and the U.S.S.R. are going to travel it. If this should come to pass, we will have taken a colossal step in correcting the critical mismatch of our civilization between technological advance and social maturation. The United States could concentrate its energies on regaining international preeminence in technology.

EIGHT

Technology and Prosperity

How can the United States prosper as future success becomes ever more dependent on technological superiority? How can we win in a world in which so many nations are competing on a highly sophisticated level? Assuming that we preserve our national security, how do we also preserve, and preferably enhance, our standard of living? If this last question were asked about individuals, we would relate living standard to income and say that the first cannot rise unless the second does. For a nation as a whole to improve its standard of living, the gross national product per capita must increase.

There are innumerable ways for an individual to make money. A sure scheme is to arrange to have oil discovered on one's land. Another strategy, satisfactory to those who have been blessed with the privilege, is to inherit great wealth and then, without insisting on a gift of uncommon business acumen, to invest it only reasonably wisely and wait. Buying and selling real estate or shares in corporations is an excellent plan too, if the buying is done when the market prices are low and the selling after they have risen dramatically. Of course, these roads to riches are paved with luck more than with talent.

Most other paths to prosperity require more than favorable accidents of birth or timing. Accumulating money is very likely to be done by surgeons who protect the health of wealthy patients, or attorneys who litigate for wealthy clients, or entertainers who mesmerize mass audiences, but skill is a must for such folk. Money can be amassed also by storing or dispensing other people's funds and taking a cut out of them regularly, as able bankers and money managers do.

None of these formulas for acquiring capital is properly categorized, however, as creating wealth. Litigants who win court cases find such activity profitable, but the losers, to almost precisely an equal extent, do not. Surgeons' cuttings and stitchings may relieve stresses in their patients, but their fees achieve the opposite. We have so far only listed ways in which money is moved about.

As a nation, we can't raise our average personal income by shifting a constant total of assets around among our own people. Nor can we count on discovering huge deposits of gold, oil, or diamonds on our land. The sure way for the United States to raise its living standards is to excel in technology. Technology can be applied to increase the resources of a nation, to generate wealth that would not exist if the technology were not employed. Technology is a tool that can multiply the effectiveness and hence the worth of time and work. Technology makes it possible to manufacture for our needs with less effort and less dissipation of valuable natural resources. (A pound of glass fiber-optics cable, made mainly of sand, can carry as much information as a ton of copper. A ten-dollar computer chip, its raw materials constituting about one percent of its cost, can make calculations in a few minutes that would require thousands of hours of effort by a human calculator.) Technology breakthroughs can lead to substitutes for resources in diminishing supply and to novel products so socially and economically advantageous as to merit the investment required to develop them. Profitable returns on investment can result from investing capital in technology because doing so can produce wealth.

I am not claiming that every advance in technology is certain to enhance society's resources. The nuclear bomb may one day eliminate all of us and all of our resources, all of a sudden. Nor do material assets automatically bring happiness. We can imagine, if we strain enough, a society that has zero technological development but where the people are kind to one another, never make war, and are blessed with excellent health, perfect weather, bounteous natural vegetation, and good streams for fishing. The members of that imaginary society can walk barefoot on the beach whenever they choose and be content with their lives.

Contrast this nontechnological society with the real world of industrialized nations. From year to year, we see a steady increase in facilities for production, transportation and communication, tools to do the work of human beings, and all the other elements that make up their physical inventories. Subjectivity and vagueness about what criteria we should apply may make it difficult to put a value on all aspects of our lives, but economic evaluations (pricings) measure well the assets that satisfy our material needs. The total economic value of those assets grows steadily.

Ensuring America's future success requires the adequate handling of many complex matters, but not everything about a successful approach is complex. Some things are straightforward. Thus, it is certain that we need copious advances in technology, made by Americans here in the United States, to increase our national output. Since America can hardly prosper by selling cheap labor to the other countries, either we excel in technology or our living standards will fall.

Is there a natural strategy for the United States to achieve superiority in technology? I am certain there is. It is to foster technological entrepreneurship. We produce business entrepreneurs at an enormous rate, but only a small fraction are involved with technology. Yet technological entrepreneuring has been the main force behind our industrial development from the beginning. It is not today at its full power. We can and should accelerate it.

In Japan, it is rare for an entrepreneurial team to set out to obtain venture capital backing to give birth to a fresh technological corporation. Americans, on the other hand, often leave established organizations to form new companies. Anyone in Japan who quits to start a new company is considered an eccentric, not a hero. The American culture, in contrast, admires such a choice. In Japan, employers think of themselves as committed for life to an employee they hire, and when young people take their first jobs in industry, they assume that they have made lifetime contracts. Extraordinary events must occur—employees must do something truly scurrilous (mere incompetence will not do it)—before a Japanese company would dismiss them.

Our broad venture-capital structure has many dimensions. The system gathers investment funds from banks, trusts, pension funds, insurance-company reserves, foundation and university endowments, wealthy individuals, investment pools for middle-class folks, public stock issues, medium- and large-size companies, and numerous individuals and organizations looking for tax deferrals or high-growth investment opportunities. A public market exists for trading shares in new, small companies. Entrepreneurs and investors in their ventures can go to that market to realize cash for their holdings or to make further investments in a broad array of young companies. Japan has nothing comparable, and Western Europe's venture-capital activities are very modest.

Effective cooperation is common in Japan among government, banks, industry, and workers' unions; its citizens save their earnings, not sharing our need for instant consumption; employees are loyal to their companies for life—these patterns work to preserve the health of Japan's established large corporations. When government and the private sector in Japan decide to seek world superiority in a new technological field, the process is one of defining roles and assigning resources to the existing corporate giants. "Japan, Inc.," a term used by Americans to sum up the Japanese nation's highly integrated planning and their deep feeling for national interest, does not include the concept of entrepreneurship. The concept does not touch it at all. The occasional Japanese entrepreneur succeeds, not because of encouragement from the system, but despite opposition. Mr. Soichiro Honda, for example, built his automobile company even as the government-business establishment, so he told me several times, put severe pressure on him not to; he was virtually directed to stick to motorcycles.

Our answer to aggressive competition from Japan or other nations should be to foster entrepreneurship. But what about our existing large technological corporations, which employ the majority of the engineers in America and produce most of the goods that the nation needs and that can be sold overseas. What is their role in our economic growth and in competitive international trade? Simply put, they will continue to be the core of our technological strength, and we must do nothing to impair their health. Those companies are the result of the entrepreneurship that launched them decades ago. Today's successful new companies will become mature, major industrial units in the future. But even if present large companies contribute as much as we can possibly expect them to, that will not guarantee U.S. technological superiority, because certain inherent characteristics of big companies that account for their success are also at the root of their many shortcomings, causing them to leave gaps, miss breakthroughs, and move too slowly. A steady, high rate of new technological entities is mandatory if the United States is to enjoy a competitive edge.

Having been intimately involved with large corporations as employee, officer, director, and consultant, I can say confidently that a billion-dollar corporation could not have succeeded without having done many things right. Its exceptional past performance and the thousands of jobs it created probably resulted from the novelty and cost-effectiveness of its products and its skill in marketing. No matter what gave rise to its growth, however, markets change. If the company does not improve its products, some competitor will offer better ones and take away its business. Moreover, any product or service is only one element in some system that uses it. New systems will arise that may no longer call for the company's components. Jet planes do not need propellers and modern radio receivers do not use vacuum tubes. The buggy-whip maker, to note the obvious, lost his market when the automobile replaced the buggy—and the horse.

Technology moves so fast that successful high-technology companies, although steadily improving their existing products, have to replace virtually all of them every ten years. They must do so to stay in business. New companies produce new products to start a business. The environment in the United States needs to be such as to encourage the contributions of both kinds of companies.

Large high-technology companies, like IBM, Exxon, and G.E., generally have an advantage over small ones in the effectiveness of each dollar spent on R&D. The broader its product line, the more will a company be able to make efficient use of its research. Only big corporations can handle big projects and operate worldwide. A new, small company cannot design and build airplanes, spacecraft, petroleum refineries, factories for mass producing automobiles, or operate a worldwide inventory distribution system or a national information network. If a large company has a good product for the domestic U.S. market, the chances are that it can manufacture or market to its advantage in other countries. A small company finds it difficult to do this. It takes money, people, and equipment stationed all around the world to make effective use of international opportunities.

America's large technological companies have the capacity to carry on enough R&D to improve and replace their products, diversify to add scope and to maximize return on investment, handle giant projects, and employ enough experts to be able to manufacture and market globally. But these strengths are not enough to guarantee our nation first place in international technology, because they are not unique to America. They are matched by the mammoth technological companies of Japan and Western Europe that are consistently aided by their governments, while the U.S. government helps only occasionally and sometimes hinders. Furthermore, for every strength of a large company, there is a weakness. I have had a number of opportunities over the years to experience directly the significant difference between managing small start-up companies and large established ones. The negatives of big organizations, I am convinced, are natural; hence, extremely difficult to counter even with the most imaginative and persistent efforts. The shortcomings are inherent in their size and maturity, the American culture, and basic human nature, and they are severe.

The worst weakness of a large corporation is its lack of true entrepreneurship. When the original entrepreneurs first launch a company, its entire net worth is at risk. The rule for managing a big established company, on the other hand, is never to put the whole net worth of the company at risk. After years of growth, the large company has many thousands of employees. Most of these want stability, not risk. Their stockholders, now typically pension- and trust-fund managers rather than venture capitalists, want steadily growing earnings, as do the banks that hold the loans. As company leaders become older, they become more conservative. For their successors they choose individuals who are like what they have become, not what they were when they started the company. A big, venerable business has enjoyed much past success, and that record can make all concerned reluctant to tinker with its winning formula, which they confuse with rigid rules. The management, without realizing it, defines wisdom as knowing well how things have been done in the past.

The financial performance of every large company is widely reported and thoroughly studied by professional analysts. To have to announce a drop in earnings, or even a lack of growth, is an embarrassment to management. A net loss instead of a good profit for a single quarter causes doubts to be immediately expressed in the business-news media and alarms employees, customers, and stockholders. An overall loss for a full year, or a deferral of a dividend, is considered a harbinger of near-term catastrophe. Top management is in jeopardy.

The priority accorded to constancy of good financial results forces a strategy of diversification to minimize the impact of negative results in one division or one major product. The size and diversity of operations means that corporate management, while able to judge the financial figures of each operating division, cannot follow with any depth the important trends, sudden changes, and problems as they arise. New opportunities stemming from technology break-throughs, manufacturing advances, and market expansions in specialized sectors are then easily missed. As the company gets huge, the upper management becomes akin to a remote financial investment manager of the shareholders' assets and a guardian of the employees' jobs. The giant company is more a social unit of the nation than symbol and substance of entrepreneurship.

When a large technological company accumulates excess cash, does it consider gambling with it to develop radically new products or to sharply reduce manufacturing costs through technology breakthroughs? Only if a project clearly will produce a relatively small negative increment to net earnings that will remain solidly positive, or if the project's costs will create no threat to the goal of a steady increase in earnings, will the management take any risk. When these results are unlikely, management will usually try to buy another company with its excess cash.

When RCA was young, still under its highly enterprising leader, David Sarnoff, it pioneered in radio broadcasting and was the world's prime developer of television. Following the Sarnoff regime, RCA suffered from less than sufficient top management, imagination, and competence. The company flunked out on seeing and responding to major trends in electronic technology and world markets in the 1960s and 1970s. Worse, while it was conspicuously losing leadership in its basic fields to new entities in the U.S. and to foreign companies, management gave priority to diversifying so as to become a random conglomerate. It acquired companies in totally different businesses (auto renting, industrial-lease financing, book publishing, greeting cards, even carpeting). It was only recently that RCA again experienced strong leadership and recovered from the threat of collapse. But the company was not strong enough to avoid being taken over by General Electric. The recovered RCA also could not come up with a research-and-development program it thought worthy of major investment. Before it was acquired by G.E., a company with an even larger cash surplus, the financially recovered RCA was busy looking for other companies to buy with its cash. Supersized G.E. apparently could not generate an imaginative, new technology-development program, and so it used its excess billions to purchase RCA.

Westinghouse, in the second half of its first hundred years, the 1930–80s, lost much of the prized position it had developed in its first fifty years. It courted financial disaster when it guaranteed deliveries of uranium at too low a price to the utilities that were its nuclear-reactor customers. For many years, its poor financial condition precluded its carrying out adequate R&D. When it recovered financially, it bought a principal cable-television company, only to change its mind a few years later and sell off the operation. Either the buying or the selling was a mistake. It repeated with robotry, buying a large company in that field, then disposing of it. Will Westinghouse use the cash from these divestments to develop major new technology? Not likely. It will probably buy still another existing company.

Rockwell International, a leading military aerospace contractor and automotive-parts manufacturer, decided to diversify into household appliances and television sets by acquiring Admiral Corporation. After some years of losses, Rockwell dropped these consumer products. Similarly, Ford bought Philco, then a leading consumer electronics company strong in TV receivers, lost money, and abandoned that business line.

When Xerox was a small company, its leadership was entrepreneurial and farsighted in its purchase of the basic patent in copiers. Exploiting a substantial period of monopoly in copiers through excellent management, Xerox became a multibillion-dollar corporation. Xerox later entered the computer business, without the competence to assess that field. It purchased a computer company not yet firmly endowed with proprietary technology or market position. The unwise, huge overpayment for that acquisition was followed by high operating losses, after which Xerox withdrew from the computer field. Xerox now is buying stock brokerage and investment banking firms.

It almost seems that the larger the company, the greater its mistakes when it seeks to diversify. Consider the record of America's off-and-on largest corporation, Exxon. The past few decades have seen much progress in earth science, satellite probing of the earth, and computer-enhanced seismic-data processing. Radical discoveries in basic chemical catalysis also have been made. These advances augur well for early corollary advances in petroleum discovery, extraction, and processing. Yet this largest of petrochemical giants chose to produce word processors and other electronic office equipment. Some years later, after taking losses that would have broken half of the one hundred largest companies in America, Exxon gave up. It also bought a quite ordinary electric-motor manufacturer under the mistaken impression that the company had a sensational electric-motor invention. It soon became evident that Exxon had paid far too much for the company, the fundamental ideas behind the invention being neither very new nor very valuable.

Examples abound of diversification errors through acquisitions by large technological companies. Fluor Corporation, with surplus cash generated by the temporary peak in building facilities for its Persian Gulf customers, bought a large mining company and lost heavily in its operations (thereby eliminating its excess-cash problem). Atlantic–Richfield, a leading petrochemical company, went into metals and minerals, later divesting itself of those operations. General Electric did something similar when it purchased Utah International, a mining company unrelated to G.E.'s area of management expertise.

There are many more startling examples of large technological corporations engaged in major diversifications into businesses well beyond their proven expertise, most often with poor or disastrous results. Almost all such activity has been accompanied by the most modest of contributions by those companies in their original fields of technological strength. The great breakthroughs were accomplished by newer and smaller companies.*

It is more difficult to spur and exploit high creativity in an old and large organization than in a new, small one. A long-established

---

* That the largest companies do not originate all technology advance is no recent development. The key ideas in the following fields were conceived by individuals not employed by large companies: atomic energy, computers, cellophane, color photography, the cyclotron, DDT, FM radio, foam rubber, inertial guidance, insulin, lasers, the Polaroid camera, radar, rockets, streptomycin, vacuum tubes, xerography, and the zipper.

unit almost certainly will have developed a substantial bureaucracy, and bureaucracy is the natural enemy of creativity. Sometimes a big company, seeking to relieve its best innovators of the burdens of the company's own red tape, will set up a team outside its regular bureaucracy and allow it to innovate in isolation. But this does not make the activity entrepreneurial. It also does not always make it successful. An entrepreneur is one who takes full responsibility for an effort, standing to gain greatly if it succeeds or be penalized severely, financially and otherwise, if it fails. A recent study showed that in the last two decades almost every large technological corporation has tried setting up small start-ups outside its organizational control system and almost all failed.

Resistance to change in large companies admittedly does have some advantages. Unjustified zeal is not likely to result in harm to a large firm, because the very bureaucracy that delays decisions to move forward with something new and good is also likely to stop something new and bad. But a price is paid. Many opportunities are missed. Large companies usually will show disdain for new small niches in the marketplace. A novel endeavor must have promise for growth in a reasonable time that will be noticeable in its annual sales report. Management is reluctant to shift leading engineers away from work to improve, even if only slightly, a billion-dollar product line and assign them instead to developing a radically new product having a mere several-million-dollar market. This is bound to rule out many exciting ventures. Their imaginative proponents will be dismayed and will contemplate leaving to become independent entrepreneurs.

As large corporations become giants, their managements often miss critical trends and technology breakthroughs. General Electric did not notice the beginning of the computer revolution, the most significant electrical-equipment development in the second half of our century. Its efforts to catch up were misguided and collapsed. IBM, today the world's foremost computer company, was not even in the electrical business when evidence that electronic computers had become practical first began to surface. Especially astonishing is that every one of IBM's present U.S. competitors in computers was nonexistent or would not have been categorized as an electrical company in the first half of the century.

Almost the same story applies to semiconductors, the basic building blocks for the computer revolution. Semiconductor products (such as the transistor and, more recently, the extremely large-scale integrated circuits on a chip) now are being produced by many companies. With the exception of AT&T, in whose Bell Telephone Laboratories the transistor was invented, all of today's major U.S. semiconductor producers were not yet in business or were not players in the electrical arena when the semiconductor era began. Regulatory restrictions made it necessary for AT&T* to offer its semiconductor technology to everyone for a modest license fee. This helped many new companies spring up, some of them headed by leading researchers who left Bell Laboratories to become entrepreneurs.

The three strongest electrical companies in the United States in midcentury—General Electric, Westinghouse, and RCA—should have been naturals to embrace semiconductors and become the leaders in supplying the world market. Not one of them set up appropriate programs. All three giants missed seeing the momentous significance of the revolution in basic electronic componentry represented by semiconductors. Semiconductor devices replaced vacuum tubes, yet none of the ten leading manufacturers of vacuum tubes became a leading manufacturer of semiconductors. (AT&T, again, is not included; it was limited to making tubes for its own use.) Silicon Valley companies, and others, sprang up to take their places. This fact by itself is amazing, as the advent of semiconductors was perhaps the single most influential technological breakthrough in all history.

---

* Bell Laboratories was a unique institution, the research arm of the nation's largest corporation. It was generously supported and allowed to probe the frontiers of science and technology from a long-range perspective; but after the breakup, AT&T, now a far smaller giant, has the more conventional need to focus the work of its smaller R&D unit, the AT&T Bell Laboratories, to support the company as it fights competitive battles. The future record of AT&T in technology research may be more like that of other large technological companies.

Producing rocket engines is a multibillion-dollar business. Some dozen large companies in existence before WW II (builders of engines for automobiles, trucks, aircraft, and ships and of electric-power-generating equipment) employed engineers who had spent their lives in the technology concerned with the burning of fuel in a metal chamber and the use of the resulting hot gas for driving mechanical or electrical apparatus. When the missile age arrived, America's industrial strength basic to rocket engines was to be found only in those companies. Yet none is today a principal maker of rocket engines. Some made a stab at producing them and failed. The managements of the rest acted as though they were unaware that a $5 or $10 billion annual business opportunity in their field of expertise had been born. Of today's four leading rocket-engine manufacturers, two (Aerojet and Rocketdyne) did not even exist, and the other two (Morton–Thiokol and Hercules) were in other fields when the opportunity to build rockets became evident.

Some large companies have a dictatorial chief executive at the top with cronies on the board of directors and a group of mediocre yes-men as his deputies. He personally makes all important decisions. Naturally, his knowledge and talents will be limited. The success of such companies is usually short-range and rests almost entirely on such financial tactics as continual merging and divesting. No such corporation is known for its technology advances.

There are occasional exceptions, large technological corporations that have not missed opportunities in their fields, that have steadily shunned unrelated diversifications and acquisitions. Such companies—Hewlett–Packard, Boeing, Digital Equipment Corporation, and TRW are examples—have consistently maintained high research-and-development budgets and applied their positive cash flow to develop new products and extend their activities within their fields of expertise. (If my including TRW appears self-serving, let it be noted that it is only in the past decade that TRW reached the size when its leadership might have been expected to follow the usual pattern of becoming an investment manager while simultaneously losing technology superiority. This was after the retirement of those of us who had originally assembled TRW and set its initial objectives and mode of operation. Credit accordingly belongs to TRW's present leadership.)

An abundance of new companies is needed to advance technology to the fullest. They will fill the gaps left by the established companies, with the result that America will excel in the world technology olympics. How, then, can we accelerate the founding of U.S. high-technology corporations?

Those who back entrepreneurs are looking for a favorable return on investment. The entrepreneurs generally have a variety of reasons for launching a new company. Getting rich is not always the most important, although I have never met an entrepreneur who rejects the idea. Technological entrepreneurs have the urge to be creative, and the new venture is unlikely to have attracted financing unless it is based on a new product or a new way to manufacture an existing one or a new idea in marketing and distribution. Without such creativity, the company will fill no need. If that point was missed by the original founders and backers, the competitive marketplace will soon force it to their attention. They then will have to become creative quickly or their company will pass out of existence.

Some entrepreneurs are in love with an idea and are hell-bent on pursuing it. Others simply are not happy unless they have the freedom to choose and do things their own way rather than in response to the directives of a many-layered management above them. If financial successes follow, they prize them as gold stars on their report cards, confirmation that they were right about themselves. Making money is welcome but still secondary.

Granted that entrepreneurship and the advance of technology are natural partners, what are the mechanisms for success? It is not enough to foster R&D and sit back, expecting technological breakthroughs and new companies to be founded to exploit them. We must help entrepreneurs find sources of capital. However, the anticipated returns on the investments must be competitive with other ways in which the capital might be employed. Venture-capital firms should include experienced people who will help organize entrepreneurial teams and counsel the managers of the companies launched with their funds.

A free-enterprise chef baking a technology soufflé is not going to get his cake to rise unless his recipe mixes sound business management with novel ideas. To advance technology is to lay a foundation for the creating of wealth, but a foundation is only the beginning of a structure. Starting an enterprise based on new technology does not automatically lead to affluence for the entrepreneur and reasonable returns to the investors. Many new high-technology corporations sink as soon as they hit competitive waters. They go bankrupt or are dissolved or sold, with appreciable losses to the original backers. They may display a glimmer of success early, only to have the light go out not much later. Roads are ways to get somewhere with automobiles, but if we want to drive to a desired destination, we must at the least arrange to be on the right road and have someone at the wheel who knows how to drive.

Once, in an advanced calculus class, a problem assigned for homework proved especially perplexing. None of us could see a way to attack it. Instead of disclosing the solution, the professor chose to keep the nasty puzzler on our agenda day after day. He would annoyingly inquire at each session whether any of us had yet figured out how to do the problem. Finally, one morning, I happily announced that I had discovered a way to solve it. I had not obtained the answer given in the book, I reported, but had arrived instead at an entirely different one. I expected the professor to send me to the blackboard to put my work up for him and the class to see. Instead, he shook his head and said soberly, "There are an infinite number of ways to do this problem if you are satisfied with wrong answers, Ramo, but there is also a way to get the right answer. That is called the solution."

In technological entrepreneuring, there are an infinite number of ways to lose. Fortunately, it is possible also to win. Most often, failure is due not to one shortcoming but to a combination. For instance, the product on which the fledgling company is based may have a fatal flaw. It may work but does not fill any real market demand. Building a better mousetrap will not cause the world to beat a path to your door if there are no mice in the area, or the existing mousetrap is satisfactory and much cheaper, or your sensational trap requires bait which is unavailable. Some new product may be excellent in all respects, but a competitor may come up with an even better one.

In addition to the possibility that the product may be overestimated, the problems of manufacturing and marketing it may be underestimated. The new company's staff may possess talents limited to the basic science underlying the product, but no knowledge about the other essential functions needed to operate a company. Making a basic discovery in science does not fit the discoverer to exploit the discovery. The aptitudes and training required for scientific research and those needed for managing a business enterprise are quite different. A research institute naturally tends to be uninterested in the demands of the marketplace. The entrepreneur, on the other hand, must be market-oriented; he must make products that people will want to buy.

Research projects at universities frequently result in technological know-how that justifies the founding of new high-tech corporations. Rocketry R&D at Cal Tech's Jet Propulsion Laboratory, for example, served in the 1950s as a basis for rocket design and production in several industrial corporations, some of which were started or staffed by former members of that laboratory. Following WW II, computer developers at the University of Pennsylvania designed the first large general-purpose electronic digital computers for the Army and later designed advanced versions for industrial computer companies. Similar situations are occurring at the moment in the field of microbiology.

Using research from universities to create high-tech industry is not, however, a formula to be counted on. Some new companies fail because their founders assume, incorrectly, that a sure way to arrive at success is to ride this train of connected events: first, unearth a new scientific phenomenon; second, develop novel technology incorporating the new science; third, design a product based on the new technology that will fill a market need that will become apparent. This scenario is often referred to as science or technology push. While building a technologically oriented business sometimes works this way, market pull is a much better bet in laying plans for a new company. In this approach, the starting impetus is a need, a market that awaits the entrepreneur who, ahead of others, sees both the market opening and how it can be met by new technology.

Over the years, I have regularly received hosts of proposals from would-be entrepreneurs seeking financial backing. Putting aside the completely nonsensical ones, I would say that ninety percent of these unsolicited propositions have been at least mildly unsound. A frequent shortcoming in the solicitations is a lack of realization that much more than an idea is required to deserve backing.

In the 1970s and 1980s, for example, I heard from many people seeking sponsorship to start a computer company. Many computer companies already exist and many are going to fail. Anyone who wants to build still another had better have original concepts. If it is technology that triggers the proposal, then the idea must be truly fresh and patentable. It must go to key aspects of science or engineering not yet conceived by others. The proprietary innovation must lead to superiority in speed, cost, or convenience, or the proposed computer must do useful things that cannot be done by other equipment. The financial plan must relate the capital investment to a rationale for believing that there will be a favorable rate of return despite the competition. The strength of the entrepreneurial team in marketing and manufacturing must be credible.

The truly fundamental essentials for success in the launching and operation of a new high-technology company are common sense and imagination. Common sense will tell you that you had better plan to do something different from the competition and be equipped to do it well. The product or the technique for manufacturing or marketing it—one or two or all three of these—must entail novel elements. Imagination is required for that.

Every year, numerous textbooks and articles are published that offer formulas for success in technological entrepreneuring. Most I find to be one-third obvious, one-third motherhood, and one-third unproven theories concocted by people who write well but have never started or managed a successful company. They are largely unnecessary for a team that joins originality with practical realism.

In the course of several decades spent in forming and operating high-technology ventures, I have been involved personally with many start-ups. I have observed overly optimistic, inexperienced enthusiasts and wise, skeptical owls, the first group proposing and the second rejecting new business plans. I have seen many successes and as many failures and have participated in both bonanzas and busts. Unfortunately, many proposals are extremely difficult to classify as good or bad. The newer the technology, the more exciting may be the possibilities, yet the harder it may be to obtain useful market information. I can best illustrate by describing a personal experience that made some contribution to the industrial world, and brought me some personal satisfactions, but was in the end a failure.

Soon after the Ramo–Wooldridge Corporation was launched in 1953, we found ourselves heavily involved with the embryonic field of electronic digital computers. Our responsibilities for the systems engineering and technical direction of the ICBM program required that we perform sophisticated mathematical analyses and led us to pioneer in the use of computers for such calculations. Meanwhile, other parts of the Ramo–Wooldridge Corporation were winning contracts to develop military computers. It occurred to us that maybe we should enter the commercial computer market. We set up a company to develop the art and science to control industrial operations by computer in real time—that is, "on-line"—while operations are underway. Typical would be a petrochemical plant where numerous materials are fed into the many steps of a continuing production process and everything about the process is constantly monitored and adjusted so the system will generate the desired products. In those days, flow rates, temperatures, pressures, timing of successive steps, opening and closing of valves, application of electric power and heat, and the rest, were determined and manipulated by human operators.

Our market research was done in long sessions at petroleum and chemical companies, papermaking factories, cement producers, steel manufacturers, electric power and distribution utilities, and the like. The product we planned was to consist not only of computer apparatus but also of systems-engineering services. Our customers knew their processes, but they did not know electronic computers, so the two staffs needed to work together to figure out how computers might improve an operation.

Our computer had to be quite different from the scientific or the accounting data-processing computers on the market. For process control, a large number of separate inputs had to come to the computer simultaneously. The computer had to be aware, through a preset memory bank for the given process, of the relationships that should exist among those inputs. The computer could then alert the human operators to change settings if they departed from proper ones, and it could figure and print out the best new settings; it could do this far faster and more accurately than any human being. The computer could also trigger automatic changes in settings, bypassing the human operator.

The existing computer companies, IBM and the others, were busy fighting each other for business in the off-line data-processing and scientific computers. That was the big volume side of the computer business, and we figured their competitive battles would go on for years. They did not employ the kind of systems engineers that we did, and they were not engaged in becoming expert in the processing industry as were we. Also, their equipment was ill-suited to the on-line control task. We were confident that we were unlikely to encounter severe competition until years after we had solidly established ourselves as the leader.

Initially, the new company was extremely successful. It was alone in the market. Then, as competitors appeared, the company still won most jobs. Its installations always improved the customer's process greatly. In a few years, the company found itself with over a hundred well-working installations, more than the total sold by all its competitors. It was the first to "close the loop" on a petrochemical process, the computer controlling the operation from the initial input of raw crude oil to the final production of refined gasoline. It was the first to implement computerized control of steel making (in Japan and Germany, ahead of U.S. steel companies). It even sold an installation to control the traffic signals in accordance with instantaneous traffic flow, so as to speed automobiles in and out of Dodger Stadium in Los Angeles.

Then a large number of competitors emerged, all intent on underbidding us. This was not because they loved losing money or because their costs were lower. Some were considering buying into what they deemed would eventually be a very lucrative business. Others would bid low by leaving out of their selling price the expensive systems-engineering support we felt was essential, which we provided. Alas, many potential customers—after they made the decision to computerize, with much help from us—fell for our competitors' sales pitch that all they would need next was the apparatus. Our expectation that there would be few competitors was a bad misjudgment. We could see no end of price fights ahead.

So we decided to quit the business. We stopped taking orders, moved our most skillful people to other projects, and sold off the remaining assets. One day, a Japanese steel company (Mitsubishi), which had installed one of our computers eight years before, decided it was time to replace it with more modern apparatus. They sawed up that pioneering unit's memory bank and sent a piece as a souvenir to each of us who had been involved in the project years before. It came cemented to a beautiful plaque proclaiming its meritorious record of service, ready for wall mounting. My chunk is hidden somewhere in the back of a closet in my office. I did not hang it up.

If I were to awaken tomorrow morning and discover myself to be far younger than when I went to bed, I would find numerous frontier fields of high technology irresistible for another entrepreneurial adventure. I would select a field by the week's end and would go out corralling the associates and capital needed to found a new company. But the role in life more becoming to me now is to help match capital with younger people's ideas and aid them in assembling entrepreneurial teams. By doing so, I am confident I am contributing my bit to the building of America's future technological strength. Let me describe some of these promising fields.

A treasure chest of scientific discoveries has been cracked open by the biological scientists, and entrepreneurial gems are pouring out. Astonishing breakthroughs are disclosing the detailed makeup and functions of animate molecules. The genetic code has been broken, and the principles of control of the development and activity of living cells are being rapidly unfolded. The ways diseases develop and the mechanisms whereby cellular structures defend against "foreign" invaders are being probed. Scientists are developing means to clone cellular materials to duplicate living organisms' vital constituents. Genetic engineering can now be carried on in an external environment, and the living materials created can be injected into the original organism. *

As this broad scientific frontier is pushed back and many more discoveries occur, rapid headway will be made in diagnosis and treatment of illnesses. Monoclonal antibodies, proteins identical to what the body naturally produces to fight disease, can be produced in the laboratory. These antibodies are magic bullets that, upon entering the body, can kill diseased cells while leaving surrounding healthy cells untouched. Engineered living matter will be produced in the future to improve human health, increase protein output in animals, and enhance crops by creating new plant forms resistant to pests and more adaptable to weather conditions. Patentable substances will give rise to new companies, as will the devices necessary to control the new materials successfully.

The spectrum of dramatic possibilities is so wide that the existing large chemical, pharmaceutical, medical-equipment, seed, and food companies are unlikely to dominate the field merely by virtue of their being large. The discoveries are too many and diverse for ready categorization. (When human skin, to take one example—actually, a specific burn victim's skin—has been duplicated experimentally and grown in the laboratory and then applied to the body as a nonrejectable transplant, no existing company is a natural to carry on

---

* Genetic engineering is the technique for rearranging DNA, the molecular building block of living cells that tells them what functions to perform. In recombinant DNA, genes are transplanted from one organism to another. For example, the gene to produce human insulin is implanted into bacteria, which then multiply rapidly and produce abundant human insulin cheaply. The process is far superior to acquiring substances generated in small quantities by human donors. Similarly, dwarfism, which affects thousands of children, can be successfully treated with a growth hormone which previously could only be obtained at great cost from the pituitary glands of cadavers.

the development from initial experiments to acceptable regular use.)

Entrepreneurs have been launching new biotech companies at a good pace in the last few years. Some have become favorites on the stock market before their product lines are established and evidence produced that they will enjoy business success. There is a clear demand for techniques that can yield positive, early diagnosis of serious diseases or that can fight those diseases. The value to the physician and the patient is so great that it is far less important to get the costs down than it is for the typical high-technology product. I do not suggest, however, that just any new biotechnology company is certain of financial success, or that any team and idea will surely attract financing. The winning entrepreneurs will be those who focus on endeavors leading to marketable products. Many start-up groups will be nothing more than research organizations. Instead of earning money, they will require transfusions of it far into the future. Moreover, the newer the basic science underlying a new company's endeavors, the more likely are the principal players to be pure scientists, with no business or applications background. Many new companies in this category probably will be acquired by large companies that will incorporate them into their research programs.

Consider next the field of scientific measurement. Those who stand out in scientific discoveries or engineering breakthroughs often cross frontiers by finding ways to measure the phenomena basic to the advances. When you observe something, you have the beginnings of knowledge, but when you can actually measure what you observe, then you have the beginnings of science and engineering. The more rapid the advance, the greater the need for specialized measuring instruments, so leading laboratories spend much of their R&D budgets on instrumentation. They buy apparatus from instrument manufacturers, but because their fields are so new, pioneers usually must create highly original measurement techniques. *

---

* One example is the most powerful microscope ever built. Called a scanning tunneling microscope, it can magnify the surface of material with a power sufficient to show how individual atoms are locked together. The new instrument, which will be valuable in research in microelectronics, DNA, and viruses, and in the creation of custom-tailored molecules, was created by laboratory researchers, not an instrument company.

The moment one research group acquires the means to study phenomena with greater speed and depth, competitors demand equally powerful tools. So when a novel instrument is built, a ready market is out there. A good entrepreneurial team starting out with instruments based on laboratory-proven concepts will have an excellent chance of finding financial sponsorship in the venture-capital world. Especially is this true for the actual conceivers of the specific instruments. Such individuals are of course innovative. If they also have an entrepreneurial bent and can make arrangements with their present employers to take the new instruments with them, they have the seeds of successful high-technology corporations. The first embodiment of a new idea for an instrument is relatively costly to create. Copies will be cheaper, and sales prospects should be excellent. The company where the measurement apparatus is first produced almost surely will not go into the business of supplying the apparatus to others. Most technological corporations toy with that possibility, but since their hands are probably full with their regular lines and the instrument business requires concentrated attention, the idea proves unattractive.

Another entrepreneurial opportunity stems from ingredients basic to technological progress: superior materials from which superior devices and equipment can be constructed, from the tiniest semiconductor element on a chip to the outer skin of a supersonic airplane. The last decade has seen a phenomenal increase in the possibilities of creating promising novel materials. Several parallel developments account for this. For one, it has become more and more evident that the performance of equipment can be enhanced greatly if the materials of which the equipment is made can be improved. The understanding of the potentials for performance improvement has increased greatly in recent years with the availability of high-capacity computers that can model the performance to be expected when superior materials become available. Sometimes it is the electrical properties that are critical. At other times, the key factor may be heat containment, corrosion resistance, light transmission or reflectivity, strength, hardness, flexibility, or reliable life under conditions of extreme temperature and other stresses.

Today, huge strides also are being made in the science of materials, in understanding just what gives individual materials their unique properties. Advanced measurement techniques have made it possible to probe the inner composition of materials, while computers permit detailed scientific calculations of the molecular structures of matter and its properties. It is becoming possible to produce a vast array of materials that do not appear in nature and to specify their properties in advance.

All this adds up to a materials revolution. The impact of synthetic matter will be far greater than the impact of plastics decades ago, what with unusual metal and carbon alloys, plastics, ceramics, composites (such as graphite fibers in an epoxy matrix), and a host of hybrids. There will be breakthroughs in techniques for fabrication of the materials as well. The consequence of the breadth and rapidity of change will make the materials field a natural for technological entrepreneurship.

As a specific example, it has been known for many years that certain materials can be made into superconductors of electricity at extremely low temperatures where they no longer resist the flow of current. Ordinary electrical conductors at ordinary temperatures, such as copper at room temperature, resist the current and soak up ten to twenty-five percent of the electrical energy flowing through them, wasting it in heat. Tens of billions of dollars' worth of generated electricity is lost annually through this resistance. The low temperatures previously needed to attain superconductivity have been so difficult to maintain, however, that the necessary apparatus has been overly expensive. The result is that superconducting phenomena have seen limited application. Suddenly now, scientists have synthesized new materials that have no resistance to electrical current at more readily achieved (less low) temperatures. If this potential is fully realized, it may improve electrical design and create a multibillion-dollar market for the novel materials.

With the wave of new materials, some of the engineers and scientists who originate them and the processes for their fabrication will separate from their present companies to start businesses. Also, some university professors involved in basic-materials science will see an opportunity to serve industry with more than mere laboratory samples. If they have an entrepreneurial itch and they present evidence to venture-capital sources of a good business plan and a competent team, they will be funded. By all-out use of the entrepreneurial route, American talent could succeed in attaining world leadership in materials. This leadership would in turn be a powerful lever for achieving leadership in products that depend on breakthroughs in materials.

We move next to what I believe will offer the greatest opportunity for entrepreneurship; namely, information technology (computer communications). To regain American preeminence in technology, we need to foster a massive number of new high-technology corporations in software and hardware based on advances in semiconductors, lasers, communications systems, computer science, robotry, automatic control, and other detailed aspects of information technology. How can I justify the establishing of more new companies when so many large established corporations and even more smaller entities are active in these fields? Won't these existing companies cover everything, leaving nothing for fresh ventures? Even if a beginner should come up with a very novel technological angle, won't the present players merely add more cards to the decks they deal, raise the ante, and swamp that new entry?

The reason for urging more start-up companies in information technology is its overwhelming potential. The number of yet uncharted dimensions of advance in information technology is even greater than the number of present players. All of man's pursuits—at work, at play, in the home, office, factory, school, laboratory, hospital, or in government—depend on information handling, and those tasks will be performed better by incorporating the steadily emerging new technology. Major advances will occur for decades ahead, and each breakthrough will give birth to an avalanche of novel applications. So vast are the possibilities that present companies will not cover everything.

Take so-called supercomputers. Scientists and engineers are always able to list critical problems no existing computer can help them solve because they generate solutions so slowly that a researcher might have to devote his entire career to working out one problem. When faster computers become available to technical experts, superior engines, airplanes, alloys, and drugs, and entirely new developments, like cheap nuclear-fusion energy, will be possible earlier. Some half-dozen American and Japanese supercomputers are on the market today, as the top of the line of some computer manufacturers or as the exclusive product of companies that do nothing but work at the leading edge of speed in computers. But existing supercomputers are only the beginning. New technologies promise radically improved yet lower-cost performance, and a large portion of those new approaches will be initiated by new companies unburdened by commitments to older approaches.

Let us elaborate on the thought that sensational developments may lie ahead by imagining a specific possibility. Two fields, information technology (computer communications) and biotechnology (microbiology and genetic engineering), probably will lead the list of technology advances likely to stimulate great industrial expansion in the coming decades. What if a significant mating of these two frontier technologies were to occur—biocomputers? Why should we expect biocomputers to be of enormous importance? Note first that we have learned how to pack millions of semiconductor devices (similar in function to the neurons of the human brain) on a single silicon chip of fingernail size. These solid, metallic chips have made possible very cheap, reliable, and small computers that can multiply two numbers in a billionth of a second, put thousands of names in alphabetical order with ease, switch connections a million times a second, and perform innumerable information-processing tasks beyond the capability of Homo sapiens.

The human brain, that compact information-handling machine—so uncompetitive with semiconductor chips for some information-processing jobs—is superior to any computer so far built or presently designable for intellectual functions like creative thought, visual pattern recognition, and associative memory. One probable explanation for this difference is this: Each neuron-like device on a semiconductor chip has at most a few connections to adjacent devices. In contrast, the ten billion neurons of the brain are amazingly generously interconnected; hundreds and often thousands of connections run from a typical neuron to distant as well as nearby neurons. The interconnections among the brain's neurons doubtless provide the basis for the remarkable thought processes of the brain, which the manmade flat chips, despite their enormous switching and computing speed, cannot equal.

Meanwhile, frontier research in biology and chemistry is giving us the capability to produce complex molecules, both animate and inanimate, which are different from any that appear in nature. It is becoming possible to engineer matter to order at a molecular level. This will create a degree of microminiaturization in design that reaches far smaller dimensions than the elements of even the densest, very large-scale integrated circuits on a semiconductor chip. The very existence of the human brain proves that, if the right biochemical molecules are formed with the right connections among them, the combination can provide the memory, logic, sorting, inferring, recognition, association, invention, learning, and other intellectual capabilities that our brains possess. Hence, we should list as a possibility that some future computers will be biochemical. When we attain the ability to create complex biochemical molecules interlinked in a pattern of our choosing, we will have opened up the potential of engineering a synthetic brain that might combine the best properties of the human brain with those of the largest, fastest semiconductor digital computers. The field is not properly labeled artificial intelligence, but rather *superintelligence*.

Let us shift and examine a factor in world technology competition critical to the United States; namely, manufacturing productivity. America starts off with a disadvantageous labor cost compared with almost all competitors, and the only practical way to overcome this handicap is to lead in manufacturing technology. But against Japan quite generally, and in specific manufacturing fields in Germany and elsewhere, the United States is firmly entrenched in second or third place. This applies, for example, in two frontiers of manufacturing technology, robotry and computer-controlled production. Our standard of living will go down if other countries win all the manufacturing technology races. We will not maintain our economic strength, even if we lead in scientific discoveries, if our businesses and citizenry are occupied mainly with selling each other insurance or shares of stock, taking in each other's laundry, suing each other, or repairing each other's foreign-made autos and appliances. We must bring advances in technology onto the factory floor.

The manufacturing technology field, I believe, can be particularly responsive to American entrepreneurship. Automation, whether handling production-scheduling information or the processing and movement of materials, requires a detailed understanding of the product, the process of manufacture, and the human components, the workers, involved. Quality control in manufacturing is attained both by designing for quality in the first place and by providing economical yet meticulous factory testing and inspection, much of it performed automatically by devices rather than people. To design and combine skillfully all the elements of a truly modern production activity is a challenging engineering task. Much analysis and invention is needed. The engineers employed by manufacturers to develop superior production technology will hold the keys to victory in our nation's bid to close the gap and excel again over other nations in manufacturing.

If controls, measurement devices, computers, fabrication machinery, and other hardware and software are worked out for one factory, they are generally useful elsewhere. Companies that improve their manufacturing skills are essentially disinterested, however, in providing their systems to others. If some of the engineers responsible for the advances possess the entrepreneurial spirit and put together a proper team, they will be able to obtain financial backing to start new corporations whose mission will be to offer production technology to a wide range of customers.

An example of this is the application of lasers to manufacturing. A laser produces light that is at one frequency, the wave fronts all in phase. Inherently, this makes the radiation unusual in two important ways. First, an extremely powerful beam can be produced and, second, it can be focused with unprecedented accuracy. In manufacturing, the intense localized heating achievable by illuminating with an energetic laser can provide surface hardening and precision drilling, cutting, and welding of materials. Additionally, remarkably fine and straight light beams can be used as tools for inspecting the dimensions and surfaces of manufactured parts for superior quality control. Moreover, the parts can be fabricated with greater precision if lasers are employed to line them up with the tools that are to form them.

To divert from manufacturing for a moment, lasers also are giving rise to technological entrepreneurship in surgery and the treatment of disease and in numerous military applications for locating and destroying targets. Light from microminiaturized lasers can be switched on and off a thousand times faster than electricity in transistors, so laser phenomena may become the foundation for faster computers. All these laser properties suggest possibilities for new high-tech companies. In the application of lasers to manufacturing technology, however, the promise of entrepreneurship is especially high because most manufacturers' staffs are not well equipped for applying lasers. If they experiment with lasers on their own, it is because they have found no outside expert to turn to. They can't depend on machine-tool builders, for instance, because, though those suppliers are skilled in design of mechanical machinery, they employ few physicists, let alone laser physicists.

So much for examples of new high-tech fields. Of the many opportunities, we have described only a few. If they are to be grasped and the nation thus strengthened in international competitive races, we shall need many technological entrepreneurs. They are not easily produced. They preferably should be found, motivated, and trained early. Universities, industry, and government all can help.

While our universities play a major part in spurring technological entrepreneurship because their R&D programs often yield advances on which new companies can be based, higher education does almost nothing directly to advance entrepreneurship. American university engineering departments educate well in the science underlying engineering, but they are weak when it comes to introducing the student to the thinking behind real-life engineering and the concept of entrepreneurship. Applying science and technology to design products which will satisfy real market requirements, which can be manufactured reliably and economically, and which will generate a satisfactory return on investment is a pursuit far from the interests and experience of most university faculties. Admittedly, any exposure a student might get in this pursuit in a university is bound to be minor compared with a lifetime of practice. But engineering graduates should not leave college, as they typically do, with only a faint impression of what actually constitutes the work of the engineering profession they are about to enter.

Few engineering schools teach much about manufacturing technology or give the student a start in the kind of thinking basic to invention. Professional engineering tasks, unlike college homework problems, are interdisciplinary, with aspects of electrical, thermal, mechanical, chemical, materials, and other physical science and technology all combined with economic and human factors. These broad but practical matters are barely disclosed to the engineering student, and their importance comes as a shock to most graduates when they first work in an industrial environment.

University business schools usually are good at presenting accounting, finance, marketing, and management methodology. They introduce the student well to quantitative financial-performance analysis. Such instruction does not develop the talent needed by successful entrepreneurs, however, any more than the education of engineers promotes creativity. Entrepreneurship is introduced so poorly in college that I have often found it confused in the minds of new business-school graduates with the preparation of a financial plan for a new business, showing estimated cash requirements.

Earlier, we cited the poor quality of primary and secondary education in math and science and the diminishing number of Ph.D.s in engineering and science and said these facts were omens of the nation's loss of technological preeminence. Our college students, the great majority not science and engineering majors, will be the influential citizens of the future. They will come to hold the majority of positions in the Congress and the state legislatures and in the executive branches of government; they will dominate industry. If the nation is to lead in deriving benefits from technology advance in the coming decades, our leaders do not all have to be engineers, but they must have an understanding of what science and technology are about. Unfortunately, most college graduates have only a single, one-year course in science, and that is usually a superficial survey course. The core curricula of even the nation's top universities (Harvard, Columbia, Michigan, California, Wisconsin, among others) require no more.

A large fraction of America's college graduates are scientific illiterates, undereducated for the technological world. The universities themselves can change this, and I think they will. As to technological entrepreneurship in particular, once its importance is recognized by the universities, I am confident that they will develop educational approaches that will bring out the creative and entrepreneurial talents of their students. Of course, government and industry must buy the idea as well, and they must extend themselves to aid the universities.

Large companies surely can do more to help. They could encourage universities by philanthropic grants specifically to develop novel instruction programs in manufacturing technology and to stimulate student interest in being creative. Since the big companies will hire most of the graduates, they will reap most of the benefits if the innovating potential of their young employees is enhanced before they arrive.

Industry can help in other ways as well. Large technological companies (which so often fail to take advantage of new opportunities) should make steady large investments in venture-capital firms whose sole business is to launch high-tech companies. The big companies should simply buy stock, be investors, but stay out of management and control, religiously keep their bureaucratic procedures out of the act but profit from the growing value of their investment and have a head start should they wish to acquire the new company at a later time. Considering the rapid advances in science and technology, a technological corporation with annual revenues in the billions of dollars might justify investing in outside venture activities at the rate of two dollars for every dollar spent in-house on R&D.

What now about the role of government in supporting technological entrepreneurship? Government policy and actions greatly affect the chances of high-technology entrepreneurs attaining their objectives, if only because the government sets the economic environment. Money supply, inflation and interest rates, currency-exchange rates, budget deficits, and other key economic factors are determined more by government actions than by free-market dynamics. Take tax policy. In the early 1970s, the government increased the capital-gains tax substantially, and new issues of common stock in high-technology ventures promptly dropped from a level of billions of dollars per year to essentially zero. Active investing in new technology is most likely to occur in a period of economic strength, with the cost of money in a favorable range, and taxation well below levels that discourage risk.

Tax policy that will create the most favorable environment for investment in new technology has never seriously been a government goal. The U.S. tax bill passed in 1986, whatever its good points, will lessen technological entrepreneurship because it increases taxes on capital gains. Japan and Germany have no taxes at all on substantive capital gains. Again, since higher savings automatically increase funds available for investment, our tax policies should encourage savings, which is not now the case.

Let me not be thought to imply that everything the government does discourages entrepreneurship. It sometimes creates direct opportunities for technological entrepreneuring. Nearly all pure research into the laws of nature at the nation's universities is government-financed. Research on the constituents of the atom is virtually entirely government-funded. The understanding of electrical phenomena in semiconducting materials was first advanced mainly in our universities; those who obtained doctorates in this field went on to the country's industrial-research laboratories, where the transistor and other semiconductor devices for switching and amplifying electrical signals were invented. The same is true of lasers; the fundamental theory originated in universities, where researchers created the scientific foundation for the first laser inventions and demonstrations, which were carried out in industry. Moreover, many of the first electronic digital-computer ideas originated at universities under government grants. Recent scientific discoveries in microbiology have also been mainly government-sponsored.

What we most need is cooperation between government, industry, and the universities to spur technological entrepreneurship. Such cooperation is now being fostered by the recently established National Science Foundation program to create new kinds of science and engineering centers at universities. Where individual academics have conventionally done isolated basic research within a single discipline, researchers from different disciplines will work in teams in the NSF centers. Although central research facilities have long existed in some American universities, in the new centers research and practical engineering will be combined and will involve industry participation. These centers surely are the most important of the Reagan Administration's modest direct and innovative activities on the technological front, and they deserve to be greatly expanded.

At Columbia University, for example, the NSF has founded a Center for Telecommunications Research. It will explore advanced communications systems that can carry all forms of information over ultra-high-speed optical-fiber lines under the control of advanced computers. The center will support fifty graduate students who will be in direct contact with industrial advisors. The financial sponsorship will be by a dozen companies as well as by the NSF. There are similar centers at the University of California at Santa Barbara (focusing on robots to control the manufacturing of microelectronic components); the University of Delaware, jointly with Rutgers University (on design and manufacturing methods for novel composite materials); the University of Maryland, jointly with Harvard University (on applications of advanced computers to the design of communications systems); M.I.T. (on engineering to improve manufacturing processes in the biotechnology industry); and Purdue University (on highly automated manufacturing systems).

In process of being set up are some ten additional centers that will deal with biology, plant science, behavioral and neural sciences, computer science, risk analysis, and materials research.

These centers will help produce engineering and science graduates with a significant beginning experience in the practical aspects of innovation. They will bring government, industry, and universities closer together, to produce a stream of promising young technological entrepreneurs.

The government can aid entrepreneurship in an entirely different way, immigration. The favorable environment in America for launching new high-technology corporations, virtually unique in the world, needs to be used to attract scientist-engineer-entrepreneurs from around the globe. The United States can become a mecca for such people. Our immigration policies should be changed to make it as easy for innovative technological brainpower from foreign countries to become American as it is for capital holders to become investors here. The more we become and are seen as a technologically entrepreneurial, free-enterprise, low-tax land, the more the cream of the world's technologists will be attracted to come here and help improve the U.S. position in high technology. Japan and Western Europe cannot equal what we can do in this area.

To foster technological entrepreneurship is essential, but our security is also a high priority. These two needs are not independent. We cannot generate a fast-flowing stream of advanced, competitive civilian products while also developing weapons systems to outdo potential enemies unless we manage both endeavors extremely well. This includes ensuring that the military systems we develop are the right ones and that we have enough competent people in the government to direct that work. Otherwise, the greater the military spending, the less likely it will be that we will maintain a strong defense, since frantic overdemand will lead to wasteful underachievement.

When the word "waste" is used in discussing military procurement, it recalls the reports of overcharging and cost overruns by weapons contractors, of ridiculous prices for simple components, and of indictments for alleged fraud. But these are not the important factors that undermine national security. True, with industry's tens of thousands of managers, purchasing agents, accountants, and other personnel, some are bound to engage in dishonest actions or display such carelessness or incompetence that mischarging will take place. A typical contractor that over a period of years produces several billion dollars' worth of equipment will have accumulated improper charges of a few million dollars. That is bad, but the loss is less than one percent of total costs. One expects this level of waste and fraud in all large organizations. The greatest of efforts is not likely to diminish it very much.

The dominant sources of inefficiency in DoD's process of acquiring weapons systems are two in number. One is the selection process that starts weapons-systems development. It is vital to match the military's requirements with the technological potential if high military effectiveness is to be achieved. Failure to do that, and concentrating instead on trying to reduce occasional dishonesty, is a bit like tolerating frequent wrong diagnoses of illnesses and hence wrong treatments while becoming agitated about overcharges for Band-Aids.

The other major factor responsible for misspending for national security arises from the highly imperfect management of procurement after projects have been chosen. Here the DoD bureaucracy, its regulations, and its paperwork lead to inflated costs and long delays in completing every project, even if it has been well selected and the contractors chosen to do the job are competent. It is no wonder that a quite simple metal part is sometimes charged at a ridiculous price when ten thousand dollars may be spent in processing highly detailed, unnecessary specifications and going through countless cost-estimating steps, approvals, and negotiations, as if a very complex piece of equipment were being purchased.

The industrial contractors match DoD's bureaucracy every step of the way with their own bureaucracies, as the only easy way of dealing with the DoD. The government and industry feed on each

other's inefficiencies, an action by one requiring a parallel or contesting action by the other, with all actions documented and preserved for later review.

An even more costly procurement practice, which only superior
management by the DoD can minimize, is the demand for ever
greater weapon complexity at an ever greater cost. This starts with
competitions that press the candidate contractors into severe "paper
invention" contests. Each competitor promises to outdo the other
in weapons performance and cites ever more speculative innovations, each of which adds to the complexity of the system being
bid on. Then, when work on the project begins, every perceived
possible shortcoming of the weapon is noted and changes in the
contract are made to deal with it. Similarly, as work proceeds,
improvements in the weapon's performance are developed and lead
to further changes in the contract. Between them, the government
purchasers and the industrial sellers endow the project with higher
cost and a stretched-out completion time, and, almost inevitably,
lower reliability and smaller quantities to be delivered in view of
the greater price. In the end, military effectiveness is impaired.

The massive U.S. expenditures on defense include many tens
of billions of dollars annually for R&D and the procurement of
technologically sophisticated hardware. With so large an operation,
it would be naïve to believe that all military projects have been
well selected. Some are bound to have originated in errors of judg-
ment and misinformation. Others might have been sound projects
when started but have become out-of-date because of unanticipated
developments. Some have resulted from overly enthusiastic sales-
manship by the military industry's marketing virtuosos and members
of Congress from their areas. Together, they apply their art skillfully
to the decision-makers within the DoD to win contracts.

Weapons selection must be made better, or else national resources will continue to be in short supply for scientific explorations,
civilian product development, and modernization of our factories.
Few congressmen will vote against a weapons system that provides
employment in their districts. The selfish-interest dealing and trading is part of our democracy. The way to minimize these negatives

is for DoD's managerial personnel to possess greater objectivity and be outstandingly capable. The earlier a sound plan to meet a true military requirement with a technological development is competently conceived in the Pentagon, explained, and stuck to, the more likely will it be that industry and the Congress will accept the plan or weapons system. On the other hand, if there are indecisive and confused signals and project justification is weak, the result will be inelegant rivalry for government funds. How can we strengthen DoD's technical management?

Wise weapons-system selections cannot be made without clear understanding of things both military and technological. Skilled career officers need to do more, however, than sit down with engineers from industry and—on the assumption that between them they will cover everything—arrive at the list of weapons systems to be procured. Interaction with the private sector is essential, but the industry has an ax to grind in its desire for contracts, and so do too many members of Congress. The free-enterprise sector cannot be allowed to team up with the Congress to decide specific weapons procurements.

The trouble is that the DoD's staff is simply not strong enough—given the complexity of the assignment—in the management of science and technology projects. As they choose and direct military weapons-system developments, the DoD's project leaders face greater challenges than do the technical executives of industry that the DoD supports. The latter must work under the former's direction, because the heads of DoD's projects have the higher responsibility for overall success. And yet we find less management strength in the DoD than in industry. Admittedly, a few high-level DoD appointive positions are held by manager-engineers of top caliber. These, typically, are individuals who have left high-paying jobs in private organizations to serve their nation, and they do so for a few years with distinction. Also, I know from personal contact that the military officer corps and the civil service always include some outstanding technology management professionals. But the number of such individuals available to the DoD is far too small.

It is easy to see why. Anyone who is unusually gifted and well

trained in directing technological work can choose from many openings to career advancement. Private positions offer greater financial
rewards and peer recognition, while government service involves
more bureaucratic frustration and a lower standard of living. Hence,
there are few generals and admirals with Ph.D.s and few civilian
scientists and engineers in the DoD whose accomplishments have
brought them membership in the prestigious national academies.
The small number of the exceptionally able in DoD operate in an
atmosphere of chaos, political pressure, and endless paperwork.
They have to devote an enormous amount of time to defending
their programs to Congress. They seldom have a chance to think
things through carefully.

To make the situation worse, the DoD retires military officers
at the very peak of their managerial strength. The retirement-pay
system (low salaries and relatively high retirement pay) makes early
retirement extremely attractive. Most weapons-systems officers elect,
or are forced, to leave the service shortly after reaching their forties.
Even the most outstanding officers, those who possess the most
gray matter and stars, are gone by their early fifties. They are likely
to take jobs in the military industry. Their competence remains
available to the national effort, but it widens the gap between the
managerial strengths of the buyer (the DoD) and the seller (the
industry).

Meanwhile, as the shortage of competent technological executives within the military has grown, the strength of the engineering
and physical-science departments of American universities, as we
have seen, is threatened. There are ways to help meet both these
critical personnel needs. The Department of Defense has long subsidized postgraduate education for selected military officers. Much
more should be done. The DoD should set up a program to support
doctoral education in American universities tied to its unprecedented managerial needs. Students in science and engineering who
obtain college degrees with distinction should be offered special
long-term contracts with the military forces. The DoD should make
available generous financial backing for those who choose to pursue
a new kind of doctorate and then become military officers com-

mitted to a substantial number of years in the service. (Also, the DoD should grant a stipend to the university for each graduate fellow placed there, to build the staff and supporting structure for the required top-grade graduate study.) The doctorate program should be custom-tailored, with innovative management and social-science courses and appropriate courses in physical science and engineering, and with practical experience in the services between academic terms.

In this way, the Defense Department could begin to create a strong staff for technological-project management. The U.S. military should include some thousand of these special doctorates. If a hundred were to leave the service every year as they move along in their individual careers, the DoD would need that many new graduates from the universities to replace them. To create ten new doctoral graduates from each of ten leading American universities would cost about $15 million per year, a mere half of a hundredth of one percent of our annual defense expenditures of $300 billion. The program would generate in future years savings of billions as a result of superior selection and management of the military's technology projects. Investment in new high-tech companies would also be increased because of the enhanced availability of financial resources now being committed to poorly chosen and poorly managed weapons programs. Higher profits in technological industry, a consequence of improving competitive performance in international commercial markets, would bring the government added tax revenue.

This ends our examples of things we can do to enhance our technological strength. Many others could have been included. We see that some measures that should prove very effective are straightforward, even easy to implement. Implementation will very likely occur in the near future as the concerned parties come to realize the potential benefits. Other needed steps will be more difficult to accomplish in our democracy, but are not impossible. It will be a while before the required majority of the public appreciates the seriousness of our loss of technology leadership and then demands that we devise and launch politically realistic programs to bring about a change. The formula for action that we cited earlier—in America things have to get worse before they can get better—will work, given enough time. But we should strive to accelerate understanding and thereby shorten the period during which the situation worsens before it is turned around.

Because so many promising approaches suggest themselves, there is reason for optimism. If we do alter America's pattern of decision-making, improve the way we determine priorities and goals, build the stature of our technology, probe the scientific frontiers aggressively, put the results to work quickly and efficiently, and even achieve world preeminence again in science and technology, will that solve all our problems? Unfortunately, the answer is no.

The business of science and technology is to discover the secrets of the universe and apply scientific and engineering skill to yield us security, prosperity, health, and happiness. Yet science and technology can never be more than tools. Poverty, disease, starvation, crime, overpopulation, ignorance, wars, and impairment of the environment cannot be cured by science and technology alone. That requires parallel social advance. The world's most serious unresolved issues are not science-technology ones; they are social, economic, and political. But those issues intersect and science-technology is right plunk in the middle of every intersection, sometimes causing or exacerbating the problems, often offering possibilities for solution, and frequently providing opportunities which, if grasped, would enable civilization to rise to new, higher levels of achievement, satisfaction, and tranquillity. Whatever we ultimately are able to do to elevate the society will occur earlier and with greater success if our science-and-technology tools are many, sharp, versatile, and effective. Wise application of science and technology should offer us a life that is steadily better as we progress, more slowly than we would like, toward one that is best.

INDEX